CHOOSING
BOOKS
for
KIDS

How to Choose the Right Book
for the Right Child at the Right Time

CHOOSING BOOKS *for* KIDS

How to Choose the Right Book
for the Right Child at the Right Time

A BANK STREET BOOK

AUTHORS
JOANNE F. OPPENHEIM
BARBARA BRENNER
BETTY D. BOEGEHOLD

CONSULTANT
CLAUDIA LEWIS, PH.D.

EDITOR
WILLIAM H. HOOKS

BALLANTINE BOOKS · NEW YORK

Library of Congress Catalog Card Number: 86-90730
ISBN 0-345-32683-0

Text design by Mary A. Wirth
Cover design by James R. Harris
Front cover photo by Mort Engel
Back cover photo: Stock Photo

Manufactured in the United States of America
First Edition: November 1986
10 9 8 7 6 5 4 3 2 1

Contents

CHAPTER III
BOOKS *for* TODDLERS

CHAPTER IV
BOOKS *for* THREE- *and* FOUR-YEAR-OLDS

CHAPTER V
BOOKS *for* FIVES

CHAPTER VIII
BOOKS *for* TEN- *to* TWELVE-YEAR-OLDS

CHAPTER IX
SOURCES *and* RESOURCES

Acknowledgements

Grateful acknowledgement is made to Joëlle Delbourgo for bringing us the germinal idea for this book; to James A. Levine for his support and encouragement in the shaping and writing of the book; to Margaret Peet for the manuscript preparation; to Ann Carlson Weeks, executive director of the Children's Division of the American Library Association, for providing us with access to children's librarians all over the country; and to the following librarians, juvenile editors, and specialists in children's literature who generously shared with us their personal "best books" choices for each developmental stage of childhood from infancy through preadolescence.

Kathleen Abbene
Ethel N. Ambrose
Christine Behrmann
Jane E. Belsches
Therese C. Bigelow
Annette Chotin Blank
Anne Boegen
Clara Nalli Bohrer
Robin A. Branstator
Muriel W. Brown
Mary M. Burns

George Burns
Margaret Bush
Eleanor Burts
Linda Ward Callaghan
Laurie Canfield
Jo Carr
Jane Dyer Cook
Pat Craig
Mary K. Dahlgreen
Judie Davie
Marjorie DeMallie

Sally Dow
Priscilla L. Drach
Margery H. Dumaine
Marion Dumond
Kathy East
Barbara Elleman
Mollie Fein
Iris Feldman
Ellen Finan
Carole D. Fiore
Adrienne Fluckiger
Maralita Freeny
Louise F. Gage
Nancy Gaut
Michele M. Gendron
Donna Gettys
Janet J. Gilles
Barbara Ginsberg
Elaine Goley
Ruth Gordon
Ellin Green
Grace W. Greene
Linda Greengrass
Beth Greggs
Ruth M. Haddow
Dona J. Helmar
Harriet Herschel
Sue Hoffman
E. Hoke
Robin Howard
Mary Alice Hunt
Coy Kate Hunsucker
Elizabeth Huntoon
Marcia Hupp
Marilyn Iarusso
Barbara Immroth
Gale Jacob
Carolyn K. Jenks
Ann L. Kalkhoff
Amy Kellman

Dr. Phyllis K. Kennemer
Gayle Keresey
Betty Kullesied
Starr LaTronica
Betty Lambert
Mildred Lee
Ilene Liebowitz
Jill L. Locke
Dean E. Lyons
Gregory Maguire
Sylvia Marantz
Lucy Marx
Barbara A. Maxwell
Florence Webbe Maxwell
Crystal McNally
Debbie McLeod
Deidre Milks
Marianne Milks
Elsie Miller
Betty Davis Miller
Sancy Milyko
Effie Lee Morris
Jacqueline G. Morris
Paula Morrow
Judy Moskal
Priscilla Moxom
Jenny Lou Opremcak
Hilda Weeks Parfrey
Caroline Parr
Susan H. Patron
Anne Pellowski
Bette J. Peltola
Linda Perkins
Barbara Ann Porte
Mary Lett Robertson
Connie Rockman
Donna Rodda
Barbara Rollock
Steven M. Rouzes
Judith Rovenger

Grace W. Ruth
Marcia B. Salvadore
Frances V. Sedney
Martha Shogren
Phyllis G. Sidorsky
Sandra S. Sivulich
Donna Skvarla
Ellen M. Stepanian
Maxine K. Stinchcomb
Dr. Margaret R. Tassia
Carol A. Tarsitano
Denise Tate

Gail Terwilliger
Divna Todorovich
Ruth Toor
Meryl Traub
Portia Tyndle
Patsy Weeks
Sally Wehr
Sue Weller
Holly G. Willett
Branch Woolls
Elisa Wrenn
Florence Yee

CHOOSING BOOKS *for* KIDS

How to Choose the Right Book
for the Right Child at the Right Time

Introduction

THE MARVELOUS BOOK

"In the beginning was the Word . . ."

The history of children's books begins with the history of people. Long before there was written language, people told stories and children listened. Many of these stories were based on history, like the accounts of the Great Flood. Others were invented to explain the mysteries of the universe. Generations of people in widely scattered parts of the globe seem to have arrived at storytelling and mythmaking independently, almost as if the need to tell and to listen is a function of being human.

As time passed, each generation remembered stories told by the previous one. Elders passed these stories along, reciting them into the receptive ears of the succeeding generation—the children—who would remember and recycle the legends to their children.

Much later, the stories were written down—first on clay, then on papyrus, still later on hide and vellum. Writing them down was a way to improve on memory, to embellish with pictures, and to preserve the story more completely intact. Many of the world's greatest books—*The Odyssey,* for example—were written long after the events which they record.

Over the years legends got changed and modified. But the

Illustration by Leo and Diane Dillon from *Why Mosquitoes Buzz in People's Ears* by Verna Aardema.

power of the events and their significance remained. Each new generation learned the history, the mythology, and the moral and religious heritage of its culture through stories. The most fascinating aspect of this passing of the literary torch is that the stories we think of today as children's literature were everybody's literature at the time. *Cinderella,* complete with glass slipper, comes straight out of Egyptian legend. *Reynard the Fox* and the other tales of Aesop go back to the year 1050. The tales of Robin Hood were sung by bards at Elizabethan theatrical entertainments. And many of the earliest novels, like *Robinson Crusoe* and *Gulliver's Travels,* were written for adults and adopted by children.

Were adults closer to childhood in olden times? Or is it simply that the divisions we made much later between adult and children's books are artificial boundaries?

Whatever the reasons, there were no books made especially for children for a very long time after the printing press was invented. Except for schoolbooks and guides to conduct, a child had to wait until he/she was a good reader to enjoy literature.

But in the 1740s the cause of juvenile literature found an advocate. An entrepreneur named John Newbery, for whom the Newbery award is named, produced the first children's book that was designed to entertain as well as to teach.

Like children themselves, children's literature had its developmental stages. Children's books have gone through many shifts and trends since the time of Newbery. Styles of writing have changed. Early children's books were heavy on morals and frighteningly graphic on the wages of sin. Later they became more whimsical and lighthearted, until sometimes they were almost simperingly sweet. For awhile fairy tales were considered too violent for the tender psyches of the young. Realistic "here and now" stories were the rage. Still later there were books that talked, or sang, or smelled good, or popped up.

Fortunately, the best children's books have persisted

through all the fads and fashions. They form a body of literature that does what the storyteller of old used to do. Books are still the single most memorable artifact of childhood. They are not only good for the child; they are a family resource beyond anything that any other medium has to offer. And children's books remain what the best of them have always been—not a lesser, watered-down version of adult literature but another and equally powerful transmitter of the culture and the values of a civilization.

Illustration by John Tenniel from *Alice in Wonderland* by Lewis Carroll.

Advertisers have always made exaggerated claims about kids' books, many of which have little to do with books' real value. Today along with the claims have come new technologies —computers and videocassettes and TV, competing with books for a child's attention and a parent's dollars. A parent is caught among a bewildering set of options. Are books going out of style? Are computers the books of the future, the new repository of our culture? Is it worth it to spend fifteen dollars for a picture book? How does one make the right choice from a bewildering array of books? These are the concerns of *Choosing Books for Kids*.

WHAT THIS BOOK IS ABOUT

Choosing Books for Kids is divided into three sections. The first section, *The Book Connection*, is a sort of appetizer. It gives you an overview on the subject of children's books—their history, our particular way of looking at books, how we made our choices, and a discussion of why and how books are important to a child.

The second section is the main course—the choices of books themselves. They're divided by age groups; each chapter will give you the titles of both old and new books that are especially appropriate for each specific stage of the child's development. For example:

In *Books for Babies,* you'll learn how and why talking and singing to Baby is the vital first step that leads to books and reading. You'll rediscover the library you never thought of as a resource—your own memory. We'll help you reconnect with those rhymes of childhood that you may not have thought of for a long time. You'll find titles of "first books"—cloth books, board books, Mother Goose, and lullabies. You'll also find resources for records and cassettes and other appropriate language-related materials made for the youngest listener. We list them and tell you why they're good for your baby.

In *Books for Toddlers,* you'll find out why toddlers are the way they are and how their development ties in with the books they need and like. There are books here that are expendable, taking into consideration the toddler's penchant for demolition. But there are also books that help the two-year-old name things and learn things and begin to enjoy language and pictures. There are books for laptime and books for a beginning bookshelf. How do you read to a toddler? This book will give you techniques that take into consideration the toddler's brief attention span, and titles that fit with his urge to be "on the go."

Books for Three- and Four-Year-Olds shows how the child's world is expanding and how books can plug into these developmental changes. It gives titles of books in which the characters do three- and four-year-old things that kids will recognize. This chapter will tell you which books mesh best with the three- and four-year-old's drive toward independence and even what kinds of books *not* to buy for this age child. In this section you'll notice the number and variety of reading material is wider, consistent with this age's wider experience with the world.

Books for Fives introduces books that will whet a child's appetite for learning to read. You'll learn about the variation of development among five-year-olds and find lists of books that satisfy both less and more mature fives. You'll find out why fives need both books that help them over social "humps" and books whose sole purpose is entertainment and stimulation of literary appetite.

In *Books for Sixes and Sevens* we talk about the new role books begin to play in children's lives at this age: why it's more important than ever to continue to read aloud to kids of this age; what books to read to children and what books they can begin to read themselves; which books fit with the sixes and sevens dawning sense of history and why folktales hit the spot for this age group.

Books for Eights and Nines focuses on developing the reading habit. It tells you what you can expect in the way of reading from an eight-year-old and why it's important to make reading a pleasure, not a hassle in the family. It offers an extensive list of books that will encourage reading for pleasure among kids of eight and nine who have varying degrees of skill in reading; it also provides suggestions for family read-aloud time.

Books for Ten- to Twelve-Year-Olds tells how ten-year-olds are different from elevens and twelves and how their reading tastes reflect it. It tells how the first stirring of adolescence may affect reading and what to do about it. How does a parent handle a child's reading "unsuitable" books? What are the good books about sexuality, romance, death? Do kids this age really read teenage novels? What should you do if your child "turns off" on books? Lastly, we offer some hints about making a smooth transition from helping kids to choose books to letting them choose their own.

Each of the chapters in the main section has a list of ten books that we consider "must" reading for the age group. It also has a checklist of pointers for parents to remember.

The last section gives you information on where to find books and lists resources connected to books that will help you and your family get the most out of your reading.

How to Use this Book

There are several ways to use this book. You may want to start at the beginning and get the feel of it before you look into specific choices of books. Or you may want to zero right in on the section that tells you about children the age of your child. You'll find the information useful whether you attack it piecemeal or read it from cover to cover. We hope that at some time you check out all the chapters. And we do think that the *Sources and Resources* chapter is an important part of your reading, because knowing what books to get is only half the battle. We know how frustrating it is to try to find books and information about them if you aren't clued in to the sources.

You not only need to know where to get books, you also need to know how to help create the climate where the book idea takes root. In *Sources and Resources* you'll read about how schools, organizations, libraries, and parent groups help the book idea flourish.

SOME THINGS TO KEEP IN MIND

Since children of the same ages are more alike than unlike, we have chosen books that we believe are most likely to be right for most kids at a specific age. But developmental age groupings are only guidelines; they're not cast in concrete. That's why we suggest that you look at the chapter before and after your own child's age. You may find in these chapters books that are perfect for your child right now. Also, keep in mind that no child will like every book on a list. A child's personal choice is very valuable. And no one knows your child's taste the way you do.

Another thing: a few of the books we have listed here are out of print. That means they may be difficult to get in the bookstore. So why did we list them at all? Because they may be in your local library. And because we feel strongly that we don't want children to miss them. It has been our experience that good books surface and resurface. What's out of print this year may be back in print next year.

HOW WE MADE SELECTIONS

Selecting books for children is a delightful task. But it is also a formidable one, given the number of juvenile books published each year. When you are also trying to make a match between books and a child's developmental stages, it adds another dimension to the search.

Fortunately, we have had a lot of help from our friends. The books listed here represent an amalgam made up of the choices of colleagues, parents, librarians, literature associations and publications, awards groups, and, of course, the children themselves.

Bank Street is especially well qualified to produce a guide for parents, teachers, and librarians for choosing books for children. As an institution devoted to the learning of children and support of families, the College has always fostered quality literature for children. Bank Street maintains a Publications Group that devotes the major portion of its time to books for children and their parents. The founder of Bank Street College, Lucy Sprague Mitchell, wrote and published in 1921 the landmark book, *The Here and Now Story Book* (Dutton), that offered children for the first time contemporary stories with realistic modern dialogue. She established the Bank Street Writers Lab, a setting for professional children's writers to share work in progress. Not only has it flourished for fifty years now, it has produced along the way such writers as Margaret Wise Brown.

Currently the Publications Group publishes quarterly reviews of new children's books. Annually they present a book award—The Irma Simonton Black Award—to the author and illustrator of a book for young children judged best by a panel of adults along with over one hundred child judges. Bank Street hosts the annual East Coast Children's Literature Conference of the Society of Children's Book Writers (SCBW). The institution also hosts the Child Study Book Committee, which publishes an annual booklist of recommended books for children.

For starters we sent out a survey to several hundred children's librarians, asking them for a list of ten books in each age category that they would want no child to miss. We got fantastic support from this group. Many librarians not only answered our printed questionnaire but also added valuable comments and opinions that are reflected in our text whenever possible. Librarians who participated in the survey are listed in the acknowledgements.

We also drew heavily on the experience of our colleagues at Bank Street. We talked to the people who teach literature and the people who teach children. We spoke to child development experts and experts in the field of writing for and about children. We spoke to the folks in our own bookstore, to our parent group, and to the kids themselves.

We looked at what respected review sources thought of specific books. Among the sources we looked at were *Parent's Choice*, the Child Study Association list, *The New York Times Book*

Review, The Horn Book, School Library Journal, and the reviews, past and present, from our *Bank Street News.*

We were aware of awards, like Newbery, Caldecott, ALA Notable Book List, and our own Irma Simonton Black Award. But we didn't always include award winners. And many of the books we included are personal favorites or special books that have not had honors but deserve them.

We also devoted more time and space to nonfiction and concept books than many booklists do. It's our conviction that good books of nonfiction are literature too.

To sum up, we chose books that we thought meshed well with children's needs and interests at various developmental stages. But the books also had to be well written and well illustrated. And our final question to ourselves was always: *Do we like this book?* All the books we've listed here are books that are not only good for kids but also that we really like.

A LAST WORD

In helping a child to choose books, it's important to be flexible. If your child goes to the library and takes the same book for three visits, let her. If she stays with certain books through two or three stages, that may be a good sign, not a bad one. If he goes through a comic book phase, it's not the end of the world. And just because the kid down the street is purported to read a book a week doesn't mean that's the norm.

A recent survey by the Business Ad Industry Study Group of the American Booksellers Association took a look at American children's reading habits and released some interesting statistics. They revealed that:

1. The average child reads 21.6 books a year, but 33 percent of the kids read more than that.

2. Boys read as much as girls, but they confess to a penchant for comic books. With both sexes, the most popular books are mysteries.

3. The older the child, the fewer books read. Not a good sign.

4. Children who are read to as tots are more likely to join the heavy reader group, as are children who are read to past the age when they can read independently.

5. The important thing, the survey concludes, is to "create a buzz" for reading in children younger than nine, the age by which most people learn to read, or fail to learn.

And here's how children choose books:

- It looks like a book I'd like.
- I read one like it before.
- My friend told me it was good.
- My teacher (or librarian) told me about it.
- I read about it somewhere.

Remember that most books are selected by kids themselves. You can't, after a certain age, choose books for them. So don't hesitate to make *Choosing Books for Kids* available to any child who can read it. In a recent survey by the Book Industry Study Group of the American Booksellers Association, it was discovered that many of the books older children read, they choose themselves. And one of the ways they make selections is by reading about a book somewhere. This book can be one of their sources.

CHAPTER I

The Book Connection

PARENTS, CHILDREN, AND BOOKS

Do you remember the names of books you loved as a child? Think for a moment and the titles of old favorites will probably come to mind. Such memories confirm how meaningful and longlasting early book experiences remain. A visit to the children's section of the library or bookstore often can lead us on a sentimental journey. Finding an old favorite, we say, "Oh, I had that! I loved it! I've got to bring it home to Jenny!"

Before you rush home with that rediscovered treasure, stop and think for a moment. Do you remember when it was that you enjoyed that book? Were you four like Jenny? Or were you six or seven? Does it really matter?

We think it does.

For Jenny at five, a book like *The Story About Ping* absolutely "hits the spot." But at two this great book would have fallen on deaf ears, and its powerful message would be wasted.

At ten, Jenny will be ready for Judy Blume's *Are You There God?—It's Me, Margaret.* Eight would be too early for her to understand the heroine's preoccupation with her sexual development.

In making book choices, we're looking at specific children's books in the light of what we know about children's *development*.

We know that kids get the book idea gradually. A toddler begins by grasping the concept that the pictures in a book aren't the real thing, but that they represent something real. In other words, it's not an apple, but it looks like an apple. When you think about it from the point of view of a very young person, this is a remarkable step, to accept the abstraction that is on a flat piece of paper and to point to it when Mommy or Daddy asks, "Where is the apple?"

At the next stage, a youngster may begin to sit still for a simple story. But, in fact, the story content of a book may be secondary to the one-to-one coziness of storytime. A very young child can sit happily through a reading of the telephone Yellow Pages if she is ensconced on a loving parent's lap, and if the reading is done with enthusiasm. The true meaning of books is still hazy. The content of the pictures may be confused with reality. The three- or four-year-old who sees scary pictures in a book may insist that the book itself be locked in a closet "so the monsters won't be able to get out."

A Horse and A Hound A Goat and A Gander

ALICE AND MARTIN PROVENSEN

Sometime between three and five, stories take on another kind of significance. Kids begin to recognize specific characters in a story. What happens to Curious George or Peter Rabbit is remembered and called up at a time when the book isn't around and related to the child's activities in a meaningful way. Books now begin to be appreciated for the story as well as for the pictures or the sound of a familiar voice. A few kids may even have an idea that those marks under the pictures have some vague connection with what the storyteller is saying.

Sooner or later, usually around age five or six, kids take another great leap forward in their relationship to books. They begin to catch on to the fact that those squiggles and lines on a book page are meaningful, and that they stand for words.

Beginning readers need simple stories to read to themselves. They need lots of pictures to accompany a text and to help them along with their decoding. They can't manage a story that is dense with written material and also has a complicated plot line. They can, however, listen with great concentration to a story that is read to them. And they can talk about it. In other words, they can understand a lot more than they can read.

As their reading skills improve, youngsters can handle more content. They begin to look for "chapter books," books with a well-defined plot, good large type, and more subtle humor or point. They understand that there are many different kinds of books and many different purposes to reading.

Finally, as kids approach adolescence they become sensitive to style. They develop personal preferences and individual tastes. They can pick out their favorite books and authors based on some experience with reading. At this point they're ready to choose their own books.

This quick overview suggests only a small part of a child's typical growth and how it relates to books. But it gives some idea of the developmental perspective which is the core of this book. We think this developmental perspective is unique. It assumes that there are optimum times for a book and a child to get together, and that this timing is important for kids.

WHY BOOKS?

Before you start looking for specific titles, let's consider your reasons for bringing books and children together. For many parents the first and only reason is the hope that sharing books will help children become good readers and succeed in school. It's true, studies do show that kids who are read to have an easier time with learning to read. In other words, reading books is good for them. But that's a rather antiseptic and limited view of the value of books. A six-year-old's mother recently complained that she had tried to do everything right to get her child ready for reading. "I brought home books, taught her the alphabet," she said, "I really WORKED at it!" Nevertheless, the child's teacher reported that this six-year-old was having trouble with learning to read. Why? It may be that the child's reading problems began before she ever arrived in the classroom. Sharing books with children isn't something you have to turn into

WORK. Indeed, that approach can turn books into objects of dread.

What some parents and teachers often overlook are the built-in reading lessons found in almost any storybook. The fact that you take time from your busy day to read to yourself or to your children conveys a message that books are important to you. If children never see you reading, you can't expect them to develop much of a reading habit. Without any formal teaching you can feel confident that sharing well-chosen books can go a long way in expanding a child's language development and sense of story, both basic ingredients for becoming more than mechanical readers of words.

Sharing time with books is qualitatively different from the usual give and take between parent and child. Taking time to share books gives you and your child a real change of pace. Unlike the day-to-day business of brushing teeth, picking up toys, and making the bus, when you open a book, both of you can take off with Gorky, a frog who can fly; or share the grief of a pig called Wilbur when his friend Charlotte dies; or thrill to the danger when Rapunzel dares to let down her hair. Such moments put parent and child on common ground, an uncommon place where reader and listener are caught up in finding out what happens next.

Time is the great friend of reading and of books. It's also a commodity in short supply in many households. Nevertheless, small children need unhurried time to look at books, both with an adult and independently. First and second graders need time for independent reading that will reinforce their newly won skills. And older children need to be helped to make time in their busy schedules of music lessons, sports, and social engagements for leisure to curl up with a good book.

WHAT IS A BOOK TODAY?

A book is a book is a book no longer holds true. Not today when books talk, sing, pull-out, pop-up; come in every conceivable size and shape, from the traditional square and rectangular volumes to the three-foot-tall Richard Scarry word book or the bunny-shaped Cyndy Szekeres books. There are books that smell when you scratch them; there are books that respond to light wands; and there are computer-generated books that insert any child's name into the text as the central character of the story. Novelty has become almost the order of the day in infant-toddler books that are now tubbable, scrubbable, and huggable hybrids that may be more toy than book. The traditional teddy bear now comes replete with built-in tape-recorded stories and movable mouth.

With the advent of economical videotape, the book has gone electronic, with professional actors such as Meryl Streep and Jack Nicolson reading classic stories for children that are further enhanced by colorful visuals. Many older children are finding delight in the "choose your own ending" mystery and adventure books. And clever packagers are flooding the market with combinations of book and audiotape, book and videotape, books with related activity books and gameboards.

While it is doubtful that any of these novel approaches to the traditional book formats have elevated the quality of children's books, it is fair to say that they do offer many new opportunities to lure reluctant readers into the reading process. But we doubt that the friendly mechanical devices will ever replace the warm and loving lap and the hand-held book.

DEVELOPING AN APPETITE FOR READING

Instead of rushing your child to find words and letters on the page, build on the pleasures to be found in the rhythm and color of language, the thrill of suspense found in a well spun story. Pause to savor the small details of exquisite illustrations that extend what the words say. In your eagerness to turn the child into a reader, don't overlook the bigger idea that reading is a pleasurable form of entertainment.

If you really hope to engage your child with reading and books, remember that reading is not just a matter of mechanics. Studies show that only a small percentage of literate adults actually read books. Why is this? Can we blame it all on the seduction of television or computers? Maybe. But, then consider the fact that most novels dramatized on TV almost instantly become best-sellers. In a sense, the TV drama seems to be a new form of read-aloud that leads many adults back to the printed page. In part, that's what reading to children can do, too. It can ease them into the world of books with an expectation of pleasure.

DEVELOPING TASTE

Not every book you bring home is going to be a hit. When kids express their likes and dislikes about books, that's a positive sign. One of the things you want them to develop is their own taste and preferences. All adults aren't fond of the same kinds of books and neither are children. Some of us can't get enough "whodunits" while others can't get past page one. What parents and teachers can do is to offer children a rich variety of books.

Variety is a friend of reading. Hans Christian Andersen and Charles Dickens were close friends in life. It's fitting that they be side by side on the family bookshelf, along with Maurice Sendak, Dr. Seuss, Shel Silverstein, Judy Blume, Mark Twain, and E. B. White. The more diverse the authors, the better for the kids.

A mix of books can also develop taste in art. Some of the best art of today and of yesterday can be found in children's books. Sharing opinions about the pictures can "tune" the eye as well as the ear.

One picture may not be worth a thousand words, but it can certainly conjure up for us whole chunks of childhood. A book that you may have loved as a child can give instant replay of another time as soon as you pick it up and see the illustrations. And since you know how important the pictures were to you, it's safe to assume they will be equally important to your children.

What's good art for a children's book? First of all, it's art that is appropriate for the age to which the book is addressed and for the subject of the book. Unrecognizably abstract animals are hard for little kids to deal with. A book on color needs to have accurately reproduced colors. An *I Can Read* book should be designed so type and illustration are clearly demarcated. An older child's book needs illustrations that recognize his/her ability to appreciate more complexity in art. Illustrations should enhance the flow of a story, not overpower or underplay it. The art needs to do more than say again what the story says. It should *add* to the words, giving them another dimension.

The chances of finding outstanding artwork in today's children's books have never been better. Maurice Sendak, Chris van Allsburg, Margot Tomes, Tomie de Paola, Nancy Eckholm Burkett, Charles Mikolaycak, Tony Chen, and hundreds of other gifted artists working in the field have done much to raise the level of children's book illustration. The trick is to get a wedding of a good story with good pictures. Some books have a great story but the pictures don't support it. Other books have wonderful illustrations in the service of a weak or silly story.

The pictures that create a world using the writer's words as a take-off point are the books that children will pore over: books like *The Tale of Peter Rabbit, Higgledy Piggledy Pop, Gorky Rises,* Burkert's *Snow White* and *The Mysteries of Harris Burdick* all lead the reader in this way, down imagination's path.

CHOOSE BOOKS THAT YOU LIKE!

Remember, a child's book isn't read once and then put on the shelf, at least not a good one. Unlike the latest adult bestseller, children's books are read and reread, "again, please, again." With young children, who can't read to themselves, this is no small issue. If you don't like the book the first time through, imagine how it's going to be the twentieth time around. Besides, kids are quick to read you and your feelings. If you dislike a book, they'll sense it and your lack of enthusiasm. Don't worry about how many honors or medals the book may have won. If you don't like the way the book looks or what it's saying or how it's saying it, look for another book. Kids read us and our feelings long before they can read words.

BORROWING, BUYING, AND COLLECTING

Like everything else these days, keeping kids supplied with books can be a costly proposition. But there are alternatives to always buying. If you haven't developed the library habit, this is the time to have a look around the children's room of the nearest library. Don't be shy. If you don't find what you're looking for, ask for help. If there's a children's librarian available, get acquainted. The children's librarian can be a great resource person and can lead you to books, records, and films you might otherwise overlook. There may be special programs sponsored by the library, not just for preschoolers, but for older kids, too.

Get your child involved in choosing the books you're going to borrow. Take some clues from the kinds of books he's attracted to and check out some of his choices. Don't worry if your child chooses what you think is a dud. Just mix in some winners. A less than great book helps kids sharpen their taste and make comparisons. If they select a book that's too long and complex, there's no rule that you have to read it from cover to cover. Read or paraphrase parts of it, rather than squashing their interest.

In addition to borrowing books, all children should have some books that are their very own—to have and to hold. Young children don't need dozens of books. In fact, owning too many can diminish their "specialness"—just as an overloaded toy box can often diminish play.

Given the high price of most picture books you may want to build a paperback library of favorites. Many of the books in this volume are available in less costly paper editions. But, keep in mind that as lovely as many of these paper books are, some are quite dreary and washed out. Often they are printed on cheap paper and have little resemblance to the original work. If the story is particularly well loved, and the illustrations are first rate, it may be worth the difference to buy the book in hardcover. When children return again and again for a specific book at the library, that's probably a book that belongs on their personal bookshelf.

In our booklists that follow each chapter, we have in most cases listed the publisher of the hardcover version of the book. You can check with your bookstore or librarian about whether the book has a paperback edition. Incidentally, kids who are having trouble reading may be discouraged by the smaller print of some paperback editions. Check out the size and format before you order.

Schoolage kids have a natural inclination and need to collect things, including books. Lined up on the shelf, the books they've read are a source of pride—something they've invested a part of themselves in and enjoy revisiting or just looking at. While the library may remain a great place to visit, especially for school projects, the appetite for ownership is quite typical.

Older children enjoy the independence of selecting their own books in the library or bookstore. Book clubs in school and the wide availability of paperbacks make building up the "collection" possible without breaking the bank. If they seem stuck on selections, take a cue from their current interests. Don't worry about pushing the "classics." You can make suggestions, but if you want them to read, let them make the selections.

THE SPECIALNESS OF BOOKS

At almost any age, a book we've enjoyed becomes a kind of extension of ourselves. If a book has moved us, tickled us, informed us, or touched our imagination, owning that book means we can return to it and to the experience, whatever it was that moved us, again and again. Isn't that what sets a book apart from a ball game, a TV show, a party and most other entertainment? In an age when obsolescence and disposability are such commonly built-in components, the permanence of a good book makes it all the more unique. Compared to most toys we buy, books offer children more long-lasting and meaningful enjoyment. Indeed, in years to come if someone should ask, "Do you remember any of the books you enjoyed as a child?" many of the books you shared with that child are likely to be recalled with a special fondness. The lucky child may even have a select few volumes with well-thumbed pages to share with his or her own children.

CHAPTER II

Books for Babies

THE FIRST TEACHERS

Father comes in carrying his son, Billy, age three months. "Do you have any books for young babies?"

"Not that young." The bookstore clerk shakes his head. "Come back in a few months."

Helpful bystander smiles and touches the father's arm. "Right now, he doesn't need *book* books," she says. "But he does need the books in your head! With babies, communication is all."

Communication Is All

From the first moment, the first hour, the first day of birth, babies need to feel you—and to hear you. Luckily, such communication seems to come naturally to most parents.

Babies may come naked into the world, but they come equipped with senses ready to be stimulated into action. For the first few years they will learn best through the senses, and they begin learning from birth.

. . .

Learning Through the Senses

Fortunately most parents also begin teaching through the senses from the first day. They hold, rock, and stroke the newcomer; they sing and babble lovingly to their new child, "What great booful big blue eyes! And nice flat ears, just like Daddy's! Blow, blow your fuzzy hair, will it blow away like dandelion fluff? Piggy wig, piggy wig, will you grow to be sooo big?"

As parents bend to or hold the baby close, crooning this type of monologue that may make bystanders cringe, they are performing some basic functions: they are using an important sensory approach through bodily touch (hugging); visual contact (eye-to-eye); the sounds of the human language; and an ineffable expression of love.

So from the first the baby is not only hearing fond words, but hearing the rhythm and inflections of language, emotional tone, and even a small story jingle: "Piggy-wig, piggy-wig, will you grow to be sooo big?"

Not much of a poem, but an important beginning, for babies are unique among mammals in that they need to *learn* human language. Kittens will mew, puppies will bark even if they never hear cats or dogs vocalize. But humans only learn human language by hearing it, only learn to speak by being spoken to. So a year of hearing human talk as much as possible is really a very short period for being initiated into the intricacies of our language.

We don't know exactly what the result is on the baby, but we do know that loving and talking are basic to baby's best development—without it, baby may not even survive. It has been discovered that some institutionalized infants whose bodily needs were adquately met, but who were otherwise left immobile in their cribs, without being lovingly held, played with, or talked to, died.

Beginning the Dance

We know that even the newest baby can fixate on our face as we feed her, can hear our voice and its rhythms. Babies only a few weeks old respond with bodily movements to the rhythms of our speech and songs. They are communicating back to us by the only means they have—moving, watching, smiling, responding. A kind of dance is born, with two partners—parent and baby.

The baby invites parental response with movements of her whole body as well as her face: the parent-partner accepts with coos, murmurings, bubbling speech, song, and bodily movements, too—cradling, rocking, and bouncing the baby. If the adult response is too strong or too prolonged, the baby slows the pace by turning her head away, frowning, even closing her eyes. Almost instinctively, the parent lowers his speech, gentles his handling of the baby, as he follows the baby's lead. And this marvelous "two-step" is carried out without either partner being completely aware of the interaction.

The Books in Your Head

Parents seem to come already equipped with "books in their heads"—stories, poems, jingles gathered from their own past experiences, or from the common culture.

Now is the time to reconnect with the world of *Mother Goose* and other traditional verses, to imprint on the baby their lilting prose, their felicitous turns of phrase, their contagious rhythms, and the joy of spoken poetry. Not only will baby benefit from hearing these enchanted words, but the parent too will delight in rediscovering some of the magical moments of early childhood.

And while you're reconnecting, by all means dip into the wealth of finger, toe, and body word games. A parent needn't feel silly if caught tweaking baby's toes while chanting,

"This little piggy went to market,
This little piggy stayed home.
This little piggy had roast beef,
And this little piggy had none.
And this little piggy cried,
'Weeeeee!' all the way home."

because this is the right time to do so. You, the parent, are engaged in a necessary and legitimate educational activity (and isn't it fun?). These little gems from our literary heritage have an advantage beyond the imprinting of lovely language—they're interactive as well. The baby as an object of finger and toe games becomes an active partner in the word play.

An Intercom System

Not only is Baby learning through this hear-and-feel sensory system, but another basic aspect of human communication is being reinforced—the baby is not a totally passive partner. As in the parent-child dance response, the baby is drawn into the process: though she has little control yet of her body movements, her partner helps her make them. She physically can contribute to the partnership.

Perhaps it will be a more passive part, as when Grandpa will chant:

Hickory dickory dock The mouse ran up the clock.	Grandpa runs his fingers up baby's tummy.
The clock struck one and down he ran. Hickory dickory dock!	Grandpa taps one tap on baby's chin, then his fingers scramble down baby's chest.

Baby pumps his arms and legs in response as Grandpa talks, just as he does when Grandma uses each of baby's hands to illustrate "Pat-a-Cake." But here Grandma is helping to further his participation.

Pat-a-cake, pat-a-cake Baker's man. Bake me a cake as quick as you can.	Grandma pats baby's hands together.
Roll it and pat it and mark it With a T [or Baby's initial],	Grandma rolls baby's hands in a circle, pulls them far apart.
And put it in the oven For Baby and Me.	Then she claps baby's hands first against baby's, then her own cheeks.

As Papa hums or sings,

Rockabye, Baby, on the tree-top,
When the wind blows, the cradle will rock.
When the bough breaks, the cradle will fall,
And down will come Baby, cradle and all,

he will rock baby back and forth. If Papa becomes aware of the words of this classic ditty, he may reject it, deciding the author was a trifle sadistic, and substitute his own made-up song, such as a take-off on "Goodnight, Ladies":

Goodnight, Baby.
Bye-bye, Baby.
Goodnight, Baby,
It's time to go to sleep.

Somehow chanting, finger-play, and babies go together. Perhaps we've always known that. In Mother Goose and company, the rhythms, cadences, and inflections of human language are more vividly exaggerated and stand a greater chance of being imprinted on receptive minds. As babies themselves begin to babble, they play with all kinds of sounds. This is why the playful sounds and repetitions in nursery rhymes have such strong appeal.

Rock-a-Bye Baby

Singing to your baby is also an age-old habit. All parents are singing stars to babies. So don't let your inability to carry a tune deter you—Baby couldn't care less.

Lullabies, of course, are perhaps the most popular of baby's songs. You can hum "Brahm's Lullabye" or, like Papa, croon "Rockabye Baby," or Mom's favorite, "Sleep, Baby, Sleep." But Baby equally welcomes a made-up lullabye or a rock favorite; the important ingredient is the sound of soothing love.

Babies also react in a more lively way to jazzier music during their "up times." As Mom dresses baby, she may sing and help Baby enact the "Puffer-Billy Song":

Down by the station early in the morning	Clapping baby's hands together
see the little puffer-billies all in a row.	Moving baby's hands across the air
See the little driver pull the little handle.	Have baby's hands make pulling mo- tions
Toot-toot, puff-puff, off they go!	Move hands far apart

Or when Baby's going outside with Dad, Dad may bellow forth his adaptation of "The Farmer in the Dell":

Down the steps we go!
Down the steps we go!
Heigh-ho! The derrie oh!
Down the steps we go!

Now, down the street we go!
Down the street we go!
Heigh-ho! The derrie oh!
Down the street we go!

Or Aunt Kate just sings a tuneless—but not wordless—monotone as she pushes Baby in his stroller:

William and Aunty go along
and *along* and along the street
'til we get to the curb.
No cars on the left, no cars on the right.
Pop! Down the curb, cross the street, up a curb.
Here we go again, along and along and along!

Traditional songs, little steam engines, big caissons, or Aunt Kate's monotones—Baby doesn't care. What is important is the feeling of being loved, of sharing. A baby equally welcomes a discourse on the stock market or the Cub's pennant chances as Father diapers him. He gazes intently at Mother as she vocalizes on his dressing experience: "Okay, honey, here comes your shirt. Sorry, we've got to stuff one arm through this hole, and that arm through that sleeve. Flap, flap, Henry's a little bird! Now comes your nightie—a nightie for a sweetie to keep him warm."

Henry may not know what Mom or Dad is saying. But he hears words from the people closest to him—and words are what he needs to hear from the day of his birth.

As Betsy Hearne, an experienced children's book reviewer, says, "The sights and sounds surrounding a very young child may not be understood, but they will make an impression." And another child expert, Nancy Larrick, is even firmer on the subject of communication with babies: "Few adults seem to realize that a baby's experience with language in the first months and years will strongly affect his or her skill in speaking, listening, reading, and writing in school."

So go ahead—enjoy your baby! Laugh with, hug and kiss her, and talk—talk, talk! Then you'll earn the highest rating as Baby's First Teacher, using "the books in your head."

An Important Transition

Sooner or later, your baby will sit up. Somewhere around the middle of the first year, Baby will be able to sit upright with or without props. Now for short periods she will enjoy sitting in your lap or in her crib and examining objects with you.

Books will be among those objects. Her first response to books probably will be the same as to other interesting items: to touch, to manipulate, to taste. She will look at the book, turn it around, pull at it, tear it, and try to eat the pages—a totally sensory approach!

Booklist for Babies

Cloth Books

Cloth books were invented because of the young baby's physical responses: they are difficult to pull apart or to tear. While they may be tasted, they can't be shredded. They are simple books.

The pictures and colors don't reproduce as well as on paper and the subject matter is limited. But since the baby is using the cloth book more as a physical plaything than as a source for naming and knowing, it adequately serves its purpose.

Make sure all cloth books are soft, nontoxic, and washable. For starters, here are a few examples:

Baby's First Cloth Book by George Ford. Random House, 1979. Bright clear pictures of things in baby's world.

Baby Talk: A Pillow Pal Book. Platt & Munk, 1982. A soft pillow book that opens to one long panorama featuring baby at play.

Baby's Mother Goose, illustrated by Alice Schlesinger. Platt & Munk, 1959. A pretty little cloth book with a few old favorite rhymes you'll be chanting to baby.

Hush Little Baby: A Peggy Cloth Book. Platt & Munk, 1982. A book for the youngest independent looker. Noisemakers built in for extra sensory appeal. Also *Baby's Mother Goose, It's Fun to Wash,* and *Pat-A-Cake.*

Kitten's Animal Friends by Carolyn Bracken. Random House, 1985. This is a combination cuddle toy and cloth book. Baby will enjoy clutching the soft kitten while the parent reads the simple story.

Little Rabbit's Garden by J. P. Miller. Random House, 1985. Part doll, part book, this is one of a series of soft dolls with little cloth paged book attached. The mechanical act of turning pages has appeal, as does the soft doll. Also *Teddy's Best Toys.*

The Me Book by John E. Johnson. Random House, 1979. A cloth book that names the parts of the body.

Spot's Toys by Eric Hill. Putnam, 1984. A soft, safe nontoxic tubbable book with the popular dog Spot pictured with his toys on every vinyl page. Also: *Sweet Dreams, Spot.*

To Name Is to Know

While still in the "search and destroy" stage, Baby often begins to notice some of the pictures, especially those that relate to exciting objects in the real world. If he is interested in dogs, he may bend over pictures crying, "Daw! Daw!" He may be looking at collies, dalmatians, sheep, or mountain goats—all four-footed animals are "dogs" to him in this initial stage of categorizing.

Old magazines fit well into this stage of teetering between tearing-and-eating and naming-and-knowing.

In this scene, Mother with Baby in her lap is leafing through an old department store catalog. Mother points out pictures Baby might recognize, commenting on the people or animals in them.

MOTHER: Look, Lovey, here's a man with a dog—just like Daddy and Tippy. Here's a kitty, too—see the little kitty drinking her milk? And here's a crib just like Lovey's crib. See Lovey's crib?"

LOVEY (tearing the page and trying to stuff it in her mouth): Gaaa, mah, dah.

Obviously Lovey is still regarding magazines and books as disposable toys. But sooner or later a magical transformation occurs. Lovey takes a giant step forward in comprehension—she sees the flat depiction of a subject on a page as representing a familiar three-dimensional object in the real world, a feat accomplished by no other creature as far as we know, with the possible exception of some members of the ape family. All children take this tremendous step, sooner or later. At first, they may recognize a picture on a block or other toy. Then they begin pointing out known objects on a printed page.

At a later date, Lovey and her mother are again looking at a cloth book.

MOTHER: What's this, Lovey? A cat? See the gray and white cat drinking milk?

LOVEY: (says nothing, but laughs)

MOTHER: And here's a man and a baby. Is that a daddy and a baby? Is he singing to his baby?

LOVEY (stabs hand toward picture): Dah—wah.

MOTHER (transported with joy): Yes, yes, Lovey! That's Dah! That's a daddy!

Lovey may have meant *Daddy,* but probably not. Mother starts reinforcing the beginning of the name-and-you-know process by emphasizing a picture and a name. Of course, Lovey may get the idea that all men are called Dah, but chances are she is still unaware of specific labels for specific people. However, she does recognize that her vocalizations excite and delight, and is thus encouraged to keep on vocalizing.

MOTHER: Hey, Dan! Come here. Lovey said "Dah" for "Daddy"! She knows you!

Daddy and Grandma enter the scene. Mother touches Dan and says, "Dah, Lovey. Here's Dah! Say Dah, Lovey."
Lovey bounces up and down and babbles energetically, "Abba, babba, mah, dah."

FATHER: Listen to her! Lovey said Mother, too! She called *Mah!*

Even though Lovey is still unaware that her babbling means something specific to her family, she soon begins to understand that specific sounds stand for specific objects.

Supporting this kind of dialogue with object books provides invaluable opportunities for the youngest child to start naming and knowing his world. Now is the time to use the best of the little hardcover books, called *board books.* Their small size, often resembling a block, are easy for Baby to hold by himself. Most are firmly stitched or glued, making them difficult for Baby to dismember. Most also have clear bright pictures, easier to identify than pictures in the cloth books. The main purpose of the board book is to show and label objects and people in the baby's environment. Good board books are an introduction to the child's lifelong process of naming and knowing.

Unfortunately, many of them are extremely cutesy; that is, they portray exaggerated, simpering, dressed-up animals in unlikely situations. Perhaps the editors feel that Great-Aunt Harriet or gruff old Grandpa George will squeal (or gruff) with delight on viewing these cloying creations. "How perfectly adorable (or charming). I just know Baby Harriet (or Baby George) will love these dear (quaint) little animals!"

The editors are often right, for unfortunately, some grandpas or great-aunts have forgotten that babies can't identify what they've never seen. How many babies are familiar with talking rabbits, let alone dressed in overalls, pushing a doll carriage? The objects in a baby's world, clearly and realistically delineated, are the ideal subjects for Baby's first books, and fortunately, there are some available.

Board Books

Baby's First Words. Photographs by Lars Wik. Random House, 1985. Part of the *Chunky Book Series,* this small cardboard book of photos features familiar clothes, objects, and actions in the child's world. Should fit baby's hands and interests just right.

Kitty's Outdoor Day. Golden, 1983. This board book is about three inches by four inches in size, with fairly thin paper pages, making it light and easy for Baby to hold. Photographs of a kitten in action are clearly recognizable: the cat is *not* dressed in human clothes but engaged in kittenish pursuits. There is a sketchy text, appropriate to a toddler's interests. If your baby is not familiar with cats, there are Golden Books about other pets in this series.

My Toys by Dick Bruna. Methuen, 1980. A board book that folds out to reveal lots of familiar toys that even the youngest child can recognize. There are many books in the Bruna Book Series, but choose carefully the simpler ones for Baby. Reserve the others for later on.

Playing by Helen Oxenbury. Simon & Schuster, 1981. Uncluttered pictures of baby with blocks, wagon, playing a pot drum, in a box, reading a book, and playing with a ball and Teddy Bear. Also: *Dressing.*

The Pudgy Books: The Pudgy Bunny Book and *The Pudgy Book of Make Believe.* Grosset & Dunlap, 1984. Good-sized books, but choose those that have the simplest illustrations. The *Make Believe* Pudgy Book, contrary to its title, is not about fantasy, but portrays real children in dramatic play.

Strawberry Block Books: The Zoo, Baby Animals, and *Wheels.* Macmillan, 1984. Again, the above in the series seem to be best suited to a baby's experiences. However, you may find others that fit your child's particular interest.

This Little Pig Went to Market illustrated by Denise Fleming. Random House, 1985. An old favorite rhyme done up in a little board book with baby-size tabs for easy turning.

Tiny Board Books: Come Out and Play and *My Animal Friends.* Grosset & Dunlap, 1981. Among the *Tiny Board Books* the above have pictures that have the best chance of being recognized by babies. Others such as *Fairyland* and *Mother Goose,* whose charming illustrations won't be identified by Baby, might please older preschoolers.

What Do Babies Do? Photos selected by Debby Slier. Random House, 1985. Part of a series of cardboard books featuring photos of real live babies doing just what babies do—sleeping, eating, looking in a mirror, and more. Just right!

What Is It? by Tana Hoban. Greenwillow, 1983. Handsome photos of familiar objects baby will recognize.

Mother Goose Nursery Rhymes

Brian Wildsmith's Mother Goose. Oxford University Press, 1982. A modern illustrator's beautiful edition of favorite rhymes.

Mother Goose by Gyo Fujikama. Platt & Munk, 1981. A popular artist fills this big book with his typical happy children.

Mother Goose: A Collection of Classic Nursery Rhymes by Michael Hague. Holt, 1984. Full color illustrations that will charm the young viewer as much as will the delightful sounds of the Mother Goose rhymes.

The Mother Goose Book by Alice and Martin Provensen. Random House, 1976. A good selection illustrated by two of today's finest artists, with well-chosen rhymes.

Mother Goose Treasury by Raymond Briggs. Coward-McCann, 1980. A noted contemporary artist's vision of the familiar verses.

Rock-a-Bye Baby: Nursery Songs and Cradle Games by Eloise Wilkin. Random House, 1981. An enduring and endearing artist illustrates these traditional poems with a cozy touch of the past.

The Tall Book of Mother Goose by Feodor Rojankovsky. Harper & Row, 1942. Reprinted. This is a fine book for lap-looking. The tall rectangular shape allows room for wiggly babies between parental arms: the details of the large clear pain-

tings on each page can be studied by young eyes. The depicted
children are engagingly realistic, yet tinged with an old-fashioned look. This Mother Goose
will be loved for years, as children grow in their appreciation
of art and verse.

Tomie de Paola's Mother Goose illustrated by Tomie de Paola. Putnam, 1985. A comprehensive
edition of over two hundred
favorite and familiar Mother
Goose rhymes, done in Mr. de Paola's exuberant and humorous art style.

Lullabies and Other Song Books

American Folk Songs for Children by Ruth Crawford Seeger; illustrated by Barbara Cooney. Zephyr Books, 1980. One of the
most popular of the folk collections, for now and later on.

· *The Baby's Bedtime Book* by Kay Chorao. Dutton, 1984. A fine
collection of songs and poems about naptime and sleep-
time, garnered from around the world. Beautifully illustrated. Also see *The Baby's Lap Book*.

Babies' Lullabies. Grosset & Dunlap, 1983. A short, inexpensive
collection, with music.

The Fireside Book of Folk Songs by Margaret Boni and Norman
Lloyd. Simon & Schuster, reprint from 1966. A new edition
of a classic book of all kinds of favorite folk songs, brilliantly
illustrated. Also: *Fireside Book of Children's Songs* by Marie
Winn and Allan Miller. Simon and Schuster, 1966. *Fireside
Book of Favorite American Songs* by Margaret Boni and Norman Lloyd. Simon & Schuster, 1973. And *Fireside Book of Fun
and Game Songs* edited by Marie Winn. Simon and Schuster,
1974.

The Funny Songbook by Esther L. Nelson. Sterling, 1984. A jolly
book of nonsense songs easy enough for beginners on
piano or guitar. Apropos to baby's livelier moments and will
be appreciated, too, by the growing child.

Music for Ones and Twos: Songs and Games for the Very Young by Tom
Glazer; drawings by Karen Ann Weinhaus. Doubleday,
1956. Perhaps the most delightful song-and-game book for
the very young. If you can get hold of it, rejoice! Keep an
eye out for any of Glazer's other books and records, too—
he is a long-time children's favorite.

Singing Bee! A Collection of Favorite Children's Songs compiled by
Jane Hart; pictures by Anita Lobel. Lothrop, Lee and Shepard, 1982. In this delightful book, the first ten or so pages
are lullabies, old and new; the next seven are finger-play
songs. The rest of this collection of 125 songs includes
Mother Goose rhymes, traditional English and American
favorites, rounds, and game songs. Guitar chords are included as well as new and easy piano arrangements. Parents
will find the introductory songs helpful for quieting and
soothing baby as well as helping her to sleep. Other songs
will fit baby's livelier moods and help parents gain confidence in communicating with their child.

Songs to Grow On by Beatrice Landeck; piano settings by Florence
White; illustrated by David Stone Martin. William Sloan
Associates, Inc., 1950. An enduring favorite; this is a fine
book for the very young.

Songs to Sing to Babies. Miss Jackie Music Company, 1983. A
gentle group of original songs that may please caregivers
seeking the unusual. Distributed by Gryphon House, P.O.
Box 211, 2706 Otis Street, Mt. Ranier, MD 20822.

Finger Games

Eye Winker, Tom Tinker, Chin Chopper: 50 Musical Fingerplays by
Tom Glazer. Zephyr, 1973. The best of the finger-play
books, this collection of old favorites and new games is easy
to learn and fun to do. Parents can involve their baby in
many of the games by moving baby's limbs and fingers,
reinforcing what baby hears by what baby does.

Finger Plays by Emilie Poulsson. Hart, 1977 reprint of early edition. This charming reprint is a reminder of our forebears'
babies' games. Whether you will copy them or be inspired
to create new ones is your decision.

Finger Rhymes by Marc Brown. Dutton, 1980. Lots of ways for amusing little ones. Bouncy, prancing words to delight the smallest ears. Also see *Hand Rhymes*.

Finger, Toe and Tummy Games: Finger Plays for Nursery and Kindergarten by Emilie Poulsson. Dover, 1971 reprint of the 1893 edition. These delightful interactive games will please babies today as much as they did almost a century ago. Like the Mother Goose rhymes they retain their magical appeal.

BABY'S BOOKSHELF

Your baby's own bookshelf should include some cloth and board books, as well as a good volume of Mother Goose nursery rhymes and a song and game book as a resource for you to use with Baby.

Baby's First Words by Lars Wik
Baby's Mother Goose published by Platt and Munk
Eye Winker, Tom Tinker, Chin Chopper: 50 Musical Fingerplays by Tom Glazer
The Me Book by John E. Johnson
Mother Goose book (illustrator is matter of personal preference —happy looking!)
Singing Bee! A Collection of Favorite Children's Songs compiled by Jane Hart; illustrated by Anita Lobel
What Is It? by Tana Hoban
    Lots of well-illustrated magazines for baby to explore and destroy

CHAPTER III

Books for Toddlers

FROM THE TODDLER'S POINT OF VIEW

Up on two feet and on the go, the toddler has a new and expanded view of the world. With newfound mobility your get-about child is no longer totally dependent on others to move from place to place. From the toddler's point of view, steps are there to be climbed, doors are there to be opened, drawers are there to be emptied. Suddenly everything that was formerly seen from afar must be turned, tasted, thumped, and thoroughly tested at first hand.

With this whirlwind of a high-energy, all-action child, is there really any interest in something as quiet as a book? Sometimes yes, sometimes no. It really depends on when, and what you offer up as reading material.

Psychologists often refer to this period as a "little adolescence," a transition stage between infancy and childhood, just as adolescence marks that in-between state between childhood and adulthood. Like teenagers, toddlers tend at times to be stormy, argumentative, and even exasperating. Although teenagers may be ready for a larger share of independence, the toddler is a long way from being able to care for himself or make many decisions—and he doesn't want to. Indeed, part of the toddler's storminess grows out of not being able to make people and things—including books—do as he commands.

Toddlers' extensive use of "no" or "mine" often has more to do with the child's limited speech than with totally negative attitudes. You and I may see a familiar face and be annoyed that we've forgotten the name that goes with that face. But consider how frustrating it would be if we found ourselves repeatedly at a loss for words.

What They Are Ready For

If you're hoping to settle in for a half hour of sit-down time with *Alice in Wonderland* or *The Wizard of Oz*—don't count on it. Hold on to these wonderful books. Their time will come. Toddlers aren't ready for long wordy stories of "Once upon a time . . ." or "Long, long ago . . ." Here and now is where the action is for young children who are just sorting out what's real and not real. They may believe that their teddy bear or the one in their picture book thinks, feels, and reacts just as they do. The line between reality and fantasy just isn't there yet. Save the flights-of-fancy books for a few years.

Much as you may long for a sit-down quiet time, ten or fifteen minutes will probably be the limit. Toddlers are notoriously changeable. Sometimes they'll bring you a book, listen for two minutes, and then take off. The truth is, bringing you a book may be more by way of making contact with you than a genuine interest in the book's content. Other times they'll snuggle up and demand instant replays—"Read it again."

While books are often part of the bedtime ritual, the end of the day is by no means the only time for stories. Nursery rhymes from the top of your head can punctuate climbing up stairs, dressing, or "rub-a-dub-dub and into the tub." Toddlers most especially love little stories about themselves and what they're doing as they're doing it. Sort of a "play-by-play" commentary throughout the day that features their favorite character—"me."

Until recently there were few books made especially for toddlers. Today bookstores are loaded with cardboard, cloth, and plastic books. While many are solid fare for little hands, many are written and illustrated with no understanding of the audience they're aimed for. At first glance these books may look alike. But remember, you can't judge a book by its cover. Too many are put together with no thought to content.

Reading material for toddlers should include books and magazines with large, clear, realistic pictures. Steer clear of illustrations that may be graphically gorgeous for a poster but much too abstract for a child to "read" visually. Avoid wishy-washy impressionistic illustrations that require an experienced eye to interpret. Cluttered pages with lots of action may be too busy for young toddlers.

Read through the text and ask yourself, "Does it make sense?" You don't need a lot of plot—in fact, many books without plots are perfect "talking" tools for getting a handle on the names of objects. But even plotless books should have logic. Objects should be sorted into meaningful categories. A story may hang on a thin thread—but the thread should be there. Take the time to read the text and consider what the book really says.

Thanks to the durable materials available for books, toddlers can get their hands on a variety of "print materials." Some might even be classed more as toys than as books. One toddler's mom was appalled by the idea of a bath book that could survive a tubbing. "Is that an idea I want to convey?" she asked. "I mean, how will my daughter know which books float and which ones can't?" She has a real point there. Of course, there have always been books that qualify more as toys than as literature. Books that turn into doll houses, costumes, murals, and puppet stages. Even books that smell! Like most novelties, such non-books tend to lose their fascination quickly, but are probably harmless—especially if there are plenty of really good books available. Drawing the line at the bathtub makes sense for toddlers. While we recommended some tub books for babies, toddlers may have a difficult time differentiating which books are tubbable and which are not.

Among the newest book-as-toy creations are musical books that automatically play a tune as the pages are turned. Turning these little books off is sometimes a problem and their novelty may wear thin before long. Perhaps more interesting and interactive are the *Music Box and Book Series* (Random House) that has a music box crank to turn along with text and illustrated pages of four sing-along favorites: *Happy Birthday, Jingle Bells, Old MacDonald,* and *Rock-a-Bye Baby.*

As a general rule the subject matter of toddler books should center on the child's own familiar world. No child needs all of the books listed at the end of this chapter for Bedtime, Naming and Knowing, Little Mysteries, Getting in Touch or How-To-Manuals. Pick and choose a good mix from each category and you'll have a rich diet of books.

A note about series: While we've included several books from popular series, it's important to note that every title in a series is not necessarily age-appropriate or valuable. Of course, publishers print series with the expectation that if you like one, you'll buy others. Look at each book and evaluate it on its own strengths and weaknesses. We couldn't include every book in each series we like, but, conversely, we're not listing books we think inappropriate, either. Knowing the child you're buying the book for, his interests, likes, and dislikes, should help you make the best choices among series and other books.

How They Use Books

What you choose may be less important than how you use it. Toddlers love the physical action of page-turning that makes things happen and new images appear. Two-year-old Rorie loves mail-order catalogues. Sitting on his grandma's lap he points to pictures, saying "mine," "me." Young Rorie is asserting his growing sense of himself as a separate and independent person. Now's the  time to cue into that "me" and "mine" by clearing a shelf for solo browsing. Put magazines, catalogues, and books intended for handling in easy reach. There may be some books you'll want to share but not leave on this shelf, such as the beautifully illustrated copy of *Very Hungry Caterpillar* that Grandma gave Rorie for Christmas. It takes time for inexperienced little hands to learn how to turn pages without ripping them. Let them practice with magazines instead of a treasured book. At this stage the book is one of many playthings toddlers want to explore. As with all their playthings, toddlers are fond of carrying their possessions from place to place. It's not really a matter of thoughtlessness or carelessness on the child's part that books get bent, torn, or tattered. Expect it. Toddlers really can't predict the outcome of their actions, so they are likely to sit or stand on a book or tear the pages quite by accident. Rather than making a big issue of it, better to separate books that can take it from those that can't.

With young toddlers, rather than fueling confrontation over ripped books, bring them out for sharing time and put special but delicate ones out of sight (and mind) for in-between times. At the same time, provide sturdy board books for independent reading. Of course, older toddlers do learn about caring for books while you're reading to them. You can give them a turn at turning the page "gently." Almost inevitably there will be "accidents" or "mistakes" with sticky hands, crayons, and rips. These are unavoidable "learning" experiences. Talk about what happened by all means but don't turn it into a major catastrophe.

Naming the World

Increasingly, the toddler's day is punctuated with words instead of grunts, screeches, and gestures. While young toddlers may have only a few words, the gradual development of speech brings with it a new kind of power. Now the toddler is actively learning to name the world of things and people. "Dis" and "dat" and the pointing finger are replaced by "ball" or "book." In fact, knowing words and being able to apply them to pictures in books gives the child power to call up an object not in sight, to give a representation of an object name.

In the doctor's waiting room, after seeing cookies in a magazine, two-year-old Rosa tried to open her mother's pocketbook, saying, "Cookie." When Mother opened her bag and said, "No cookies here today," Rosa went to another woman's pocketbook and said, "Cookie?" After checking every pocketbook, Rosa sat down and thought a bit. "Cookie in kitchen," she said.

Rosa's story gives us a transparent view of a young child's

thinking process at work. If cookies are usually found in mother's pocketbook, why not cookies in other pocketbooks? Using just one word has enabled her to clarify a small piece of information. Indeed, although Rosa knew what a cookie was before she could say "cookie," the ability to use the word facilitates a giant leap in saying what she likes and dislikes, wants and doesn't want. No wonder, then, that toddlers find books with objects to name fascinating reading. While your idea of a good book may be a plot with a beginning, middle, and end, toddlers have different needs. Just two, Rory simply can't sit still for wordy storybooks or far-flung fantasy. For two-year-old Rory the real world of people and things holds more than enough magic and mystery. "Object" books that mirror the child's own here-and-now world of home and family are just the right size "stories" for young listeners.

TODDLERS' BOOKLIST

Name and Know Books

Early Words by Richard Scarry. Random House, 1976. For the young toddler a book like *Early Words* is a good match on several levels. Printed on cardboard pages, this sturdy book can take rigorous and repeated use. It's a book you can share together and yet feel comfortable about leaving in easy reach for solo time.

Essentially, there's no plot here. Each double-page spread follows Frannie the bunny through the day—from waking up to washing, dressing, eating, playing, and bedtime. This sequence of events is told by the pictures. For the naming and knowing toddler, the fun comes in naming and finding all the clearly illustrated objects in Frannie's bedroom, bathroom, kitchen, and back yard.

Unlike many of Richard Scarry's wonderful books for older children with busy pages full of characters and objects, this one is clearly for a young child. Objects that are related to each other are together on one page, but there is plenty of space around them and less clutter, so objects are easily recognizable and nameable.

Using the book together you can play little games of "Where's the cup?" or "Can you find Bunny's toothbrush?" As the toddler's language grows, change the game to "What's that?" or "What do you wear on your head?"

Babies by Gyo Fujikawa. Grosset & Dunlap, 1963. A cardboard book showing babies being washed and changed, eating, laughing, crying—just as babies do.

Baby Animals, photos by Gerry Swart. Golden, 1978. Bright pictures for toddlers who may know some zoo animals.

Baby Strawberry Book of Cars, Trucks, Trains, and Planes, illustrated by Lawrence Di Fiori. McGraw-Hill. Not to be confused with the Strawberry Shortcake licensed character. Nothing "sweet" here—just a sturdy cardboard book with almost no text, but lively double-page spreads showing various forms of transportation. A good source for the get-about child who seems to have a natural affinity for things that go.

Baby's Things. Platt & Munk, 1978. A clean, clear board book of photos of things familiar and not so familiar. In spite of its title, this one is better for toddlers who can recognize objects, such as scissors and yarn.

Blue Hat, Green Hat by Sandra Boynton. Simon & Schuster, 1984. An amusing little book tots will love "reading" with you while learning their colors, too.

Busy Houses by Richard Scarry. Golden, 1981. A cardboard book with busy animals doing everyday household jobs.

Color Book by Richard Scarry. Random House, 1976. Mr. Paint Pig colors the zany world á la Scarry, one color to a page.

Harriet at Play by Betsy and Giulo Maestro. Crown, 1984. A board book featuring that busy little elephant Harriet. Part of a series that goes a step beyond "naming the world" by embedding familiar objects in a simple story line. Also *Harriet at Work* and *Harriet at School.*

I Spy with My Little Eye by Lucille Ogle and Tina Thoburn. American Heritage, 1971, and *I Hear,* American Heritage, 1970. These are classic "naming" books full of small but clear objects in the child's world. The older toddler will love to play the "I Spy" game. You give a clue about an object: "I spy something round and red and bouncy." Then the child points to the object—a ball.

My First Book of Things by John E. Johnson. Random House, 1979. A sturdy cardboard book with objects classified under Things to Eat, Wear, Play With, etc.

This Is Me by Lenore Blegvad, illustrated by Erik Blegvad. Random House, 1986. Charming illustrations coupled with a minimal story in rhythmic verse make this little chunky book a perfect fit for toddlers learning to name familiar things.

Trucks by Harry McNaught. Random House, 1976. A totally wordless cardboard book of trucks—just one to a fold—with enough other things happening to make it interesting.

Trucks illustrated by Art Seiden. Platt & Munk, 1985. Wonderfully uncluttered pictures of vehicles for young transportation enthusiasts. More for looking than reading.

Words to Grow On by Harry McNaught. Random House, 1982. There are many details on every page in this "naming" book with objects that go together on large double-page spreads. Handsome, clear illustrations.

Familiar Events

Slightly older toddlers are ready for a little more story than naming books provide. They can relate to small plots that trace familiar events. Most of these books are of sturdy cardboard for safe keeping and independent "reading."

Remember, they understand a great deal more than they can say in words. Don't underestimate the pleasure (and learning) they gain from the sound and rhythm of words and the snug satisfaction of a warm lap and relaxing time together.

I Can Do It by Myself illustrated by June Goldsborough. Golden, 1981. This book plugs right into the toddler's deep-felt desire for independence. For the "me do it" set, this book follows a small child through a typical day picturing all the little things he or she can do. Indeed, this technique of reciting daily events can be used to personalize the toddler's own day. Sure, it's not what you'd call "literature" by any means. But its clear illustrations are on sturdy cardboard pages that also promote solo "reading" and support good "can-do" feelings.

Dad's Book by Jan Ormerod. Lothrop, Lee and Shepard, 1985. One of a small series of books that feature Dad on center stage with Baby. Very little text but lively pictures. Also: *Reading, Sleeping,* and *Messy Baby.*

Reading

Jan Ormerod

Good Morning, Baby Bear by Eric Hill. Random House, 1984. Simple one-line text tells sequence of the day from getting up, washed, fed, and on to play. Part of series of *Baby Bear Books* with clear, pleasing illustrations. Also *Baby Bear's Bedtime.*

I Can—Can You? by Peggy Parish; illustrated by Marylin Hafner. Greenwillow, 1980. A series of small cardboard books that illustrate small boys and girls playing, dressing, eating, socializing, and learning. Each page makes a simple statement about what the pictured child is doing and then asks the child listener if he can do that, too. Short but right on target for interaction between parent and child, with room for plenty of personal input by the child.

I'm King of the Castle by Shigeo Watanabe; illustrated by Yasuo Ohtomo. Putnam, 1982. All about playing alone in the sandbox. Big, clear illustrations.

In Our House by Anne Rockwell. Crowell, 1985. More than a naming book, here's a tour of the Bear family's house. Each room is introduced and then followed with a busy picture of the many activities they do in that room. A good talking book.

I See by Rachel Isadora. Greenwillow, 1985. Gorgeous illustrations and utterly simple text about familiar sights in the child's world. Each sight is named and followed with an action statement that rings true.

Let's Eat by Gyo Fujikawa. Grosset & Dunlap, 1975. A cardboard book with clear illustrations of things we eat. More than just a naming book, this one invites opinions. "What do you like best?" Picky eaters might get a lot of negatives out of their system as they point to things they don't like. Fujikawa includes a good mix of multiracial faces in his cast of male and female children. He touches on what animals eat and ends with an all-time favorite eating occasion—a birthday cake!

Marmalade's Nap by Cindy Wheeler. Knopf, 1983. Delightfully simple story about a little cat's need for a nap. Probably won't change anyone's mind about naptime, though.

My Back Yard by Anne and Harlow Rockwell. Macmillan, 1984. Part of a series of *My World* books done in small format for small hands. For the country or suburban child (foreign territory to the city child) with a simple catalogue of familiar things in back yards—trees, birds, laundry drying, sprinkler, sandbox, and swing.

My Daddy by Mathew Price, illustrated by Jean Claverie. Knopf, 1986. A cardboard book with sturdy lift-down flaps that reveal a father and child playing familiar games. Also see *My Mommy.*

Playing, Dressing, Friends, and *Family* by Helen Oxenbury. Simon & Schuster, 1981. A popular series of small books for little hands about daily events—pictures are humorous but a little washed out for young toddlers. Try one; if it's a hit, they'll like the series.

Sam's Lamp, Sam's Ball, and *Sam's Bath* by Barbro Lindgren, illustrated by Eva Eriksson. Morrow, 1983. This series features young Sam in simple stories for the very young with clear pictures, minimal text, and rare but welcome touches of humor.

Shopping Trip by Helen Oxenbury. Dial, 1982. With simplicity, charm, and humor we follow the young toddler on a shopping trip for shoes, slacks for mom, and on to the grocery store and restaurant. No words but plenty of talk here. Also: *Beach Day, Good Night, Good Morning,* and *Mother's Helper.*

The Snow by John Burningham. Harper & Row, 1975. One of a series of small books with limited storyline. In this case the plot traces the typical events of a snowy day: rolling a snowball, riding a sled, getting cold and ending the day with hot chocolate, and the hopes that there'll be snow tomorrow.

Tuffa and the Snow by Binette Schroeder. Dial, 1983. A boy and his dog romp in the snow.

What Do Toddlers Do? Photos selected by Debby Slier. Random

House, 1985. A sturdy cardboard book featuring photos of toddlers on the move, picking flowers, swinging, climbing, banging pots, and other well-loved and familiar activities.

Animal Books

There are dozens of animal books done in cardboard and picture book formats. Since the youngest child may persist in calling every four-legged creature a "doggie," it's puzzling that many illustrators get carried away with the opportunity to paint far-from-familiar beasts. For toddlers, start with the familiar world of animal pets and farm creatures, and then go on to wilder beasts they see in the zoo or circus.

Animal Sounds illustrated by A. Battaglia. Golden, 1981. Action-packed pictures with clear illustrations and simple question-and-answer text.

Baby Animals by Harry McNaught. Random House, 1976. Painterly illustrations of mother and baby animals.

A Children's Zoo by Tana Hoban. Greenwillow, 1986. Ten familiar zoo animals and birds, each presented in a gorgeous color photograph with only three accompanying words to describe it, makes this book a wonderful springboard for discussion with the youngest child.

Doggies by Sandra Boynton. Simon & Schuster, 1984. A combination counting and sound book with a new variety of dog added to each page making a new "doggie" sound.

Farm Animals, Zoo Animals, and *Pets* by Valerie Greely. Bedrick/Blackie Books (distributed by Harper & Row), 1984. Three handsome books with painterly illustrations that are nevertheless clear and tasteful. These would make good follow-up reading after a trip to the farm or zoo.

I Am a Bunny, I Am a Kitten, and *I Am a Puppy* by Ole Risom. Golden, 1970. Very simple stories about each animal in large format on cardboard pages.

I Am a Little Cat by Helmut Spanner. Barrons, 1983. Christine's cat follows her through the day from sunup to sundown. Charming illustrations on sturdy stock. Also: *I Am a Little Dog, I Am a Little Lion,* and *I Am a Little Elephant.*

Miffy at the Zoo by Dick Bruna. Methuen, 1975. After a trip to the zoo this little book will be a real favorite. One of a series, this one is less abstract and more "readable" for the youngest readers. A small book for small hands, the vivid illustrations are highly stylized, but recognizable.

Moo, Baa, La-la-la by Sandra Boynton. Simon & Schuster, 1984. Part of *Little Simon Books Series.* This one has a little upside-down humor that young listeners who are "in the know" about animal sounds will enjoy.

My Day on the Farm by Chiyoko Nakatani. Crowell, 1976. A small child's first trip to the farm with the sights, sounds, smells, and feelings all captured with one line of text to the page and painterly but "readable" illustrations.

Getting in Touch

Anyone who lives with an inquisitive toddler knows that little children use all their senses to explore the world. They need to smell, touch, taste, shake, and hear in order to fully experience things you and I take for granted. It's from such experiences that words such as *round, smooth, sticky, hard, big,* and *small* take on meaning. While books aren't a substitute for the real thing, they can help extend and focus the child's sensory awareness.

For the child, it's a giant leap to go from a three-dimensional round, rolling, crunchy, juicy, red apple to a flat picture of an apple on a page. Yet the ability to read pictorial symbols on a page comes rather early and represents a first step toward reading more abstract symbols such as words. The more experience a child has with the "real" things, the better able he will be to bring meaning to spoken or written symbols.

Big Ones, Little Ones by Tana Hoban. Greenwillow, 1976. A wordless book of lush black and white photos featuring big and little creatures—good for looking at and talking about together.

Gobble, Growl, Grunt by Peter Spier. Zephyr, 1971. A parade of lively, colorful, familiar animals, each presented with the sound the animal makes. Also see *Crash! Bang! Boom!,* where the sounds that are made by people and things in the kitchen, living room, and other settings well known by the young child are delightfully portrayed.

Hush Kitten by Emanuel Schongut. Little Simon Book, 1983. Two active little cats romp in crackling leaves, pop balloons, break dishes, rip paper, and make other noises.

It Looked Like Spilt Milk by Charles G. Shaw. Harper & Row, 1947. Here's a book that can change the way children look at the clouds in the sky. Told in a simple pattern that children catch onto quickly, this is a book they'll enjoy hearing, looking at, and playing.

Little Bunny Follows His Nose. Golden, 1971. Part of a series of novelty books in the *Scratch and Sniff* series. Many have more nose appeal than literary merit, but it's a novelty some tots will like.

Max, the Music Maker by M. Stecher and A. Kandell. Lothrop, Lee and Shepard, 1980. A handsome photo essay about young Max who makes music with pots, pans, and other found objects in his house.

Noisy by Shirley Hughes. Lothrop, Lee and Shepard, 1985. Familiar sounds in and around the house are explored in rhyme and charming pictures.

The Noisy Book (1939), *The Indoor Noisy Book* (1976), *City Noisy Book* (1976), and *Country Noisy Book* (1976) by Margaret Wise Brown; illustrated by Leonard Weisgard. Harper & Row. These books are classic examples that extend the child's sensory awareness. In the series a little dog, Muffin, for one reason or another, can't see, but can hear all sorts of sounds. All of the books in the *Noisy* series invite plenty of noisy listener participation and creative play with sounds and words.

Pat the Bunny by Dorothy Kunhardt. Golden, 1962. A classic with a variety of textures glued into place for making firsthand connections between words and touch. Other books by Kunhardt explore touch, sound, size, and smell.

Pat the Cat by Edith Kunhardt. Golden, 1984. A sensory book for the very young. It begins with patting a furry cat, but moves on to other activities that fill the day of a family with children.

Taste the Raindrops by Anna G. Hines. Greenwillow, 1983. A delicious little story about a child who longs to go out in the rain. Full of sensory language, plenty of negatives, and a happy ending!

The Touch Me Book by P. and E. Witte; illustrated by H. Rockwell. Golden, 1961. Sponges, wood, furry feeling things—a different sensory experience on every page.

BOOKS FOR OLDER TODDLERS

At two and a half, going-on-three, children have a broader interest in the objects and activities of the world around them. They also have a greatly enlarged command of language. So, they're better able to make themselves understood and to understand others. Books with a simple story line and oft-repeated phrases, as in *The Three Bears,* are just right for listening and chiming in on. Given the child's own playful ways with language, books like *The Three Bears* or *Jamberry* make for delicious fun.

Little Mysteries

Probably the most complex stories for older toddlers are little mysteries in which one character is searching for something or someone. The "problem" is right up front on the first page and neatly resolved on the last.

Angus and the Cat by Marjorie Flack. Doubleday, 1931. Angus, a small Scottie dog, has grown large enough to do many things, but he is very curious to learn more about cats. So, when a cat arrives at his house, Angus is given a merry chase that ends up in a budding friendship. Also: *Angus Lost* and *Angus and the Ducks.*

The Box with Red Wheels by Maud and Miska Petersham. Macmillan, 1949. Here's a classic little mystery with barnyard animals trying to figure out what's inside the strange box with red wheels.

Brown Bear, Brown Bear, What Do You See? by Bill Martin, Jr.; illustrated by Eric Carle. Holt, 1983. Repetitive question-and-answer format should appeal to older twos. A handsome book of colorful animals.

Sam Who Never Forgets by Eve Rice. Puffin, 1980. Sam the zookeeper feeds all the animals and never forgets. One day it seems as though he has forgotten the elephants, but all turns out just like the title. Older toddlers will enjoy the surprise and repetition of the refrain.

The Very Busy Spider by Eric Carle. Philomel, 1986. A spider begins to spin a web, and on each page a barnyard animal tries to distract her from her task. Spider perseveres to make a beautiful and useful finished product. Stunning pictures and a chance for the child to participate in the story by chiming in with the animal sounds.

The Very Hungry Caterpillar by Eric Carle. Philomel, 1969. From tiny egg to beautiful butterfly, the story of a tiny caterpillar as it eats its way through the week. With brilliantly painted fruits and goodies that are punched with holes just the right size for the fat caterpillar and small fingers to poke through.

Where's My Baby? by H. A. Rey. Houghton Mifflin, 1943. A mother and baby animal book. Each page features a mother animal and verse that asks, "Where's my baby?" When the reader opens the fold-out page, there's the baby. This one's a classic.

Where's My Easter Egg? by Harriet Ziefert; illustrated by Richard Brown. Puffin Books, 1985. A lift-the-flap book with a big idea. Behind each liftable is another kind of creature with an egg peculiar to its species. Hide-and-seek game with a little information.

Where's Spot? by Eric Hill. Putnam, 1980. The dog Spot is lost and hasn't eaten his dinner. What follows is a peek-a-boo game of lifting flaps on every page until Spot is at last found. While the mystery may be obvious to you, this is probably the child's first experience with problem solving in a book format. In the real

Eric Hill

world most problem solving is done on a trial-and-error basis. Here, the delight comes in lifting little pages and discovering where Spot will be found. The first read-through is full of surprises. Subsequent readings become a game of recall and "knowing" who's behind what gate or door. Although part of a series, this is the youngest and most appropriate one for toddlers. Also see *Spot at Play.*

William, Where Are You? by Mordicai Gerstein. Crown, 1985. When William hides at bedtime, his parents go hunting under, inside, behind, and everywhere. Part game, part book, the half pages lift to reveal many surprises, including William under the covers in his own little bed.

Day-to-Day Life

Big World, Small World by Jeanne Titherington. Greenwillow, 1985. Side by side, Mama's world and young Anna's world are juxtaposed in a charming book that mirrors the toddler's view.

Geraldine's Blanket by Holly Keller. Greenwillow, 1984. If your toddler's security blanket is coming undone, here's a lovely solution Geraldine works out. A charming little story young listeners will see themselves in. Also: *Too Big.*

Happy Birthday, Sam by Pat Hutchins. Greenwillow, 1978. It's Sam's birthday but he's still not quite as big as he wishes— until a special gift from his grandpa arrives.

Hush, Little Baby illustrated by Aliki. Prentice-Hall, 1981. Aliki's painted woodblock illustrations are a beautiful accompaniment to this old folk song you've probably sung since you were small. Open the pages and sing with your toddler!

I Can by Sue Tarsky; illustrated by Katy Sleight. Random House, 1985. Here's a bit of upside-down humor to giggle and talk about. Using a question format, the child listener/looker sorts out the appropriate "tool" from an assortment of absurd ones.

I Can Build a House by Shigeo Watanabe; illustrated by Yasuo Ohtomo. Putnam, 1982. Toddlers will see the humor and enjoy bear's triumph in building a play house. Also: *I Can Ride It.*

Jesse Bear, What Will You Wear? by Nancy White Carlstrom, illustrated by Bruce Degen. Macmillan, 1986. Lilting verse and delightful illustrations that put a little humor into the sometimes tedious business of getting dressed in the morning, and ready for bed at night.

Just Like Daddy by Frank Asch. Prentice-Hall, 1981. Bear and his daddy go fishing. Step by step we follow the two with Little

Bear doing everything just like Daddy—until the surprise ending, which will give Mom a smile. Sweet and simple.

Lily Goes to the Playground by Jill Krementz. Random House, 1986. A new look in boardbooks, Lily's trip to the playground is done in photographs in a full size format. Also: *Jack Goes to the Beach.*

The Little Panda Bear by Koichi Ono. Little Simon Book, 1982. A simple story about a panda bear who decides home is best of all. Flocked cover may have special touch appeal.

Look, There's My Hat! by Maureen Roffey. Putnam, 1985. An amusing little book with cut-out frames that enhance the story. Also provides little "lessons" in size relationships with a sense of humor and story.

Max's New Suit by Rosemary Wells. Dial, 1979. This is a situation that the very young child can relate to. Also see *Max's Ride* for some early fun and humor.

Marmalade's Yellow Leaf by Cindy Wheeler. Knopf, 1982. When summer ends, Marmalade the cat's fancy is caught by a flying yellow leaf—nothing else will do. Also: *Marmalade's Picnic.*

My Shirt Is White by Dick Bruna. Methuen, 1984. A very simple book about color with just one item of clothing and one color on a page.

On Mother's Lap by Ann H. Scoll; illustrated by Glo Coalson. McGraw-Hill, 1972. For Michael one of the best places in the world is on Mother's lap with his blanket, his boat, and his puppy. But when his new baby sister cries, Michael isn't sure there's room.

Sam's Ball by Barbro Lindgren, illustrated by Eva Eriksson. Morrow, 1983. A little drama in which young Sam almost loses his ball to a clever kitty, but ends up playing together happily. Also: *Sam's Teddy Bear.*

Thumpity Thump Gets Dressed by Cyndy Szekeres. Golden, 1984. Here's a little story about a bunny who can't seem to find just the right thing to wear to go with the weather.

When We Went to the Park by Shirley Hughes. Lothrop, Lee and

Shepard, 1985. A little girl and her grandfather count the familiar things they see as they walk through the park.

When You Were a Baby by Ann Jonas. Greenwillow, 1982. A look back at all the things your toddler couldn't do when she was a baby. Something of a comfort to the often frustrated tot who still can't do many things, but can begin to appreciate what she can do now. Also: *Holes and Peeks.*

Will That Wake Mother? by Martha McKeen Welch. Dodd, Mead, 1983. A story in photos about some mischievous kittens and their mother who loves them, even when they're naughty.

Old and New Favorites

Ask Mr. Bear by Marjorie Flack. Macmillan, 1958. Danny wants a present for his mom's birthday and asks each of the animals what they would suggest. Plenty of repetition and a happy bear hug ending.

Bears by Ruth Krauss; illustrated by Phyllis Rowand. Harper & Row, 1948. A rollicking little poem about bears that will please the ears and eyes. This is one they'll learn to chant with you. Also: *I Can Fly.*

Jamberry by Bruce Degen. Harper & Row, 1983. A delicious romp through all kinds of berry patches, in rhythm and rhyme toddlers will gobble up.

The Little Red Hen illustrated by Amye Rosenberg. Golden, 1984. Toddlers will begin chiming in once they get the hang of this old favorite with so many opportunities to say "Not I!"

Milton the Early Riser by Robert Kraus, illustrated by Jose and Ariane Aruego. Simon & Schuster, 1972. Like most toddlers, Milton the Early Riser can't wait for everyone to wake up and get the day started. Milton waits so long he falls asleep. Oversized book with plenty of action and amusing details to look at.

Mr. Gumpy's Motor Car by John Burningham. Crowell, 1976. Mr. Gumpy takes all the animals for a zany ride. Toddlers who have a natural affinity for puddles will love it.

The Three Bears by Paul Galdone. Houghton Mifflin, 1972. Here's an oversized beauty of that classic with delightful action-filled illustrations. Even the steam on the porridge is just right! Also: *The Little Red Hen.*

How-to-Cope Books

There are "how-to-cope" books on a variety of touchy topics for toddlers. While it's doubtful that little ones can learn "how-to" from any book, these little manuals may stir some friendly conversation toward that end. Here are several that may be useful.

The Baby by John Burningham. Harper & Row, 1975. One line of text to a page, yet this tells it all—what baby does, how the "big" sib helps and sometimes feels. No romanticizing about baby, but not mean-spirited, either. If there's a new baby in the family, this one may help.

Betsy's Baby Brother by Gunilla Wolde. Random House, 1975. Betsy is not altogether happy with her new baby brother. This is no romantic vision of siblinghood. It ends on the upbeat but presents the resentments honestly. Also: *Betsy and the Doctor* and *Betsy's First Day at Nursery School*.

The Checkup by Helen Oxenbury. Dutton, 1983. Part of a series that features slightly mischievous children who "accidentally" end up getting adults in ticklish tangles. In this case, the doctor ends up on the floor. These aren't for everyone; in fact, they may be as much for adults as for kids. Also: *Eating Out* and *The Important Visitor*.

Come Play With Us by Anne Sibley O'Brien. Holt, 1985. When Rachel's father takes her to the daycare center, she's not too sure about wanting to stay. A short but comforting little story that includes Daddy's return. Lovely illustrations on cardboard pages. Also: *I Want That* and *Where's My Truck*.

Going to the Doctor by Fred Rogers, photographs by Jim Judkis. Putnam, 1986. A photographic preview of what to expect on a trip to the doctor's office for a checkup. Also see *Going to the Potty*.

How Do I Put It On? by Shigeo Watanabe; illustrated by Yasuo Ohtomo. Philomel, 1979. Taking a cue from the toddler's upside-down sense of humor, here's one about the often difficult business of getting dressed.

No More Diapers by J. G. Brooks, et al. Delacorte, 1977. A picture book that documents toilet training. Also see *Once Upon a Potty* by A. Frankel and *The Toddler's Potty Book* by A. Allison.

Throw A Kiss, Harry by Mary Chalmers. Harper & Row, 1976. Harry, the cat, is just as independent as big toddlers love to be. This is a satisfying little story about a cat who doesn't always listen.

The Very Little Boy by Phyllis Krasilovsky; illustrated by Ninon. Doubleday, 1962. A reassuring story about a very little boy who was too small to do many things but who grew and grew, much as your toddler will do. Bound to please the young and restless. Also: *The Very Little Girl.*

What A Good Lunch! by Shigeo Watanabe; illustrated by Yasuo Ohtomo. Philomel, 1980. Here's a humorous book about table manners. Like the books in the *I Can Do It All by Myself* series, this one features Bear learning the hard way. In this case it's about using his spoon, slurping spaghetti, and putting jam on his bread.

You Go Away by Dorothy Corey; illustrated by Lois Axeman. Whitman, 1975. Here's an issues book close to the heart of toddlers and their separation problems. In this gentle little book there's a quiet reassurance that Mom and Dad not only go away, but come back, too.

Bedtime Stories

Books for bedtime don't need to be about going to sleep. Any one of the books in this chapter may become part of your toddler's good-night ritual. However, no child should miss the bedtime classic, *Goodnight Moon.*

Goodnight Moon by Margaret Wise Brown; illustrated by Clement Hurd. Harper & Row, 1947. What makes this book so right for even the youngest listener? Perhaps it's because it embodies the eternal concerns of the child: a desire for power of her own, a need

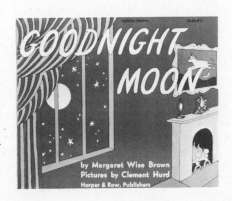

to know and name her environment, and a comforting reassurance that all is well in her small world as the child slips into that other state called sleep.

Goodnight Moon offers this support. A little rabbit sitting up in his bed puts away the familiar objects in the small world of his bedroom by saying goodnight to each—"goodnight kittens and goodnight mittens." There's a "quiet old lady whispering hush" as she rocks in her chair, but she is not putting *him* away to bed; he is putting *her* away by saying goodnight first. As the little bunny says goodnight, he names all the fascinating things in that cozy room. He is reinforcing his knowledge of and comfort in his intimate environment—naming and knowing are among the first steps in learning. A "young mouse," as it scampers through each picture, fascinates children. Soon, when asked, "Where is the mouse?" small fingers point to it unerringly; another characteristic of the very young is their ability to discern tiny details.

Goodnight Moon stands above the rest in its unique quality of art, text, and depth of meaning. The pictures, in the style of the thirties, are representational, yet imbued with magic. Subtle action flows from page to page—the little old lady raises a "shushing" finger, then leaves; the mouse scampers about; the moon rises as the room gradually darkens; the kittens romp until they, the rabbit (and usually the listener) close their eyes. Black-and-white pages alternate with pictures full of off-beat color. The meticulous details are another joy to babies and toddlers.

Finally, the language seems deceptively simple but is profoundly effective. Even the choice of vowels has a slumberous quality—try saying "Goodnight Moon" fast. The "o's" almost demand a drawl.

The whole brief text is a tone poem that takes us from the particular—"goodnight bears, goodnight chairs"—to the large unknown—"goodnight stars, goodnight air, goodnight noises everywhere"—that permits the small rabbit to let go of his day in comforting reassurance. Read *Goodnight Moon* aloud. Not only will the magic of the art and felicity of the language give you pleasure, but you will catch a glimpse of the underlying reassurance and strength this enduring favorite bestows on its very young audience.

Baby Bear's Bedtime by Eric Hill. Random House, 1984. A very simple story about Baby and Mother Bear at bedtime.

A Child's Goodnight Book by Margaret Wise Brown; illustrated by Jean Charlot. Addison-Wesley, 1943. In this small gem of a book, the child learns how many animals sleep. Ms. Brown's simple but enchanting text closes with a prayer. The illustrations may seem stylized to modern eyes.

Close Your Eyes by Jean Marzollo; illustrated by Susan Jeffers. Dial, 1978. Here's a story within a story. It's a rhythmic lullaby accompanied by a charming wordless story, featuring Dad putting his child to bed.

Goodnight, Horsey written and illustrated by Frank Asch. Prentice-Hall, 1981. A girl begs Daddy for a horsey ride. In her imagination he turns into a real horse. After the ride, he gradually assumes human characteristics as he fetches her some water, or reads a bedtime story. Then, fully human, they both sleep. Simply told and illustrated, yet very effective with toddlers.

Goodnight, Little ABC by Robert Kraus; illustrated by N. M. Bodecker. Windmill Books, 1982. One of a set of four tiny books, just made for toddler hands and equally toddler-appropriate in language and art.

Patsy Scarry's Big Bedtime Story Book by Patsy Scarry; illustrated by Cyndy Szekeres. Random House, 1980. A loving collection of small stories about small creatures as cozily comforting as a security blanket. A story a night is just right.

Ten, Nine, Eight by Molly Bang. Greenwillow, 1983. A gentle nighttime counting book featuring a black father and child counting backwards from ten little toes to one big girl all ready for bed.

. . .

THINGS TO REMEMBER WHEN CHOOSING BOOKS FOR TODDLERS

- Look for clear uncluttered pictures that are easy to "read."
- Little stories that reflect the child's own world are most appropriate for now.
- Books for independent reading should be of sturdy materials since turning pages is still difficult.
- Choose books you won't mind reading and rereading.
- A supply of magazines for browsing is still fascinating.

THE TODDLER'S BOOKSHELF

Early Words by Richard Scarry
Goodnight Moon by Margaret Wise Brown
Marmalade's Nap by Cindy Wheeler
Pat the Bunny by Dorothy Kunhardt
Sam Who Never Forgets by Eve Rice
Shopping Trip by Helen Oxenbury
Taste the Raindrops by Anna Hines
The Very Hungry Caterpillar by Eric Carle
Where's My Baby? by H. A. Rey
Where's Spot? by Eric Hill

Books for Three-
and Four-Year-Olds

A COMING-OUT TIME

Three- and four-year-olds are at last emerging from the frustrating chrysalis of their own inabilities. Despite a marvelous development from birth to two, the two-year-old still struggles to gain
mastery over her physical skills and her competence in verbal
communication.

Now at three and even more at four, she can use language
to express most of her needs, emotions, and ideas; she can run,
jump, spin, and climb more freely. At last she can be independent of the helping hand, the guiding voice. Or so she thinks.

A SENSE OF POWER

Of course, the three- or four-year-old isn't really independent.
He still needs physical and verbal help. However, the child with
developing abilities feels a strong sense of power and often
resists adult help and advice. Thus he is drawn to books of
fantasy that depict "power to the young!" Even though he
knows he really isn't all-powerful, such books satisfy his innate
sense of his emerging capabilities. Charlotte Pomerantz's *Piggy
in the Puddle* is a good example. It is full of the tongue-twisting

rhymes and nonsense words so beloved by the very young, like *fuddy-duddy, fiddle-faddle, mooshy-squooshy.* Plus the enchantment of having the disobedient, mud-puddling pig-child responding to adult orders with a resounding NOPE. The solution? The authoritarian family finally follows the plump little pig into the puddle.

This book, with its clearly delineated pictures full of color and humor, meets many a four-year-old's ardent wishes:

- to be disobedient to adult authority
- to be independent
- to indulge in forbidden play places
- to have power over the adults
- to win out over them
- to play with language in an inventive, rhythmic way

INDEPENDENCE, STEP ONE

Closely related to his sense of power is his sense of growing independence. The four-year-old favors books about independence as he stretches out to do more things on his own. While the three-year-old also appreciates the independence theme, for her, independence is firmly rooted in the dependable home base. For her, independence and dependence are changeable themes. *The Runaway Bunny* by Margaret Wise Brown is a little classic on the dependence/independence theme. Although the Bunny relishes the idea of running away, there is the reassurance that no matter where he runs Mother will be there.

Some of the first independent book choices children make are linked to their exposure to television. Strolling down the aisle in the supermarket, they reach for books whose covers display their favorite television characters. Big Bird and the whole Sesame Street gang are very successful in leading children to books. While they are not great literature, and should not be the only books available to young children, they do serve the purpose of helping kids connect to books.

· · ·

THE THREE-YEAR-OLD

Are You My Friend?

The three-year-old, while still most comfortable in the known world of home, is beginning to reach out for a playmate. The four-year-old is even more interested in beginning to develop social relationships. And both are adjusting to the sometimes painful realization that "all mine" must adjust to "yours and mine." Both are beginning to understand on their different developmental levels that attaining such a desired relationship requires a compromise between "my way" and "your way"— between "all mine" and "yours and mine."

The three-year-old seems most comfortable with one other child, though she often changes from one playmate to another. Most three-year-olds show more interest in the social side of play rather than in the subject of play or the materials used in the activity. Much of their social activity consists of talking, of describing what they *will* do rather than what they *are* doing. They tend to move quickly from one activity to another.

Parents sometimes think a three-year-old is being selfish when he or she refuses to share or wants all the blocks. Actually, the young child is still in a stage where he can only see his own needs; he doesn't yet understand that those outside of him have equally strong desires. This comprehension develops slowly— it often continues into adult life. One way to help the young child to understand reciprocity is to hear books about the trials and joys of making friends. *Will I Have A Friend?* by Miriam Cohen is a charming depiction of this strong urge to find a friend.

Imaginary Friends—Petey Dink Did It

During the third year, the child often develops quite a resistance to ordinary routines, which can lead to fixed battle stations with Mom on one side and stubborn three-year-old Jimmy on the other. Experts suggest that avoiding, as much as possible, the occasions for such confrontations, or letting another adult carry out the detested routine, are probably the most successful tactics. Jimmy isn't your enemy. He's just trying out his powers of independence, and he often fails. One face-saver for him is to produce a constant companion, invisible to others, on whom he shifts the responsibility for failure.

"Petey Dink" was young Paul's inseparable but invisible companion. When the bathtub water overflowed, Petey Dink did it. Petey Dink also was responsible for the torn jacket, the broken toy, the lost teddy bear. At first, Paul's parents feared their son was becoming a liar and didn't want to acknowledge his fantasy friend. Then they came to see that Petey Dink sprang from Paul's gradual acceptance of his parent's ideas of right and wrong. Paul was learning which actions were acceptable, but he still didn't want to admit his inability to perform them at all times. Hence, Petey Dink.

At times the imaginary friends can be useful tools for parents, too. Emily Winograd was told by her small daughter Posy that the yard mess was caused by Gemema (Posy's invisible friend). Emily replied, "You tell that Gemema that she and you can't play in the yard again until you both pick up the mess." Often great friction can be avoided by the absence of direct commands.

Imaginary friends are also great companions for the solitary child, or for the imaginative child who loves dramatic play. While parents needn't kowtow to this phenomenon, which may also be present in the fourth year, they shouldn't order its banishment. One way of coping is to share stories of imaginary friends with the young child. Barbara Shook Hazen's *The Blackboard Bear* is a good example of this genre.

Finally, imaginary friends, like old soldiers, just fade away as the growing child's power struggles lessen.

Sibling Rivalry

Three-year-olds love to pretend they are something else.

"Grrr," growls Melissa, crawling over the rug toward Baby. "I'm a hungry tiger looking for my dinner."

For that brief moment, Melissa is a tiger, and her jealousy of Baby takes tangible form. No use arguing that she really is a sweet little girl who loves her baby brother. She isn't and she doesn't. Better to enter the fantasy yourself, saying something like, "Wow! What a ferocious tiger! I'd better get Baby out of its way. I hope that tiger can wait 'til I get its delicious dinner ready."

Later on, perhaps as a bedtime story, Melissa's Mom or Dad may read her a book like *Nobody Asked Me If I Wanted a Baby Sister* by Martha Alexander, not only as a catharsis, but to let her know she's not alone in her fantasy and/or jealousies.

Little Baby Me

Most threes also love to hear about their own babyhood even if they don't have younger siblings usurping their rightful place. Robie Harris and Elizabeth Levy's book *Before You Were Three* speaks to this desire; part of the book is for the child, part is directed to the parent. So does a children's book called *Big Boy, Little Boy* by Betty Jo Stanovich.

Not only do three-year-olds like to hear about their babyhood and how much more competent they are now, but at times they return to it. Often when a new sibling or other child arrives whom they fear might replace them, threes and fours regress to a more helpless state. Parents need to comfort the uncertain regressor, and gently encourage his recognition of great advantages he has over the newcomer. Scolding would just reinforce the child's conviction that he is being rejected. A funny little book called *Pig Pig Grows Up* by David McPhail might help restore his composure.

That's Scary!

Another three-year-old characteristic is a growing fear of the dark, of scary animals, of strangers, and strange situations. Some experts believe you can have a dialogue with youngsters about these fears. With three-year-olds you might ask, "What would you like to do to that monster?" as a device for letting the child verbalize her fantasies or subduing these terrors. Or you may ask, "What do you want *me* to do to that scary thing?" This enables you to enter the fantasy and act out the child's wishes. Of course, just offering comfort and loving presence can be reassuring, as shown in the beautiful little book, *Sometimes I'm Afraid* by Sylvia Tester. One father told his ghost-fearing son that he, the father, had painted the whole room with ghost-preventative paint. When asked how long the paint's effect would last, Father replied, "One hundred and forty-two years." Satisfied, his son slept.

But isn't this lying? asks the conscientious parent. Wouldn't it be better to assert that there are no ghosts?

Better, perhaps. But as effective? Probably not. The three-year-old's fears arise from emotional fantasy: we enter that world to allay them as briskly as possible. Since the child isn't dealing with facts, facts usually won't satisfy him. And soon enough, these fears will pass.

Is It Real or Unreal?

If the child's fears are based on real experiences, of course, we must be more realistic in our assurances. But even then, real experience is still so limited for a three-year-old that emotional and physical comfort is the most effective relief.

Books play a strong role in relating to and assuaging these fears. The danger lies in presenting the child a fantasy that is too threatening for him at this developmental stage. For instance, Maurice Sendak's classic story, *Where the Wild Things Are,* in our opinion, is not suitable for three-year-olds and most four-year-olds, though it is fine for most fives and sixes, who are mature enough to recognize their own "wild things" and accept the fantasy. It may terrify the three-year-old. Three and even four-year-olds, for all their fine new knowledge, are still not sure what is real and what is not. Even more sophisticated older children often reveal confusion over the reality of ghosts, monsters, witches, and werewolves.

A fantasy story about wild animals that is enjoyed by many three-year-olds is Marie Hall Ets's *In the Forest.* Here the wild animals such as bears, elephants, and monkeys, who go for a walk in the forest with a little boy, are presented as friendly and fun-loving—and in the end are clearly seen as imaginary. This story gives the young child the opportunity to draw *just close enough,* not too close, to animals usually seen as wild and scary.

Fairy Tales

Bruno Bettelheim's fine book *The Uses of Enchantment* has had a noticeable impact on teachers, parents, and publishers. He explains the ancient fairy tales in terms of their powerful appeal to the unconscious needs of children and praises their absence of watering down. The result has been the republishing of these tales with gorgeous illustrations. (The publishers and buyers of these new editions evidently skipped over Bettelheim's statement that these tales should not be illustrated.)

Unfortunately, most of these familiar fairy stories are *not* for younger children. The inability of threes and fours to discriminate between the real and the unreal can cause anxious reactions if the more sophisticated fairy tales are presented.

Folktale Fantasy

However, some folktales are just right for the younger children. *Folk* tales are often like fables and deal with ordinary folk, while *fairy* tales involve princesses, kings, queens, cruelty, and adult love. Fairy tale themes are also more sophisticated.

Folktales are also full of fantasy and magic, but some are very acceptable to the three- and four-year-old. Why? Because young children readily identify with both the theme and the characters.

The common criteria for choosing appropriate folktales are a limited amount (or lack) of violence; simple language and straightforward unfolding of the plot; a theme that is related to the emotions and/or interests of this age group; an uncomplicated plot and easily remembered refrains.

The Little Red Hen fulfills these requirements. Even though the basic activity (the steps in bread-making) are largely unknown to today's child, the process is so clearly set forth that even three-year-olds comprehend it. The theme of accomplishing by oneself is relished for the independence shown by the heroine, and the story's ending satisfies the desire for fairness, for deprivation of the selfish ones, and triumphant success of the determined hen. The story also contains repeated phrases: "Not I," said the Cat; "Not I," said the Dog; "Not I," said the Pig; as well as the action and statement of the feisty Red Hen—"Then I'll do it myself." And she did.

These dependable phrases also give the three-year-old an opportunity to join in the reading of the story. The parent can ask the child, "Then what did the dog (cat, pig) say? What did the Little Red Hen answer?" The child's happy response gives the child not only pleasure, but the deep satisfaction of "reading" with Mom or Dad.

Finally, there is no violence in this classic little folktale.

The Child in a Fur Coat

Youngsters of this age accept animal protagonists as surrogate children. An animal (or "child in a fur coat") may do things that might be threatening to the listener if a real child did them—run away to Mr. McGregor's garden like Peter Rabbit, stay out all night like the little duck Ping, or live by themselves like The Three Little Pigs. Animal actions are one safe step removed from human reality.

Also, small children seem to have a natural affinity with animals. Even babies are fascinated by dogs and cats. Perhaps the simple lifestyle of the family dog is more akin to, and therefore more comprehensible to the lifestyle of a three- or four-year-old. Adult lifestyles often must seem fairly weird to a child of three.

Furthermore, using the animal-as-child characters avoids the problems of racial, socioeconomic, and religious representations. Animals are neither rich nor poor, Hispanic, Caucasian, black, or Asian. The author can concentrate on the developmental stages of emotional, physical, and personal development that appeal to all children. The best animal-as-surrogate-child stories are imaginatively flavored with the real lifestyle of animals. Peter Rabbit may wear a coat with buttons, but he lives under the roots of a tree and is in danger of becoming a rabbit pie.

An engaging example of the child-in-the-fur-coat fantasy is Robert Kraus's *Leo the Late Bloomer,* just right for young threes in its few words, its bright pictures, and its comforting story. Leo the tiger is slow at just about everything. He doesn't talk much, he eats sloppily, and can't read or write or draw. Of course, three-year-olds aren't expected to be readers and writers, but some of them may wish they could be. Leo's development at an easy pace can be very reassuring.

Other Interests

Your three-year-old's interest in language and stories is continually growing. Playing with words often strikes a funny bone.

> "Hush, tush toot!" yells Jeffrey, dragging a spool train across the floor. "Heebie, jeebie, peebie," calls David, making silly grimaces as he pushes a truckload of blocks. Roger's contribution causes gales of laughter as he dances about shouting, "Boopy, roopy, poopy!"

The combination of nonsense syllables with the implied scatology is a surefire rib-tickler for three-year-olds. Of course, Mother Goose has appealed to very young children for centuries, not because of what the rhymes say, but because they have such clear rhythm and are sprinkled with catchy words such as "Hickory dickory dock," "Diddle, diddle dumpling," "A diller, a dollar," and so on. For the same reason, Maurice Sendak's *Chicken Soup with Rice* (in the Nutshell Library) can be enjoyed endlessly. The silly words trip off the tongue and include easy repetitions that invite the child's participation.

What about the fun of upside-down situations and preposterous incongruities? Young children can enjoy these because *they know better* and like to indulge in a sense of superior knowhow. Books of this type, however, are not often written with the aim of appealing to children as young as three, who need to be very sure of what's right-side-up before they can appreciate what's upside down. One that can often be enjoyed by threes, however, is Irma Simonton Black's *Is This My Dinner?* As the girl in one picture holds up a tiny raw fish and asks the question, the three-year-old knows—horrors!—that this is certainly not any dinner he or she would want. And knows, also, that the grass in the next picture would be impossible.

Besides humor, these children are interested in real life information. Domestic animals, farm life, simple stories of what workers do, all kinds of transportation, information about the seasons, and more exotic animals have great appeal. One of the favorites about winter is Ezra Jack Keats's *The Snowy Day,* not a story with a plot but an account in simple words and glowing pictures of a little boy's fun in the snow.

Threes still love stories, either real or made up, about themselves and their doings, told by a friendly adult. When the adult's ingenuity runs dry, she can sometimes substitute the child's name for a book character, such as Davy in *Davy's Day* by Lois Lenski. And let the child just look at the pictures over and over and point to what he sees and knows, and give it a name. Threes still have that yearning—experienced also when they are younger—to label their world. All the informational books with their pictures of trucks and cars, and animals wild and tame, are wonderful for this labeling urge. Or try Anne Rockwell's *First Comes Spring,* a book about all the seasons and chock-full of little animal people busy indoors and out in an engaging variety of activities.

Finally, the wide assortment of bedtime books offers soothing assurance to close the day's activities and slide into sleep. Threes as well as twos love the lullaby rhythms of Margaret Wise Brown's *Goodnight Moon*—the perfect good night book for young children—and incidentally a book the parent can never tire of reading. A mother or father not accustomed to reading aloud to a child could well start with this book—a wonderful way to begin modeling for son or daughter the importance and pleasures of reading.

THE FOUR-YEAR-OLD

Go, Go, Go!

A four-year-old is chock-full of energy. His motor drive is turned to "high" as he speeds around his kingdom, rushing from activity to activity. He often dashes recklessly into dubious situations. At times he seems "out of bounds," physically and emotionally. He loves or he hates; he is hilariously laughing one moment, then downcast or in tears the next.

He loves stories that are "out of bounds," too, reveling in absurd situations, extravagant language. A story like *The Gingerbread Man* is a favorite: the impudence of the hero, the catchy refrain, "You can't catch me, I'm the Gingerbread Man," expresses his feelings of power and of exaggeration. Another newer favorite, Paula Fox's *Hungry Fred,* is full of the silly situations and exuberant tall-tale flavor of the four-year-old's speech. Four-year-olds exaggerate their own reports—"That building is a million miles high"; "She eated all the beans in the world"— and love to hear similar language in stories.

Safe-Scare and Silly Words

Four-year-olds are enchanted by foolish silliness and scary situations (if they aren't too scary) in their own stories and in stories read to them. That they want everything to end in safe security is a reflection of their own need to have boundaries. The wise parent will check the fear-factor of the fantasy and the safe-and-sound-ness of the ending.

Some parents may not agree with this advice. "Doesn't Bruno Bettelheim, the noted psychiatrist and author, believe children need to have their fears—unconscious or not—confronted and dealt with in story fantasies?" Sure they do, but, as with children's medicine, they need to be taken in small doses. *Peter Rabbit,* the classic by Beatrix Potter, is a prototype of this need to face fears but return to safety. In this little literary gem, Peter not only disobeys, escaping in the nick of time, but also must take the consequences—in this case, chamomile tea. Yet there is an atmosphere of safe-scare. Peter is not a child, though he acts like one. His milieu is quite separate from the everyday world of the listener, and his peril is different from any faced by four-year-olds. Yet they respond to the danger and the suspense. Anxiety rises in the listener and is satisfied by the return to the cozy rabbit home.

Other classics, such as *Alice in Wonderland* and most fairy tales, are not suited to the four-year-old's developmental stage, but will be cherished when he is older and able to read them for himself.

Again, some parents challenge these suggestions, feeling that their child is mature enough to cope with scary fantasy. This may well be so; parents usually are good judges of their child's capabilities. But sometimes we parents and other concerned adults mistake verbal facility and glibness with mental and emotional maturity. In this age of constant exposure to television, videodisks, tapes, and VCRs, children may not only be more fluent in language but also more proficient in expressing information. Yet they still may have only a superficial understanding of what they hear or see. They parrot others' words rather than understand them. We must be careful not to be fooled by the facile language; children still develop through recognizable emotional, social, and physical stages, just as they have always done. If, bemused by the maturity of their speech, we fail to recognize their emotional immaturity, we will do them a disservice. They still need books that speak to their developmental levels.

Who? What? How Come?

Four-year-olds are bursting not only with energy, but with curiosity as well. Adults are bombarded with their questions: "Why don't dogs talk? Where do bugs live? How come the moon follows us when we walk on the beach?" The more the children race, gallop, and climb around in the natural world, the more they wonder.

Sometimes our best bet is to wonder with them. Recently a woman recalled the day her child wanted to watch a worm, but mother was too busy to stop. Later she sadly admitted she forgot what the hurry was, and regrets not joining her child in wonderment. Are we too busy to watch a worm with our child?

A book such as May Garelick's *Where Does the Butterfly Go When It Rains?* helps both parent and child stretch their minds by observing the small wonders around them.

Four-year-olds want to sort out these puzzles in order to clarify their new experiences and concepts. Sometimes their questions and answers may make us smile, but they are good evidence that they are making reasonable deductions from their limited knowledge.

Real Answers

The four-year-old seeks information about his world. His curiosity begs for more facts. Children of this age have a wide range of questions, from "What does this machine do?" to "Where did that puddle go?" In spite of the effort to eliminate sexism, most experts feel that boys are particularly interested in vehicles, while most girls' interests center more on people.

School Bus by Donald Crews is one of the newer books that supplies information about these large vehicles. Stunning posterlike illustrations show the bus in action and at rest, with a minimum of text. In contrast, Richard Scarry's *Cars and Trucks and Things That Go* is full of details in the busy scenes of vehicles at work. Both threes and fours enjoy these books.

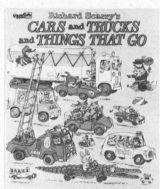

They also are drawn to Gunilla Wolde's *Tommy* or *Betsy* books, that show young children in some of the dramatic play activities that enlarge their learning. It is through role playing and by acting out their interpretation of the world around them that young children attempt to understand their experiences.

Luckily, there are good books of information for this young age. Most are in picture-book format. Some may have a slight story line, but most are straight information and range from ABC books to depictions of trucks, planes, snow, or insect life. You probably will be able to find a book relating to the particular interests of your child, whether about puddles or the work of machines.

Wanna Play?

The social drives of the four-year-old are even stronger than they were at three. Now the child is more interested in group play, rather than in confining herself to one friend at a time. In order to accomplish her heart's desire, she must not only further increase her understanding of the other child's needs but also be willing to yield some of her own self-centered desires.

One playground scene emphasizes how cooperation strengthens intergroup ties. Four youngsters are clustered around a slide: Mia, at the top of the ladder, is giving directions. "I'll be the doctor; Toby, you be the daddy; Jayne, you be the mommy; and Jon can be the baby." But her players object, and the roles are exchanged. Toby is now the doctor, Jon is the dad, Mia is mommy and Jayne, the baby. Mia is reluctant to give up her role at first, but accepts it when Toby starts to walk away. Her desire to play with the others is stronger than her need to have a preferred role. And in a short time, the dramatic play changes shape, and all become shipmates on a tugboat.

Books about friends, such as Arnold Lobel's *Frog and Toad* series, are very appealing to these children who are beginning to value good intergroup relations.

Story Plots

The fast-changing content of dramatic play suggests that four-year-olds enjoy the social interaction of peers even more than the drama itself. It also emphasizes the energy and speed of four-year-old shifts of play. Thus, books where the action moves right along have great appeal. Four-year-olds like plotted stories, but the plot must be clear and simple, the action swift and direct, and suspense and thrills should be quickly and satisfactorily resolved. A book like Esphyr Slobodkina's *Caps for Sale* exemplifies this simple direct plot.

How Does It Taste, Feel, Smell?

Young children learn primarily through their senses. As babies, they touched, tasted, and shook things. Now they still explore in hands-on experiences. They explore their accumulation of knowledged in dramatic play: this is how a horse gallops, this is what firemen do, a storekeeper does this.

In the stories that are read to them, children respond to sensory words—words that describe how things taste, feel, look, sound. A book such as *One Morning in Maine* by Robert McCloskey conjures up the smell of salt water, the feel and look of sea fog. In the *Noisy Books* by Margaret Wise Brown, a little dog explores the world through his senses.

Children love concrete verbs and descriptions. They love knowing just what Peter Rabbit eats in that famous garden, and how the little bunny moves—lippety, lippety. These specific details make a story come alive for three- and four-year-olds. One of the problems in many of the little books sold in the supermarket is the lack of these vivid details. Too often the books are tacked on to merchandise the publisher is trying to sell, and little attention is paid to the quality of the text. Their usual fate is to be discarded after a quick read-through. Take time to examine a book's text as well as its art. Do *you* like the style? If not, chances are your child won't either.

I Feel Bad

By now, four-year-olds may have encountered illness or death, if not of a human, then of a pet. The younger children often think death is reversible—some still do at four. Their awakening empathy with others allows them to be aware of others' pain or illness. In earlier times, children often were sent away to stay with Aunty when death or serious illness struck a household. Today many parents and educators, feeling that such events shouldn't be hidden from children, explain sad events as simply as possible, and try to answer children's questions. There are books about death that even four-year-olds can understand, such as Edith Stull's *My Turtle Died Today*.

This Is My Family

Three- and four-year-olds enjoy sharing household chores. While the three's part may be minimal—matching spoons to the number of family members at the table, or helping to stir the cake mix—fours usually want a "real" job. While they may have spells of rebellion, they like the importance of being the mail or wastebasket collector. Look for books that highlight family co-operation such as *Washday* by Susan Merrill.

Sell that Baby!

Fours may have more problems adjusting to a new baby than do their older siblings. Young children are just emerging from babyhood themselves, and often feel threatened by the new arrival. Will this newcomer get all the attention, all the cuddling that was formerly given to the four-year-old? It may seem that way to the child. Books are a great help in this situation. *The New*

Baby by Fred Rogers (TV's "Mister Rogers") may offer a fine way to talk about the feelings young children have about a new baby in the family.

Another positive way to handle this situation is to include the four-year-old as much as possible in baby-related activity. A wonder book in this category is *100 Things to Do with a Baby* by Jan Ormerod. While intended for an older child, it is fine for parent and four-year-old to look at together.

Some books relate to the young child's problems and joys with older sibling relationships. In *Big Brother* by Charlotte Zolotow, a small girl finds she can be friends with her brother.

Relations with Older Relations

There are more books than ever about the relationships of a child with an older family member. Amy Hest's book *The Crack-of-Dawn Walkers* relates the special feelings of a small child toward her grandfather—also more than a hint of sibling rivalry. Arnold Lobel's *Uncle Elephant* tells of an uncle in the parenting role and *Aunt Nina's Visit* by Franz Brandenberg is a delightful depiction of a child-loving aunt. *Daddy and Ben Together* by Miriam Stecher and Alice Kandell shows the warm feelings between a boy and his father, while in *A Chair for My Mother* by Vera B. Williams, a small girl strives to please her mother. Among the old and new books on all kinds of family relationships, you will find those that are relevant to you and your child's particular circumstances.

Who Is Like Me?

Perhaps the greatest need of most young children is to understand their limitations, their needs, their delights, and their fears. In exploring these areas, the child is discovering not only who she is, but also that others are like her, too. Sometimes just discovering she is not alone in her fear of spiders, for instance, is a tremendous relief.

Many books for this age help children begin the lifelong voyage of self-identity. The books range from *Bedtime for Frances,* Russell Hoban's mischievous little badger's amusing stalling at bedtime, to *Two Homes to Live In: A Child's Eye View of Divorce* by

Barbara Shook Hazen. This book speaks in a young child's voice about the puzzling upsets that divorce may create. Susan Hill's *Go Away, Bad Dreams* and *When Small Is Tall* by Reit, Hooks, and Boegehold are two paperbacks that help children identify with others who feel as they do—scared of nighttime fantasies or powerless in an adult world.

The world of the four-year-old is expanding all the time. Conscious of his widening universe and powers, he tends to grandiose demands: "I want that! Give that to me!"

This shows in his desire for books, also. Left to himself, he will grab all kinds of books—"I want this one and that one." Caring adults will have to tread a delicate path between overfree choices of books and too-limited choices prescribed by rote. We hope this brief survey of three- and four-year-old characteristics will lead parents and teachers to the kinds of books that relate to the developmental needs of their children.

This is also the age group where there is an explosion of good picture books for children. Keep in mind that while three- and four-year-olds will enjoy the booklist that follows, it is also appropriate for most five-year-olds as well.

Booklist for Threes and Fours

Power, Independence, and Safe-Scare

The Tale of Peter Rabbit by Beatrix Potter. Warne, 1902. *Peter Rabbit* has been mentioned briefly a number of times already. It's hard to keep him out of any discussion of good books for preschoolers. But let's look more closely now at the importance of this little rabbit character for children who are savoring a sense of power and independence, who want a little suspense and danger (not too much) in their stories, and who are constantly asking—in spite of their bravado—"Who is like me?"

Peter is indeed like most young growing children. He doesn't really mean to disobey, and to get himself into so much trouble—but that urge to explore the world, to dare, to go beyond bounds, pulls him into Mr. McGregor's garden in spite of himself. "Thank goodness," thinks the child listener, "I'm not the only one who does things like this!"

And "Hurray for Peter," the child might continue to feel. "He got himself out. He listened to the sparrows and wriggled out of his jacket in time, and found a place to hide. He wasn't going to let Mr. McGregor get him!"

The daring Peter, in spite of his naughtiness, is someone to care about, to admire—and his mother is the embodiment of comfort and understanding. She gives Peter Chamomile tea, but she doesn't scold or punish. She knows that danger has given him all the punishment he needs. What blessed security and love and safety to come back to, after such a scare! What more does a four-year-old need in a story?

Well—more, of course. There is always the story's language to consider. Young listeners need the concreteness that will help them visualize the story, see it as a little drama before them; and they are lucky if the story can charm them with its interesting words and its flowing, storytelling style, full of simple action verbs to carry them along. Beatrix Potter is a master of all these fundamentals. She tells the reader exactly what vegetables Peter eats in the garden. She writes the sound of Peter's sneeze "Kertychoo!" and the sound of Mr. McGregor's hoe, "scr-r-ritch, scratch, scratch, scritch." True, she uses a few adult expressions ("implored him to exert himself") and names some things not entirely familiar to present-day American children, such as a "gooseberry net," but perhaps these only make the story more interesting. Children are drawn to writers who do not condescend to them.

Curious George by H. A. Rey. Houghton Mifflin, 1941. This little monkey, a "child in a fur coat," has been with us for a long time delighting children from about three to seven with his antics. And no matter what scary situations he gets himself into, he's always rescued by his protector, "the man with the big yellow hat." If you think your three-year-old would be too disturbed by the jail scenes in this book, wait until he's four, or try one of the other stories: *Curious George Takes a Job, Curious George Rides a Bike,* or *Curious George Gets a Medal.* (And there are still more.)

Harry the Dirty Dog by Gene Zion. Harper & Row, 1956. Harry is sick of baths and decides to really end them. He buries his bath brush and runs away, and has a fine time. But he gets himself so covered with black dirt that he is not recognized by his family when he returns. He has lost his identity —a frightening situation! But all turns out well. Before choosing this book, parents should keep in mind that Harry's natural color is white with black spots, more acceptable than when he becomes black with white spots. Dark-skinned children have been known to turn away from this story.

Mike Mulligan and His Steam Shovel by Virginia Lee Burton. Houghton Mifflin, 1939. The small outmoded steamshovel proves its worth in a hectic feat of digging a cellar all in one day. Of course, it can't get out afterwards, but there's a happy end to this dilemma. A story filled with suspense, likable people, and names that are fun to say.

Pierre by Maurice Sendak. The Nutshell Library, Harper & Row, 1962. Children love to shout "I don't care!" over and over along with the cocky Pierre, who gets himself into dire trouble—but out of it in the end. This is a game, a poem, and a fantasy that does not confuse.

Piggy in the Puddle by Charlotte Pomerantz; illustrated by James Marshall. Macmillan, 1974. Full of the sense of power over adults and nonsense wordplay beloved by the very young.

Rosie's Walk by Pat Hutchins. Macmillan, 1968. Rosie, the small hen, walks through this book concerned only with her own business, while a hungry fox follows close but never quite succeeds in nabbing her.

The Runaway Bunny by Margaret Wise Brown; illustrated by Clement Hurd. Harper & Row, 1942. A little classic on the dependence/independence theme. Although the bunny relishes the idea of running away, there is reassurance that no matter where he runs, Mother will be there.

The Three Billy Goats Gruff by Peter Christen Asbjornsen and Jorgen Moe; illustrated by Marcia Brown. Harcourt, 1957. About the blustering, courageous goat who knocks to pieces the dangerous troll under the bridge. Delightful repetitions and refrains that stay with a child for years.

Whistle for Willie by Ezra Jack Keats. Viking, 1964. No dire trouble here. Just a small boy in his father's hat who longs to be able to whistle, and finally succeeds.

Absurd Situations, Extravagant Language

Clifford the Big Red Dog by Norman Bridwell. Four Winds, 1963. Clifford is outrageously funny to young children as he goes bungling around causing all sorts of damage.

Chicken Soup with Rice by Maurice Sendak. Nutshell Library, Harper & Row, 1962. Endlessly enjoyable silly rhymes, and easy repetitions that invite the child's participation.

Drummer Hoff adapted by Barbara Emberley; illustrated by Ed Emberley. Prentice-Hall, 1967. A folk rhyme about the building of an old type of cannon. Its lines pile up and repeat until "Drummer Hoff fires it off" in a huge explosion of sound and color. Wonderful rhyming words—and at the end a picture of the cannon outmoded and overgrown with flowers.

Hungry Fred by Paula Fox; illustrated by Rosemary Wells. Bradbury, 1969. Hungry Fred eats up everything, including his house, in a story of exuberant exaggeration.

In the Night Kitchen by Maurice Sendak. Harper & Row, 1970. A chance to identify not only with the daring exploits of bold Mickey but with his loud and bold chants, such as "I'm not the milk and the milk's not me!" Children go for the book's large print and the stars everywhere in the pictures.

Is This My Dinner? by Irma Simonton Black; illustrated by Rosalind Fry. Whitman, 1972. The three-year-old can recognize the absurdity of the questions asked here about what's suitable for dinner.

Jamberry by Bruce Degen. Harper & Row, 1983. Every conceivable rhyme for every kind of berry ("Quickberry! Quackberry! Pick me a blackberry!") in this roistering little book jam-full of word play and fantastic pictures. Enjoyable for threes as well as fours and older.

Magic Michael by Louis Slobodkin. Macmillan, 1949. Michael pretends to be all sorts of animals and things. Funny, lively rhymes and crazy pictures. Present of a bike turns him back into a boy.

Millions of Cats by Wanda Gag. Coward, McCann, 1928. An old story loved for many reasons, including the presence of all those millions and billions and trillions of cats and their absurd feats of eating, drinking, and fighting. Enough exaggerations here to satisfy the most exuberant preschooler.

The Temper Tantrum Book by Edna Mitchell Preston; illustrated by Rainey Bennett. Viking, 1969. A book full of rages in pictures and words that may be just right for certain moods for the younger preschoolers.

Monsters, Goblins, Witches in the Dark

Are There Spooks in the Dark? by Claudia Fregosi. Four Winds, 1977. A boy and girl shoo away spooks supposedly hiding in the closet and under the bed. Stylized pictures convey more fun than fright.

The Berenstain Bears in the Dark by Stan and Jan Berenstain. Random House, 1982. After reading a scary mystery story, Sister and Brother have a bad night. Papa helps by locating an old night-light he had used when he was a child afraid at night. Illustrated in bright, cartoon-style pictures.

Chasing the Goblins Away by Tobi Tobias; pictures by Victor Ambrus. Warne, 1977. The goblins surrounding Jimmy's bed at night are a revolting and horrible lot (to these adults' eyes). You'll have to judge whether or not your four-year-old can take it—even though Jimmy does succeed in routing the creatures all by himself, with his father's encouragement.

Clyde Monster by Robert L. Crowe; illustrated by Kay Chorao. Dutton, 1976. Perhaps too tricky for a three and even for some fours. The gentle-looking monster boy here is afraid that *people* will creep into his cave at night! His gentle monster parents help.

Go Away, Bad Dreams by Susan Hill; illustrated by Vanessa Julian-Ottie. Random House, 1985. An understanding mother finds a way to help her son with his bad dreams.

I Won't Be Afraid by Joan Hanson. Carolrhoda, 1974. A little boy comforts himself with his belief that he won't have any of his fears when he's six years old.

I'll Protect You from the Jungle Beasts by Martha Alexander. Dial,

1973. A little boy and his teddy bear walk in an imaginary woods, where the growls of beasts come closer and closer. The boy isn't afraid, oh no, but begins to feel weak and is glad when the teddy bear lifts and carries him to the safety of home and bed. An endearing little fantasy that says every child needs protection at times.

Moonlight by Jan Ormerod. Lothrop, Lee and Shepard, 1982. The little girl gets ready for bed and is tucked in, but alone in the dark she is afraid, runs back and forth to Mother and Daddy for comfort, then finally falls asleep. Wordless book, easy to follow.

Sometimes I'm Afraid by Sylvia Tester; illustrated by Frances Hook. Children's Press, 1979. The fears here are not too scary for a three-year-old, and there's comfort in the parental protection and the beauty of the pictures.

There's a Nightmare in My Closet by Mercer Mayer. Dial, 1968. A little boy in bed at night hears the nightmare creeping toward him from the closet, bravely gets up, shoots it with his popgun. The nightmare cries, won't be quiet. The boy tucks him in bed and crawls in with him. A second horrible creature begins to come out of closet, but boy is asleep.

Who's Afraid of the Dark? by Crosby Bonsall. Harper & Row, 1980. Although the little boy in this book assures his dog that there's nothing to fear in the dark, four-year-olds will get the point that the boy is really reassuring himself.

Books About Death

The Dead Bird by Margaret Wise Brown; illustrated by Remy Charlip. Young Scott Books, 1938. This beautiful classic about the children who have a little funeral in the woods for a dead bird may be just right for some fours who have lost pets. Others may appreciate it when they are a little older.

My Turtle Died Today by Edith Stull; illustrated by Mamoru Funai. Holt, 1964. The birth of kittens helps to remove the grief in this beautifully illustrated book for the very young.

Nana by Lyn Littlefield Hoopes. Harper & Row, 1981. Her grandmother is dead, but the little girl finds many happy reminders of her as she wanders through house and garden.

Someone Small by Barbara Borack; illustrated by Anita Lobel.

Harper & Row, 1969. A rich little story on several levels. About family life and getting along with a little sister; also about the death of a pet bird, and the children's way of saying good-bye.

When Violet Died by Mildred Kantrowitz; illustrated by Emily A. McCully. Parents Magazine Press, 1973. When Amy and Eva's bird dies, they bury it and invite the neighborhood children to the funeral. Afterward, as they look at their cat who is about to have kittens, they realize that though nothing lasts forever, they can take comfort in knowing that new life goes on.

Siblings: Jealousies and Getting Along

Abby by Jeannette Caines; illustrated by Steven Kellogg. Harper & Row, 1973. Kevin is sometimes impatient with his little adopted sister, but means well. This story gives the reader an intimate view of a few hours in a black family.

Amy and the New Baby by Myra Berry Brown. Watts, 1965. Amy has some negative feelings about the new baby's arrival, but her parents help her to feel better about it.

A Baby for Max by Kathryn Lasky; in the words of Maxwell B. Knight; photographs by Christopher G. Knight. Scribner's, 1984. In this sensitive, beautifully photographed account of the arrival of a sister for Max, there are joys as well as fears and frustrations.

Big Brother by Charlotte Zolotow; illustrated by Mary Chalmers. Harper & Row, 1982. A small girl finds she can be friends with her brother.

Betsy's Baby Brother by Gunilla Wolde. Random House, 1975. Betsy learns how to go through the whole diapering process for her baby brother, and decides that though he is often a nuisance, he is also cuddly and sweet.

David's Waiting Day by Bernadette Watts. Prentice-Hall, 1977. The emphasis in this very beautiful book is not on the sibling relationship but on the long and exciting day of waiting for Mother to come home from the hospital with the new baby. A refreshing look at the old story from a slightly different angle.

Do You Have the Time, Lydia? by Evaline Ness. Dutton, 1971. It's easy for the big sister to get so involved in other things that she forgets her responsibilities for the little brother.

Everett Anderson's Nine Months Long by Lucille Clifton; illustrated by Ann Grifalconi. Holt, 1978. Everett Anderson has been a beloved character for several years now. Here we see him a little troubled in the new family situation. His mother has remarried and a baby is on the way. Thanks to the loving parents, things are probably going to turn out well. A beautiful book to look at and to hear read aloud.

Faye and Dolores by Barbara Samuels. Bradbury, 1985. Three short stories about two sisters getting along at home. The older one can be annoying at times, but also helpful. Very much like real life.

I Want a Brother or Sister by Astrid Lindgren; translated from the Swedish by Barbara Lucas; illustrated by Ilon Wickland. Harcourt, 1978. Mother's love is what helps in this appealingly illustrated book.

If It Weren't for Benjamin (I'd Always Get to Lick the Icing Spoon) by Barbara Shook Hazen; illustrated by Laura Hartman. Human Sciences Press, 1979. The younger brother has his frustrations, but there is fondness too.

Katie Did! by Kathryn Osebold Galbraith; illustrated by Ted Ramsey. Atheneum, 1982. Mother is busy with the new baby, and Mary Rose gets into trouble she blames on her doll Katie. Fortunately Mother begins to realize that Mary Rose needs some loving attention.

My Brother Fine with Me by Lucille Clifton; illustrated by Moneta Barnett. Holt, 1975. When little brother runs away, his older sister decides he really isn't much of a nuisance after all.

The New Baby by Fred Rogers. Putnam, 1985. In this book "Mister Rogers" talks with children (as he does on TV) about some of the feelings they may be having about a new baby in the family. Fine photographs of family scenes.

A New Baby Is Coming to My House by Chikiro Iwasaki. McGraw-Hill, 1972. A little girl awaits the arrival of the new baby. Her thoughts and moods are caught very suggestively in the artist's soft watercolor illustrations.

Nobody Asked Me If I Wanted a Baby Sister by Martha Alexander. Dial, 1971. A little boy tries to give his baby sister away, until he discovers he is the only one who can get her to stop her crying.

On Mother's Lap by Ann Herbert Scott; illustrated by Glo Coalson. McGraw-Hill, 1972. The little Eskimo boy who's rocking on his mother's lap finds plenty of room there for his dolly and boat and puppy, but claims there's no room there for Baby. Mother makes room for both children and they all rock away comfortably. "There's always room on Mother's lap."

Peggy's New Brother by Eleanor Schick. Macmillan, 1970. Peggy doesn't want a new brother as much as she wants a dog, but when she discovers that she can stop the baby's crying when no one else can, she decides it's all right to have a little brother.

Peter's Chair by Ezra Jack Keats. Harper & Row, 1967. A picture book in Keats's striking collage style about Peter's feelings of displacement when his furniture is painted over for the new baby sister. For a wide age range.

Pig Pig Grows Up by David McPhail. Dutton, 1980. Almost before he realizes it, Pig Pig finds himself a little more grown up —in a funny, comforting story.

Sisters by David McPhail. Harcourt, 1984. A little sister and a big sister—how they are different in their tastes and how they are alike.

Someone Small by Barbara Borack; illustrated by Anita Lobel. Harper & Row, 1969. This book, which we have listed under *Books About Death,* is full of themes about family life, including the rivalry feelings of a little girl when her sister is born.

We Are Having a Baby by Viki Holland; photographs by the author. Scribner's, 1972. In spare text and vivid photographs the story is told of the arrival at home of a new baby brother, and the four-year-old sister's ups and downs over the event. A book for a child to pore over.

Family

All Kinds of Mothers by Cecily Brownstone; illustrated by Miriam Brofsky. McKay, 1969. Here they are, in great variety—tall or short, fat or thin—what they like to cook, what they like to do. Whatever their differences, they all love their children.

Busy Monday Morning by Janina Domanska. Greenwillow, 1985. Gorgeous illustrations show a little peasant boy helping his father with all aspects of the haying throughout the days of the week. The few words are those of a Polish folk song.

A Chair for My Mother by Vera B. Williams. Greenwillow, 1982. After a fire in their house, a small girl works hard to save money for a beautiful present for her mother.

Daddy and Ben Together by Miriam Stecher and Alice Kandell; illustrated with photos. Lothrop, Lee and Shepard, 1981. Daddy and Ben learn a great deal about each other during the week they spend without Mother.

A Father Like That by Charlotte Zolotow; illustrated by Ben Schecter. Harper & Row, 1971. A little boy who has never known a father describes in detail the kind and sympathetic father he wishes he had. His mother gives him a new thought: he can be just like that when he grows up.

Gone Fishing by Earlene Long; illustrated by Richard Brown. Houghton Mifflin, 1984. An early morning fishing trip for the big daddy and the little boy. Full-page pictures and one line of text on each page.

Leo the Late Bloomer by Robert Kraus; illustrated by Jose Aruego. Windmill, 1971. Leo the tiger, a child in a fur coat, is the slow one in the family—slow to talk, read, write, and draw. But no need to worry. He suddenly does learn, when he's ready.

Make Way for Ducklings by Robert McCloskey. Viking, 1941. Don't leave out this old favorite about the duck family in Boston's Public Garden. What child will ever forget the ducklings and their mother crossing the street with a policeman's help?

Our Garage Sale by Anne Rockwell; illustrated by Harlow Rockwell. Greenwillow, 1984. The whole family works to put on a garage sale of old things no longer wanted. The little boy sells his old puzzles and truck and can buy himself a model airplane kit and some bubble gum.

A Piano for Julie by Eleanor Schick. Greenwillow, 1984. Julie longs for a piano like grandmother's. The day comes when her parents can buy one, and it is moved into Julie's home. Julie learns "Twinkle, Twinkle, Little Star" and Daddy sits down and plays "music that sounds like moonlight." The soft, muted pictures may appeal very much to some children and less to others.

The Quarreling Book by Charlotte Zolotow; illustrated by Arnold Lobel. Harper & Row, 1963. Even young children want books that show them what real life is like—the quarrels as well as the love. This book is especially appealing because of the story form in which the quarrel mounts and then unwinds in the end.

Something Special for Me written and illustrated by Vera B. Williams. Greenwillow, 1983. The shopping trip for the birthday present from her mother ends up in an unusual and wonderful present for the little girl.

The Summer Night by Charlotte Zolotow; illustrated by Ben Schecter. Harper & Row, 1974. Mother is away for a day and a night, and Father takes care of the little girl. She's restless at bedtime and her father stays with her—reads to her and walks with her in the yard, way past the usual bedtime. Very comforting inside view of a house, going-to-bed rituals, and an understanding father.

Thunderstorm by Mary Szilagyi. Bradbury, 1985. How comforting it is for a mother, a little girl, and their dog to settle down on a couch together while a loud thunderstorm rages. Dramatic pictures.

Washday by Susan Merrill. Seabury, 1978. The whole family helps on this washday, exuberantly pictured on fresh green and blue pages full of active people.

Friends

Addie Meets Max by Joan Robbins; illustrated by Sue Truesdell. Harper & Row, 1985. Very lively illustrations and just a few words tell this story of making a new friend. Addie had been so sure she wouldn't like the new boy next door, but it didn't take long for her to find out that they could have fun. Very true to life.

Best Friends by Miriam Cohen; illustrated by Lillian Hoban. Macmillan, 1971. Here are the ups and downs of being best friends during a kindergarten day.

Cheer Up, Pig! by Nancy Jewell; illustrated by Ben Schecter. Harper & Row, 1975. Children will identify with the feelings of this lonely little pig, and will find the solution to his problem comforting.

Corduroy by Don Freeman. Viking, 1968. This great favorite about a forlorn little teddy bear has many things to say to young children. Perhaps it is loved chiefly for the happy ending when the teddy bear and the little girl who has bought him realize that at last each one has a friend.

Friends by Helen Heine. Atheneum, 1985. The friends in this fantasy are a rooster, a pig, and a mouse, who spend happy days together. They even manage to ride a bicycle and sail a boat. Of course, they have a few troubles, but "Good friends stick together," they always say, as they make things right again. Eye-catching pictures in rich colors.

Frog and Toad Are Friends by Arnold Lobel. Harper & Row, 1970. Five chapters, which can be read as separate stories, tell of small episodes in the days of these two delightful friends. See also *Frog and Toad Together, Frog and Toad All Year,* and *Days with Frog and Toad.*

George and Martha by James Marshall. Houghton Mifflin, 1972. These two great lumbering hippo friends in human clothes have become very popular with children. In the five very short stories in this book the hippos learn how important it is to be honest with each other.

The Golden Egg Book by Margaret Wise Brown; illustrated by Leonard Weisgard. Simon & Schuster, 1947. In this gorgeously illustrated book, friendship is the happy outcome.

May I Bring a Friend? by Beatrice Schenk De Regniers; illustrated by Beni Montresor. Atheneum, 1964. Children as young as three and as old as seven warm to this book, not only for the fun of the animals who come to tea, but for the good king and queen who welcome "any friend of our friend." The flowing lines with their natural rhymes are wonderful for reading aloud.

Play with Me by Marie Hall Ets. Viking, 1955. In this delicately illustrated small book, a lonely little girl tries to make friends with some animal creatures such as a frog, a turtle, a chipmunk. Chasing them brings no results, but when she sits quietly and waits, they know they will be safe and come to her.

Rollo and Juliet Forever! by Marjorie W. Sharmat; illustrated by Marylin Hafner. Doubleday, 1981. Two cats are "friends forever," but one day make each other very mad. Of course, this can't last. Gradually they find their way back to friendship.

Sam and Emma by Donald Nelson; illustrated by Edward Gorey. Parents Magazine Press, 1971. How two friends (pictured as cat and dog) manage to continue their friendship in spite of personal traits that get in the way.

Steffie and Me by Phyllis Hoffman; illustrated by Emily McCully. Harper & Row, 1970. This lively and very human story of the friendship of two girls, one black and one white, about five or six years old, should appeal to many fours, particularly if they have preschool experience and thus can visualize the schoolroom where much of the story takes place.

Timothy Goes to School by Rosemary Wells. Dial, 1981. How comforting it is when Timothy finds a friend after what seems to him an unhappy start.

Ton and Pon: Two Good Friends by Kazuo Iwamura. Bradbury, 1985. The big dog and the small dog (substitutes for children) cooperate in finding ways to carry a heavy basket of apples to a friend for her birthday. See also these two learning about cooperation in *Ton and Pon: Big and Little.* Both books have what the three-year-old needs: large, uncluttered pictures and just a few words of story.

Will I Have a Friend? by Miriam Cohen; illustrated by Lillian Hoban. Macmillan, 1967. Anxiety about the first day of school ends in happiness.

Older Relations and Friends

Aunt Nina's Visit by Franz Brandenberg; illustrated by Aliki. Greenwillow, 1984. A delightful depiction of a child-loving aunt.

Big Boy, Little Boy by Betty Jo Stanovich; illustrated by Virginia

Wright-Frierson. Lothrop, Lee and Shepard, 1984. David is both a big boy and a little boy in his relationship with his grandmother.

Coco Can't Wait! by Taro Gomi. Morrow, 1984. Coco and Grandma live several hills away from each other in what looks like a Caribbean country. One day each sets out to visit the other, but the bus passes right by the trolley. They try again—but their car and truck pass each other on the highway. Finally they have a happy meeting in the middle of the way. Very few words and large exciting pictures in brown and purple tints.

The Crack-of-Dawn Walkers by Amy Hest; illustrated by Amy Schwartz. Macmillan, 1984. The special feelings of a small child toward her grandfather on an early morning walk.

Grandfather and I by Helen E. Buckley; illustrated by Paul Galdone. Lothrop, Lee and Shepard, 1959. The little boy especially enjoys going out with Grandfather, because Grandfather is willing to go slowly, and stop, look, and listen whenever the boy wants to.

Grandma and Grandpa by Helen Oxenbury. Dial, 1984. Simple, clear pictures about playing with grandparents. Just right for many three-year-olds.

Grandmother and I by Helen E. Buckley; illustrated by Paul Galdone. Lothrop, Lee and Shepard, 1961. Mothers and fathers and grandfathers have good laps, but grandmother's is just right for all sorts of occasions.

Grandpa by Barbara Borack; illustrated by Ben Schecter. Harper & Row, 1967. Games they play, walks they take, and oranges they eat together. A great loving pair, these two.

I Have Four Names for My Grandfather by Kathryn Lasky; photos by Christopher G. Knight. Little, Brown, 1976. Whether it's Poppy or Pop, Grandpa or Gramps, the little boy has lots of fun with him. Few words and very expressive photographs.

I Know a Lady by Charlotte Zolotow; illustrated by James Stevenson. Greenwillow, 1984. The old lady who lives alone gives the neighborhood children flowers from her garden, and invites them in for treats on Halloween and Christmas. Everyone loves her. Large, colorful pictures.

Pet Show by Ezra Jack Keats. Macmillan, 1972. This story of the show has a lot to say to young children, not only about a group of friends but also about the good relationships of adults and children in this community.

Uncle Elephant by Arnold Lobel. Harper & Row, 1981. An uncle steps into the parenting role when he is needed and turns out to be not only a comfort but a lot of fun.

A Secret for Grandmother's Birthday by Aliki. Greenwillow, 1975. A brother and sister cat love their indulging grandmother and make secret plans for her birthday—gifts they make all by themselves.

A Special Trade by Sally Wittman; illustrated by Karen Gundersheimer. Harper & Row, 1978. When Nelly is very small, her neighbor, Old Bartholomew, pushes her in her stroller every day. But time passes and Old Bartholomew becomes lame and needs a wheelchair. So Nelly is the one who pushes. "Kind of like a trade." Abundant small pictures accompany the simply told story.

Wilberforce Goes on a Picnic by Margaret Gordon. Morrow, 1982. When the little bear Wilberforce and his brother and sister go on a picnic with the grandparents, all of them have fun but also get into some troubles. The pictures show a lot more happening than is told in the story.

Just Like Me

Alfie Gives a Hand by Shirley Hughes. Lothrop, Lee and Shepard, 1984. Alfie goes to a birthday party and takes along his little security blanket. It's in his way, but he hangs on to it until he needs a free hand to help the little girl who needs him. The pictures of small youngsters at a party have the great charm of real life. Try also *Alfie's Feet,* in which Alfie delights in his new boots.

Amifika by Lucille Clifton; illustrated by Thomas Di Grazia. Dutton, 1977. The little black boy, Amifika, misinterprets the conversation he overhears and thinks there will be no room for him when his daddy comes home from the army, so he runs away and hides. A very loving father finds him.

Bad Thad by Judy Malloy; illustrated by Martha Alexander. Dutton, 1980. Thad is called "Bad" over and over during the day for troubling things he does in spite of himself. But at bedtime, it's easy to see how much his parents love him.

Bedtime for Frances by Russell Hoban; illustrated by Garth Williams. Harper & Row, 1960. A mischievous little badger's amusing stalling at bedtime.

Benjamin's Book by Alan Baker. Lothrop, Lee and Shepard, 1984. Children will sympathize with the little hamster whose efforts to fix up the damage he caused only make it worse.

A Big, Fat, Enormous Lie by Marjorie Weinman Sharmat; illustrated by David McPhail. Dutton, 1978. When the little boy lied about eating the cookies, his lie seemed to him like a big, fat, enormous creature hanging around with him. He got rid of it finally by telling his parents who ate the cookies. A situation that will have a lot of meaning to most children of four and older.

The Carrot Seed by Ruth Krauss; illustrated by Crockett Johnson. Harper & Row, 1945. This little book has been around for a long time now, but is there a child of three or four or even older who can fail to identify with the story's determined little planter? It doesn't seem to matter how many times one hears this book.

Daddy by Jeannette Caines; illustrated by Ronald Himler. Harper & Row, 1977. A story especially for all those children who, like Windy, go to Daddy's apartment every week to spend a happy Saturday with him.

Even If I Did Something Awful by Barbara Shook Hazen; illustrated by Nancy Kincade. Atheneum, 1981. Mom doesn't approve of the "awful" things, but her love is always there. A warm, reassuring book.

Lester's Overnight by Kay Chorao. Dutton, 1977. It's not easy to have to spend a night away from home. Auntie Belle is very kind but her food is not like the food at home, and she has purple soap and doesn't read goodnight stories. All little children who have felt strange away from home will sympathize with Lester.

Noisy Nora by Rosemary Wells. Dial, 1973. A noisy little mouse learns a lot in this story about the love her parents have for her in spite of her jealous, noisy behavior.

SH H H H! by Suzy Kline; illustrated by Dora Leder. Whitman, 1984. After a child who's been "shushed" all day explodes in yells, shrieks, and screams in her back yard, she's willing to be quiet again. Youngsters will love the great noisy words, and identify with the girl's feelings.

Some of the Days of Everett Anderson by Lucille Clifton; illustrated by Evaline Ness. Holt, 1970. A small black boy plays in the rain, feels lonely and afraid of the dark. One of a series of fine books.

Two Homes to Live in: A Child's Eye View of Divorce by Barbara Shook Hazen; illustrated by Peggy Luks. Human Sciences Press, 1978. This book speaks in a young child's voice about the puzzling upsets that divorce may create.

Umbrella by Taro Yashima. Viking, 1958. Children who long to use their own new umbrellas can identify with Momo, the little girl in this colorful, bright picture book.

Very Shy by Barbara Shook Hazen; illustrated by Shirley Chan. Human Sciences Press, 1983. It's a comfort to Nancy to discover that she's not the only one who feels self-conscious.

When Small Is Tall by Seymour V. Reit, William H. Hooks, Betty D. Boegehold; illustrated by Lynn Munsinger. Random House, 1985. Small creatures win out in these three short tales based on Aesop.

Imaginary Playmates

A Birthday for Frances by Russell Hoban; illustrated by Lillian Hoban. Harper & Row, 1968. Jealous Frances makes up an imaginary Alice to sing Happy Birthday to, when it is her little sister Gloria's birthday. The story may be a little too long and wordy for the attention span of fours, but no harm trying it. The appeal of the theme may outweigh all the difficulties.

Blackboard Bear by Martha Alexander. Dial, 1969. Feeling left out, a little boy draws a blackboard bear who comes to life for him—and he doesn't let the older boys ride the bear or even touch him.

Goodnight Horsey by Frank Asch. Prentice-Hall, 1981. When the little girl's father, pretending to be a horse, takes the girl for a ride before she goes to sleep, she imagines him changing into a real horse she can ride out in the country. The pictures, which might confuse a young three-year-old, show the father taking a horse shape and galloping across the pages. Of course he changes back into a father at the end.

The Horse in Harry's Room by Syd Hoff. Harper & Row, 1970. Harry has a fine time with the imaginary horse in his room. No one believes him, but this doesn't matter to Harry. The horse even stays when Harry offers to let him go where he can be free. So Harry knows he can have him as long as he wants him. The pictures suggest an imaginary, not a real, horse.

Me and Neesie by Eloise Greenfield; illustrated by Moneta Barnett. Crowell, 1975. Neesie, the imaginary playmate, looks very real in these pictures, but when Janell starts school, she can't find Neesie any more.

Action, Suspense, Happy Ending

Ask Mr. Bear by Marjorie Flack. Macmillan, 1932. This simple repetitive story has just the right pace and amount of suspense for the young three-year-old, and its happy ending is unforgettable.

Blueberries for Sal by Robert McCloskey. Viking, 1948. Sal and her mother are out blueberry picking and who should they encounter but a shy mother bear and her cub, also out for berries! Presented with a sense of fun rather than danger. Stunning black-and-white pictures.

Caps for Sale by Esphyr Slobodkina. Addison-Wesley, 1947. How will the peddler get back his caps from the monkeys in the trees? A favorite story full of suspense and lovely repetitions.

Danny and the Dinosaur by Syd Hoff. Harper & Row, 1958. This easy reader tells the story of a dinosaur who steps out of the museum and plays with Danny all day. The dilemmas the two of them encounter delight the four-year-old.

Eddy B., Pigboy by Olivier Dunrea. Atheneum, 1983. The Pigboy outwits Mama Pig in a picture-book story outstanding for both simplicity and satisfying action.

Grasshopper on the Road by Arnold Lobel. Harper & Row, 1978. Children of about four and older should enjoy the adventures of this daring insect, as shown in Lobel's short text and soft-hued pictures.

Little Bear by Else Holmelund Minarik; illustrated by Maurice Sendak. Harper & Row, 1957. The four gentle stories here about Little Bear (who is a little child to readers) all involve very small dilemmas and very comfortable endings. Try also *Father Bear Comes Home, Little Bear's Friend, Little Bear's Visit,* and *A Kiss for Little Bear.*

The Little Engine That Could by Watty Piper; illustrated by George and Doris Hauman. Platt & Munk, 1954. For the sake of its refrain, "I think I can, I think I can," "I thought I could, I thought I could," if for no other reason, children love this old story.

Madeline by Ludwig Bemelmans. Viking, 1939. Not only Madeline's cry in the night and her stay at the hospital, but the scenes of Paris and the story's words tripping along in easy verses draw children over and over to this intriguing book. For fours and older.

The Mystery of the Missing Red Mitten by Steven Kellogg. Dial, 1974. An amusing small tale of the search for a mitten, with intriguing guesswork involved. Illustrations are more appropriate to four-year-olds, since guesses are made to look as real as the realities.

The Snuggle Bunny by Nancy Jewell; illustrated by Mary Chalmers. Harper & Row, 1972. The lonely little bunny hunts for someone to snuggle with and finally finds him—a lonely old man. A cozy story, with just enough suspense.

Swimmy by Leo Lionni. Pantheon, 1963. The inventive little black fish solves a problem and makes life safer for all the little fish his size. Marvelous sea-life pictures.

Mouse Soup by Arnold Lobel. Harper & Row, 1977. The short stories told here by a mouse to save his skin are "easy to read" but also satisfy the younger child's need for small dilemmas and speedy action. See also the seven short stories in Lobel's *Mouse Tales.*

Three Rounds with Rabbit by William H. Hooks; illustrated by Lissa McLaughlin. Lothrop, Lee and Shepard, 1984. Very short stories with repeated phrases just right for the young child to chant—all about how Little Rabbit can outwit Terrible Tiger.

Sensory Books: Taste, Feel, and Smell

The following are some picture books outstanding for use of concrete, sensory details in their texts:

I Dance in My Red Pajamas by Edith Thacher Hurd; illustrated by Emily Arnold McCully. Harper & Row, 1982. About the lively time a little girl has when she visits her grandparents.

Gilberto and the Wind by Marie Hall Ets. Viking, 1963. Wind—how it sounds, what it blows, what it breaks, and what a little boy can do with it. Some fours may have learned to love this beautiful book when they were a little younger. If not, don't let them miss it.

Lordy, Aunt Hattie by Ianthe Thomas; illustrated by Thomas di Grazia. Harper & Row, 1973. In the flowing cadences of southern black speech, Aunt Hattie tells Jeppa Lee about things to do on a hot summer day.

Mr. Gumpy's Outing by John Burningham. Crowell, 1971. Full of expressive action verbs that are a delight to children. Also: *Mr. Gumpy's Motor Car.*

One Morning in Maine by Robert McCloskey. Viking, 1952. Family happenings on the beach, in a story conjuring up the smell of salt water and the feel and look of sea fog.

Wait Till the Moon Is Full by Margaret Wise Brown; illustrated by Garth Williams. Harper & Row, 1948. One of the classic stories by this author who was so attuned to the sensory world of childhood.

Goodnight Stories and Poems

The Animals' Lullaby by Trude Alberti. World, 1967. Where does the seal sleep, and the bear cub, and the little beaver, etc.? Finally, where does the child sleep? Lilting four-line verses on each page.

Animals Sleeping by Masayuki Yabuuchi. Philomel, 1983. Captivating illustrations show how various animals sleep. Simple text.

Bedtime Bear's Book of Bedtime Poems selected by Bobbie Katz; illustrated by Dora Leder. Random House, 1983. A comfortable size little square book with a great array of small poems by outstanding poets, including some by Robert Louis Stevenson and some choice Mother Goose.

Bedtime Story by Jim Erskine; illustrated by Ann Schweninger. Crown, 1982. Simple text and muted pictures are just right for go-to-bed time.

Big Bedtime Story Book by Patsy Scarry. Random House, 1980. A collection of little stories about small creatures. Good bedtime reading.

A Child's Goodnight Book by Margaret Wise Brown; illustrated by Jean Charlot. Young Scott Books, 1950. If you are looking for a book that has a little prayer in it and an angel picture, here it is. After we hear about all the creatures who are going to sleep, then the children say their prayers and climb into bed. A poetic book.

Goodnight, Goodnight by Eve Rice. Greenwillow, 1980. All over the town people are saying goodnight to each other—to family, to friends, to pets.

Goodnight, Mr. Beetle by Leland B. Jacobs; illustrated by Gilbert Riswold. Holt, 1963. On each one of these lavishly colored pages there's a goodnight to a familiar creature—a beetle, a fly, a sparrow, a rooster, and so on—in a very natural rhyming scheme. So short that it can be read again and again.

Go to Bed: A Book of Bedtime Poems selected by Lee Bennett Hopkins; illustrated by Rosekrans Hoffman. Knopf, 1979. A variety of short poems to read aloud about the coming of night—about stars and moon, teddy bears, bedtime, and dreams.

Hush, Little Baby by Margot Zemach. Dutton, 1975. This familiar lullaby can be either read aloud or sung.

More Night by Muriel Rukeyser; illustrated by Symeon Shimin. Harper & Row, 1981. A noted poet for adults explores dreams and night in a way that many young children can understand.

Mother, Mother, I Want Another by Maria Polushkin; illustrated by Diane Dawson. Crown, 1978. The restless child here who wants "another" and "another" is a young mouse. Mother invites in other mouse mothers to help her get her child to sleep.

Night Again by Karla Kuskin. Atlantic–Little, Brown, 1981. The bedtime ritual in poetic prose and a round picture on each blue page. (The blue color darkens as the little boy settles down to sleep.) For what age? Certain children of any young age may dearly love certain pages, if not all of the quiet, lyrical book.

Patrick Goes to Bed by Geoffrey Hayes. Knopf, 1985. For a very young child, a small book with small uncluttered pictures, about some of the things Patrick Bear does and asks for before he can go peacefully to bed.

Sleepy Book by Charlotte Zolotow; illustrated by Vladimir Bobri. Lothrop, Lee and Shepard, 1958. A quiet book with few words about how and where bears and pigeons and other creatures sleep; finally where little boys and girls sleep.

Ten, Nine, Eight by Molly Bang. Greenwillow, 1983. This is a lulling book that counts backwards from ten, beginning with ten toes, nine soft friends (the playthings), eight square window panes, etc. Easy rhyming words and clear pictures full of color.

Wake Up and Goodnight by Charlotte Zolotow; illustrated by Leonard Weisgard. Harper & Row, 1971. This book begins with morning, then moves into night, when "the golden sun is down" and it's time for everyone to sleep deeply and say goodnight. A lyrical book that creates a sleepy atmosphere.

Where Did You Put Your Sleep? by Marcia Newfield; illustrated by Andrea Da Rif. Atheneum, 1983. Annie stalls about going to bed, but her father helps resolve the conflict. An imaginative goodnight story.

Vehicles and City Streets

The following are notable for their clear, colorful pictures. The
ABCs and counting which appear in some of them can be
ignored if the child is not yet interested in them.

The ABC of Cars and Trucks by Anne Alexander. Doubleday,
1971.
Airport by Byron Barton. Crowell, 1982.
The Big Book of Red Trucks by George Zaffo. Grosset & Dunlap,
1964.
The Big Red Bus by Ethel and Leonard Kessler. Doubleday,
1969.
Big Red Fire Engine by Rose Greydanus. Troll Associates,
1980.
Busy Day, Busy People by Tibor Gergely. Random House, 1973.
Cars by Anne Rockwell. Dutton, 1984.
The City by Douglas Florian. Crowell, 1982.
City Seen from A to Z by Rachel Isadora. Greenwillow, 1983.
Freight Train by Donald Crews. Greenwillow, 1984.
The Giant Nursery Book of Things That Go by George Zaffo. Garden
City, 1959.
The Little Auto by Lois Lenski. Walck, 1934. See also *The Little
Airplane* and *The Little Sailboat.* These small books with their
simple stories and pictures are still useful for the youngest
children, though written long ago.
People Working by Douglas Florian. Crowell, 1983.
Planes by Anne Rockwell. Dutton, 1985.
Pumpers, Boilers, Hook and Ladder: A Book of Fire Engines by Leon-
ard Everett Fisher. Dial, 1966.
Richard Scarry's Best First Book Ever. Random House, 1979. Books
by Richard Scarry are loved by children for their great array
of clear and brightly colored little animal people and ob-
jects. Fascinating for looking at and "labeling," whether or
not the story themes are followed. Also: *Early Words, Richard
Scarry's Best Word Book Ever, Richard Scarry's Busy, Busy World,
Richard Scarry's Cars and Trucks and Things That Go, Richard
Scarry's What Do People Do All Day?*
School Bus by Donald Crews. Greenwillow, 1984.
Traffic: A Book of Opposites by Betsy Maestro. Crown, 1981.

Train Whistles by Helen Roney Sattler; illustrated by Giulio Maestro. Lothrop, Lee and Shepard, 1985.

Truck by Donald Crews. Greenwillow, 1980.

Trucks by Gail Gibbons. Crowell. 1981.

Trucks by Anne Rockwell. Dutton, 1984.

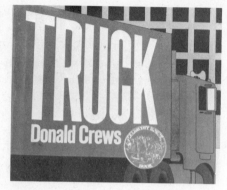

Truck Song by Diane Siebert. Crowell, 1984.

Animals, Insects, Farms

All Ready for Winter by Leone Adelson; illustrated by Kathleen Elgin. David McKay, 1952. Short questions and answers about what happens to various creatures when winter comes—birds, mice, turtles, horses, squirrels, butterflies, etc. Attractive picture-book format. Highly appropriate for young children.

The Animals of Buttercup Farm by Judy Dunn; photos by Phoebe Dunn. Random House, 1981. Excellent, clear photos, and an appropriate text for very young children.

Big Red Barn by Margaret Wise Brown; illustrated by Rosella Hartman. Addison-Wesley, 1956. Wonderful to read aloud about the animals and their day in and around the big red barn. Worth hunting for in the libraries.

Busy Monday Morning by Janina Domanska. Greenwillow, 1985. A little Polish peasant boy accompanies his father each day of the week to complete the haying process. Rhythmic words of a folksong, and magnificent large pictures.

A Chick Hatches by Joanna Cole and Jerome Wexler. Morrow, 1976. Clear photos and language detailing one of the wonders of life.

Farm Alphabet Book by Jane Miller; illustrated with photos. Prentice-Hall, 1984. Superb color photographs depicting the farm and its animals.

Farm Animals by Nancy Sears. Random House, 1977. Familiar domestic animals shown in large, clear pictures.

Good Morning, Chick by Mirra Ginsburg; pictures by Byron Barton. Greenwillow, 1980. A chick hatches and explores the farmyard, having some dangerous encounters but always returning to safety. Large bright pictures and story full of the repetitions pleasing to the young child.

Greeneyes by A. Birnbaum. Capitol Publishing Co., 1953. Story of a kitten's growth, very satisfying to young children, who can easily identify with the kitten.

The Little Duck by Judy Dunn. Photos by Phoebe Dunn. Random House, 1976. This and the other animal books by this team can be highly recommended for superb photography and content that is interesting and suitable in every way. See also *The Little Dog, The Little Lamb, The Little Rabbit,* and *The Little Goat.*

Look—A Butterfly by David Cutts; illustrated by Eulala Conner. Troll Associates, 1982. Vivid illustrations and a few well-chosen words make this book a rich sensory experience for a young child.

Sleepy Bear by Lydia Dabcovick. Dutton, 1982. Here is the simply told, gentle story of a bear's hibernation.

The Very Hungry Caterpillar by Eric Carle. Philomel, 1969. This very favorite book could be listed under several categories. While it mainly reveals the transformation from caterpillar to butterfly, it also tells a story beautifully organized to cover the days of a week while the caterpillar eats its way (leaving holes in the pages) through a fantasized assortment of delectable foods.

Where Do Bears Sleep? by Barbara Shook Hazen; illustrated by Ian E. Staunton. Addison-Wesley, 1970. The question is asked and answered not only about bears but also many other creatures, and at the end the human child. Colorful pictures.

Where Does the Butterfly Go When It Rains? by May Garelick; illustrated by Leonard Weisgard. Young Scott, 1961. A book of questioning about creatures in the rain.

Whose Mother Are You? by Robert Kraus; illustrated by Jose Aruego. Macmillan, 1970. This story has been a childhood favorite for a long time. Each time the question is asked, the child sees only the tail of the next animal to appear.

• • •

Nature

A Book of Seasons by Alice and Martin Provensen. Random House, 1978. Here the authors of the beautiful Maple Hill Farm books illustrate seasonal changes. Simple text.

First Comes Spring by Anne Rockwell. Crowell, 1985. A picture book chock-full of little animal people busy indoors and out in all sorts of activities during the four seasons.

Grandmother Lucy in Her Garden by Joyce Wood; illustrated by Frank Francis. Collins World, 1974. A little girl accompanies her grandmother as they walk about the garden in the spring, planting flowers, picking pussywillows, and noting other signs of spring. A beautiful, large picture book.

Owly by Mike Thaler; illustrated by David Wiesner. Harper & Row, 1982. Owly's mother helps him find answers to his many questions about stars and waves and other things in the universe that can't be counted.

Rain by Peter Spier. Doubleday, 1982. How to enjoy the rain (when you're dressed for it). In this wordless picture book two children have a lively time investigating what happens in the rain.

Song of the Seasons by Robert Welber; illustrated by Deborah Ray. Pantheon, 1973. Very small, lyrical book centering around a tree in the four seasons, text consisting of a simple four-line verse for each season.

A Tree Is Nice by Janice May Udry; illustrated by Marc Simont. Harper & Row, 1956. Everything about trees and their uses in a large colorful picture book that has been a staple for years now.

The Snowy Day by Ezra Jack Keats. Viking, 1962. Simple words and glowing pictures tell of a little black boy's fun in the snow.

Water Is Wet by Penny Pollock. Putnam, 1985. Simple text and candid black-and-white photographs show children using and exploring water in all its forms.

Concepts

By definition a concept is "a general idea or understanding." So, what's a concept book? Most usually it is a book that takes a single idea and expands the child's understanding of that idea. At its simplest level, a concept book begins with a familiar object, say a truck, and then illustrates the infinite variety of things we call trucks. It takes a general notion and focuses the child's attention to more specific views. Although concepts are better learned with concrete experience, these sometimes abstract ideas can reinforce slippery words and ideas that children are trying to pin down.

Books by Tana Hoban These stunning photographic picture books help children develop their perceptions and concepts and also are a great deal of fun to look at. Most suitable for threes and fours are the following—watch for new ones appearing almost every year:
Published by Macmillan:
Circles, Triangles, and Squares
Look Again!
Over, Under, and Through
Push-Pull, Empty-Full
Shapes and Things
Published by Greenwillow:
Is It Larger? Is It Smaller?
Is It Red? Is It Yellow? Is It Blue?
Little Ones, Big Ones
Take Another Look
Round and Round and Round

Kitten from One to Ten by Mirra Ginsburg; illustrated by Giulio Maestro. Crown, 1980. Good rhythms and friendly pictures create a charming book for youngsters, who'll enjoy enumerating the animal groups.
Little Blue and Little Yellow by Leo Lionni. Obolensky, 1959. Three-year-olds will tell you this is a favorite story about two friends—a blue spot and a yellow spot. But much of the attraction of the book lies in the visual demonstration that blue and yellow, when they are together, make green.

Daily Life and Its Events

Books by Anne and Harlow Rockwell, published by Macmillan. The little books in this series cover everyday activities of young children in a very satisfying way in both pictures and text.
Can I help?
Happy Birthday to Me
How My Garden Grew
I Love My Pets
I Play in My Room
My Barber
My Back Yard
Sick in Bed
The Supermarket
When I Go Visiting

Books by Harlow Rockwell, published by Greenwillow:
My Dentist
My Doctor
My Kitchen
My Nursery School

Books by Gunilla Wolde The popular Tommy and Betsy books first appeared years ago. The following are some of the most recent and up-to-date, showing children in everyday activities:
Published by Random House:
Betsy and the Chicken Pox
Betsy's First Day at Nursery School
Betsy and the Doctor
Betsy and Peter Are Different
Published by Houghton Mifflin:
Tommy Builds a House
Tommy Cleans His Room
Tommy Goes to the Doctor
Tommy Takes a Bath

The Berenstain Bears Visit the Dentist by Stan and Jan Berenstain. Random House, 1981. Many children already know the

Berenstain Bears and will feel comfortable exploring the dentist's office and equipment with them.

The Birthday Party by Helen Oxenbury. Dial, 1983. Birthday fun in typical three- or four-year-old fashion. Other books in this series, such as *The Check-Up, Eating Out,* and *The Car Trip* show youngsters and adults in various realistic situations. Sometimes unpleasant! You may want to check them first.

A Child Goes to School: A Storybook for Parents and Children Together by Sara Bonnet Stein; photos by Don Connors. Doubleday, 1978. An informal, helpful introduction, in stories and photographs.

Come to the Doctor, Harry by Mary Chalmers. Harper & Row, 1981. This small book about Harry the Cat might help some children overcome some of the fears they may have about visiting the doctor.

Davy's Day by Lois Lenski. Walck, 1943. This classic little tale, perhaps hard to find now in the libraries, takes Davy through the day from the time he arises until he goes to bed.

Everybody Has a House and *Everybody Eats* by Mary McBurney Green; illustrated by Louis Klein. Addison-Wesley, 1961. A classic about everyday activities.

Going to Day Care by Fred Rogers. Putnam, 1985. Real life photographs of children being cared for in other people's homes and in day-care centers. "Mister Rogers" helps both parents and children understand the activities and practices.

Moving by Wendy Watson. Crowell, 1978. The little animal person, Muffin, doesn't want to leave the old house when the family must move. Eventually he is persuaded.

Nursery and Folktales

The Gingerbread Man, illustrated by Karen Schmidt. Scholastic, 1985. The much-loved impudent hero, whose catchy refrain expresses his sense of power. See also in this series *The Bremen-Town Musicians, The Little Red Hen,* and *The Three Billy Goats Gruff.*

Gone Is Gone by Wanda Gag. Coward, McCann, 1933. This old tale about the peasant husband and wife who change places for a day is very accessible to fours in Wanda Gag's telling.

Children love the small book, the spare text, and the clear black-and-white pictures.

Henny-Penny, a picture book by William Stobbs. Follett, 1968. Here are all the traditional characters, in bright pictures, and all the details of Foxy-Woxy's killings, for the four-year-old who doesn't shy away from such things.

The House That Jack Built illustrated by Rodney Peppé. Delacorte, 1985. Fascinating large pictures bring this intriguing old accumulative tale to life for even quite young children.

Margaret Wise Brown's Wonderful Story Book: 25 Stories and Poems, illustrated by J. P. Miller. Golden, 1979. Not a book of traditional nursery tales but a classic collection for fours and older that seems to belong with these tales. Not to be missed.

Millions of Cats by Wanda Gag. Coward, McCann, 1928. We have listed this under another category, *Absurd Situations,* but it deserves a place here also, even though it is not an old folktale, strictly speaking. But this story of the man and woman who wished for a cat and had their wish fulfilled a zillion times over has been delighting children for some fifty years now.

One Fine Day by Nonny Hogrogian. Macmillan, 1971. A tale from the Armenian about a greedy fox. For fours and older.

My First Book of Nursery Tales by Marianna Mayer; illustrated by William Joyce. Random House, 1983. Contains five old favorites, including *The Gingerbread Man.*

The Little Red Hen illustrated by Paul Galdone. Clarion Books, 1973. Irresistible pictures and a familiar old tale—just the right combination to please older threes and fours.

The Old Woman and Her Pig, pictures by Paul Galdone. Whittlesey House. McGraw-Hill, 1960. The very lively drawings make this old rhyme easily comprehensible to young children and a delight.

The Old Woman and Her Pig and 10 Other Tales by Anne Rockwell. Crowell, 1979. This sequel to the book just listed above has the same pleasing format, and many of the stories will be found suitable for fours.

Pancake Pie by Sven Nordquist. Morrow, 1984. Old Festus, eager to celebrate his cat Mercury's birthday by baking his favorite pie, keeps running into absurd difficulties. Children will love the zaniness of text and full-color illustrations with their tiny unexplained monsters. A rib-tickler.

The Tall Book of Nursery Tales, pictures by F. Rojankovsky. Harper & Row, 1944. A Companion to *The Tall Book of Mother Goose.* Lively bright pictures and a wide variety of stories.

The Three Bears and 15 Other Stories by Anne Rockwell. Harper & Row, 1975. Some of these stories can wait for slightly older listeners, but fours will be attracted to the abundant, colorful pictures.

Walt Disney's Three Little Pigs retold by Barbara Brenner. Random House, 1982. In this excellent version of an old favorite, the wolf isn't scalded to death, but is scared off—a more humane ending that fits a four-year-old's sense of justice via deserved punishment but a safe ending.

Poetry

The best poems for children as young as three and four are probably to be found in Mother Goose and in the best-loved picture books. See those that have already been listed under *Goodnight Stories and Poems,* as well as the following:

Drummer Hoff by Barbara Emberley
Jamberry by Bruce Degen
Madeline by Ludwig Bemelmans
Magic Michael by Louis Slobodkin
May I Bring a Friend? by Beatrice Schenk de Regniers
Nutshell Library by Maurice Sendak
Song of the Seasons by Robert Welber

In addition, there are a few books suitable for young children, featuring short poems or riddles that catch attention through their rhythms and rhymes or humor, or the small ideas they are presenting:

Blackberry Ink, poems by Eve Merriam; pictures by Hans Wilhelm. Morrow, 1985. Short poems with tricky sounds and rhythms to catch the interest of the youngest listeners. Most are just for fun, and great for chanting along with the reader.

Catch Me and Kiss Me and Say It Again by Clyde Watson; illustrated by Wendy Watson. Collins, 1984. Charming catchy verses and delightful pictures.

City Green by Eleanor Schick. Macmillan, 1974. Very short un-rhymed poems about city life. Plenty of pictures.

It Does Not Say Meow, and Other Riddle Rhymes by Beatrice Schenk de Regniers; illustrated by Paul Galdone. Seabury, 1972. Just the right combination of rhymes, guesses, and bright pictures for the three-year-old.

Listen, Children, Listen: An Anthology of Poems for the Very Young edited by Myra Cohn Livingston; illustrated by Trina Schart Hyman. Harcourt, 1972. An inviting small book—six inches by eight inches—with small black-and-white drawings and appropriate small poems.

Nibble Nibble by Margaret Wise Brown; illustrated by Leonard Weisgard. Young Scott Books, 1959. A large book with soft green illustrations for the short verses about various small creatures. Full of sounds fun to hear and fun to say.

Poems to Read to the Very Young selected by Josette Frank; illus-trated by Eloise Wilkin. Random House, 1982. A very wel-come new edition of a large book that has long been a favorite for its format and well-selected poems.

Ring a Ring o' Roses: Stories, Games and Fingerplays for Preschool Children. Flint Public Library, 1979. Some of these rhythmic finger-plays may be just what the youngest three-year-old would enjoy most.

Whispers and Other Poems by Myra Cohn Livingston; illustrated by Jacqueline Chwast. Harcourt, 1958. This small book with its small poems and pictures may be hard to find, but it is highly suitable and worth a search.

Mother Goose Books

The market is now overflowing with Mother Goose books, some featuring the very familiar rhymes, others including the lesser known; some illustrated in lyrical old-fashioned style, others aimed at contemporary tastes for brilliance and abstraction. The choice is up to the adult and the child. In our suggestions here, we are covering highlights of the range, from the old-fashioned to the new in illustrations, and we emphasize the collections that contain at least a good body of the most familiar rhymes.

A Treasury of Mother Goose compiled by Oscar Weigle; pictures by Harold Berson. Grosset & Dunlap, 1967. Here are the familiar rhymes, illustrated in both black-and-white and soft color, with an old-fashioned storybook look.

Grey Goose and Gander and Other Mother Goose Rhymes compiled by Anne Rockwell. Harper & Row, 1980. A book for a child to hold easily, with uncrowded, imaginative pictures to look at, in color. Both familiar and unfamiliar rhymes.

The Mother Goose Book by Alice and Martin Provensen. Random House, 1976. The two Provensens, well known for their Maple Hill Farm animal books, have produced a handsome large collection of rhymes traditionally illustrated and grouped according to topics.

Mother Goose Nursery Rhymes illustrated by Arthur Rackham. Viking, 1975. This full collection of familiar rhymes is illustrated in both black-and-white and color, with the well-known delicate Rackham touch.

Mother Goose, rhymes selected and illustrated by Michael Hague. Holt, 1984. Mainly the classic nursery rhymes, pictured in a bright, active style.

The Mother Goose Treasury by Raymond Briggs. Coward, McCann, 1966. A very large book with 408 rhymes and 897 illustrations in both black-and-white and color; in its style aiming to appeal to contemporary children. The large pictures, especially, are full of swirling action.

The Real Mother Goose, introduction by May Hill Arbuthnot; illustrated by Blanche Fisher Wright. Rand McNally, 1916. A large book of over three hundred rhymes. Here is the old look treasured by many adults.

Ring-a-Ring o' Roses: A Picture Book of Nursery Rhymes by Raymond Briggs. Coward, McCann, 1962. Just a few rhymes with full-page colorful pictures delightfully full of details. A picture book as well as a rhyme book, for the beginner.

The Tall Book of Mother Goose by Feodor Rojankovsky. Harper & Row, 1942. This abundantly illustrated collection of familiar rhymes has been one of the favorites for years because of its intriguing tall shape.

Tomie de Paola's Mother Goose by Tomie de Paola. Putnam, 1985. In this book the well-known picture-book artist illustrates over two hundred rhymes in brilliant color and in the pleasantly stylized technique many children now associate with his name.

THINGS TO REMEMBER WHEN CHOOSING BOOKS FOR THREE- AND FOUR-YEAR-OLDS

- Is this right for my particular child?
- Will he or she understand the theme?
- Will it scare or comfort him?
- Does it relate to his interests or needs?
- Does it answer some of his questions?
- Is the language as fresh as possible?
- Are the pictures interesting, well done, and enticing enough to pore over?
- Will I enjoy reading it many times?
- Do I approve of its messages, hidden or overt?

If you feel that most of the answers you give are positive, then you have probably chosen a good book. And good books will last long in the memory of your impressionable child.

TEN BOOKS ALL THREE- AND FOUR-YEAR-OLDS SHOULD KNOW

The Carrot Seed by Ruth Krauss
Curious George by H. A. Rey
Freight Train by Donald Crews
Gilberto and the Wind by Marie Hall Ets
The Little Red Hen
Make Way for Ducklings by Robert McCloskey
May I Bring a Friend? by Beatrice Schenk de Regniers
Poems to Read to the Very Young selected by Josette Frank
The Snowy Day by Ezra Jack Keats
The Tale of Peter Rabbit by Beatrix Potter

CHAPTER V

Books for Fives

How are books for fives different from books for fours? In some ways, not at all. Many of the best-loved preschool picture books will remain favorites that fives will want to hear again and again.

How Fives Are Different

However, in selecting new books for fives, the text can be longer and the language less simple. The attention spans of fives are growing like the rest of them, so they can sit still longer and deal with a more complex story than preschoolers. In terms of format, fives love very big and very small books; either extreme is appealing. Big books seem to prove how grown up they are and little books are just the right size to have and to hold.

Depending on your child, you may find some books in the next chapter (on sixes and sevens) that will fit some fives very well. Those words "depending on your child" are the key to matching individual kids with the right books. If you have an early reader in the family, the easy-to-read selections in the next chapter will be of interest right now. On the other hand, not all books, even in this chapter, will be just right for every five-year-old.

While a good story should be at the heart of the books

you choose, try to serve up a rich and varied mix of books. What better way is there to whet the appetite for learning to read? With a wide range of prereading experiences the preliterate child can discover that books come in all flavors. A book like *Caps For Sale* is amusing, *Little Toot* is exciting, *Millions of Cats* is entertaining, *A Baby Sister for Frances* is touching. Some books, such as *Nibble, Nibble,* are good for the sheer delight of the language. Occasionally you may even share a book that's "not so good." Indeed, by sharing a few klunkers, five-year-olds start comparing those they like with those they don't, which is all part of the process of shaping their literary taste and preferences.

FANTASY FOR FIVES

A children's librarian recalls that her eldest child, the original Mr. Good, seemed to get vicarious pleasure from the adventures of Max in Maurice Sendak's *Where the Wild Things Are.* For her mischievous younger son, however, Max's drama hit a bit too close to home. He didn't even want to be in the same room with that book. Why should he be so frightened? Isn't this child unusual? Not really. Most fives still engage in a certain amount of magical thinking. Like Ramona, the kindergarten heroine of

Beverly Cleary's *Ramona the Pest,* fives are not absolutely sure (especially when the lights are out and they are alone) that the animals inside the Big Book of Wild Beasts will stay inside the book. While fives are gaining a better understanding of what's real and not real, the line is not firmly fixed by any means. So steer clear of fantasies that may fuel their fears. Save the scarier folk and fairy tales for a bit later. A few years from now most of those classics, Grimm and otherwise, will provide vicarious flights of adventure, courage, and the joy of good triumphing over evil. However, at this stage, kids still need more benign fantasies along with realistic storybooks about people, animals, and how things work.

FIVES AND THEIR EXPANDING WORLD

Let's consider those things that typically touch most five-year-olds.

Entry to kindergarten marks a turning point in the lives of most fives. Even if they have attended nursery school, going to "big" or "real" school sets the experience apart from whatever has gone before. For most kids this is the first full day of being away from the familiar world of home and family. Besides, kindergarten is different and so are everyone's expectations. You don't "just play" in real school; you do "work."

For those who have been to nursery school, the transition may be easier; nevertheless, school is different. Kindergarten classes tend to be larger, so fives have to share the teacher's attention with more kids. When the teacher reads a picture book like *Mike Mulligan,* she's apt to read to a whole group. As one of many, the kindergarten child must learn to wait for a look at the pictures or an answer to a question. It is no longer a one-to-one arrangement or a private reading. In other words, there are larger demands for independence.

Not only do adults expect more from the child, the five-year-old also begins demanding a little more say in being his own boss. So fives sometimes come off as fresh or sassy. Yet at the drop of a hat their big schoolchild image can collapse. After trouble on the school bus or the playground, for instance, your big, bold, and boisterous Bobby may fade into a tiny, timid tot in need of some old-fashioned tender loving care. While the big world of school with its social and intellectual demands is now a daily adventure, home and family continue to be the secure base returned to each night.

For fives, books that reflect their own journeys out into the big world are very satisfying, especially when all ends happily ever after. *The Story About Ping* is an adventure story that speaks directly to the hearts of five-year-olds—to their struggles with authority and their feelings about independence and dependence.

THE PARTICULAR APPEAL OF ANIMAL STORIES

Animal stories such as *The Story About Ping* offer the child listener the vicarious thrill of being scared with just enough distance to feel safe—a kind of safe-scare. Cast in a fantasy world, characters like Ping, the duck, can play the part of a child in feathers (or fur) and do things that would be too frightening if he were a flesh-and-blood child. Through such characters, one step removed from reality, the child can try on a whole range of feelings without fear. With Ping the child can spread his wings, taste adventure, sense the danger, and finally face with courage the consequences of his actions. With *Curious George* he can be as mischievous as a little monkey and still get home safely.

Often animal stories make a more comfortable fit than realistic fiction. It doesn't matter if a child is male or female, white or black, Chicano or Asian, the child in fur is easy to identify with and more universally appealing.

FROM FANTASY TO REALITY

Fives also love stories about real boys and girls they can identify with easily: Kids with families, friends, and problems that ring true. Realistic fiction helps the still essentially egocentric child see that she is not quite so unique—that other people feel shy, have fights and make up, get lost and found again. Such books as *Let's Be Enemies* and *Rosa Too Little* give kids a sense of commonality with their peers and enhance their understanding of themselves and others.

Unfortunately, some of the "problem" books lack much in the way of literary style or grace. While they may fill a special need of the moment, they should not be the child's only experience with books. Big messages are often taught better by indirect means, rather than hammering directly at a sore spot.

Look for books that have more than a lesson to preach. It's something like feeding their bodies. You don't just serve up vitamins from a bottle. Good nutrition comes along with taste and eye appeal. In other words, there's something to chew on and savor. It's the same with books. Kids need more than messages. They grow from stories that move them and amuse them and illustrations that engage their eyes and imagination.

THE BIG WORLD AND THINGS THAT GO

Stepping onto the school bus or off for a day at the beach, fives are becoming increasingly aware and curious about the people, places, and things they see. Books can't replace excursions out into the big world. But books can expand those experiences and give them an unhurried close-up view of many fascinating things they have seen along the way. Sometimes a boat like *Little Toot* becomes the leading character of such tales. In other cases, the information is straightforward but essentially visual. Don't overlook the possibility of browsing through adult books that are heavy on illustrations and photographs. You don't need to read the text. Often just the captions will do, or simply talk about what's there on the page. Try to relate it to what you've seen on your travels—how it's alike or different.

STORIES WITHOUT BOOKS—A TWO-WAY STREET

From their earliest days onward, children enjoy listening to stories about themselves and of "long, long ago when Grandma was a little girl." These oral histories, often a mix of fact and fancy, are among the all-time favorites of children fortunate enough to grow up with in-house storytellers.

By four or five, the repertoire of such storytimes will also include the classic folktales such as the "Three Little Pigs,"

"The Three Bears," and "Little Red Riding Hood." While pictured versions of these are readily available, perhaps the most memorable tellings are those from the head and the heart. There's something to be said for following a story without benefit of someone else's visual input. In other words, the listener must make his own pictures in his mind's eye. Indeed, this is how most folktales were originally intended to be told—in the oral tradition, which should be part of every child's literary heritage.

Nor should this oral tradition be a one-way street. Fives who have developed a sense of story love to take a turn at retelling their own version of *The Three Bears and Goldilocks.* Some may need a little help here and there to keep the story going, but don't be a stickler for details. When they get to an inevitable, "I forget," pick up the thread and let them get back in when they can. Being a listener gives you a ringside view of the child's mind at work.

Sometimes your young storyteller may enjoy having you write down the story she's telling. Seeing the words they say transformed into lines and squiggles on paper helps kids understand the connections between printed and spoken words.

In addition to the classics, a number of "modern" folk-style tales are just right for fives. Take the time to preread old tales. Some tellings that are too Grimm for most fives will be enjoyed at eight or nine. You have to know your own child. Check the list at the end of this chapter of both classic and modern tales to get you started.

FITTING BOOKS INTO THE FIVE'S BUSY DAY

At the end of a busy day away, fives may really need unwinding time. Active, big-muscle action needs to be balanced with some quiet sit-down time with you and a good book. Although kindergarteners also enjoy browsing through books alone, the pleasures of being read to offer both teller and listener a real change of pace from the world of work-a-day demands. It's a time for one-to-one sharing, a bit of that often hard-to-find "quality" time that's joyful for its own sake.

While entertainment is at the heart of the matter, a great deal of significant learning is also built into these read-aloud moments. You don't have to get hung up on teaching kids to read letters and words. True, there are some fours and fives who can read, but the greater majority of bright (and even super-bright) kids learn to read at six, seven, and even eight. No one has proven that sooner is better. In fact, some studies show that early-to-read kids read no better than average starters a few years down the road. Indeed, if the labor of learning to read has been bumpy, the price for reading early may be at the expense of the most basic kind of learning—a love of books and reading. Rather than concentrating on "how-to," five-year-olds should be building "want-to" attitudes by hearing books that entertain, amuse, move, and touch them. When young kids grow up with a rich diet of wonderful books, the appetite for learning how to read falls into place quite naturally rather than having to be hammered in by others.

GETTING INTO THE READING MODE

Of course, while you're reading to fives there are certain "readiness" skills that you can be aware of and stress. Before they can read, kids need to learn how books "work." Watch a toddler or young preschooler open a book. It may be upside down and they may start in the middle or back. By five, kids who have been read to know books begin at the beginning and the story moves from left page to right.

You can now draw their attention to the text, reinforcing the idea that we read the words on the page from left to right. No big speeches needed. Just put your hand under the words and move it along as you read. In a way you are modeling the eye motion, left to right, and the sweep from the end of one line to the next.

Take time as you read to look at the pictures and encourage your child to tell about what's going on. What does he think is going to happen when Goldilocks falls asleep and the Three Bears come home? How does he think Peter Rabbit felt as Mr. McGregor was checking the flower pots? Naturally, you're not going to do this on every page and interrupt the flow of the story, but meaningful pauses can deepen the pleasure, suspense, and appreciation of picture books.

Unlike most adult "best-sellers," picture books are meant to be savored. You don't just read them once and put them on a shelf. Probably one of the best measures of a book's success is the frequency with which it is requested. In part, kids really love repeat performances because they know what's going to happen next. Try to remember your own excitement in hearing *Jack and the Beanstalk,* and that delicious moment when the giant cried, "Fee, fi, fo, fum." It's from repeated hearings of well-loved stories and books that kids also develop a basic skill needed in reading—that is, a sense of story. This is where reading comprehension begins—in the listening mode. Kids who are experienced listeners bring that story sense of what happens first, next, and last to the books they will ultimately read independently.

In the course of sharing books prereaders are likely to start pointing out letters or even "sight" words they know. The letters that start their own name, a "STOP" sign in an illustration, the oft-repeated name of a character or repeated refrain, as in, "I think I can, I think I can," or "Hundreds of cats, thousands of cats, millions and billions and trillions of cats," are bound to catch the eye of the preliterate child who is just on the threshold of reading. By all means, encourage such "discoveries." They represent big leaps in learning. But DON'T dive in and turn every page into a reading lesson.

FOLLOW-UP GAMES TO PLAY

Once fives settle down with their storybooks it is sometimes difficult to call the storytime to a halt. One way to get on with it is to look for an active play idea that comes from a story they enjoyed.

Almost any book can launch a puppet dramatization that leads kids to retell a story in their own words. *The Little Red Hen* offers some wonderful roles and allows the child players to step out of themselves and into the heads of different characters.

A supply of paper, crayons, paint, and clay can lead to original illustrations and sculptures that extend a story book.

After reading *The Carrot Seed* or *Jack and the Beanstalk,* why not start a carrot-top garden or some beans sprouting?

Children love making their own color, counting, and alphabet books. They can draw their own illustrations or cut and paste photos found in old magazines. Staple together eight to ten pages of paper from an oversized note pad and they are in business. How about a personal book of *Cars* or *Cats* or *Things I Like to Eat?*

Using books to stimulate active play can go a long way in building fond associations with books. It prolongs a happy shared time to some indepandent time, a welcome way of getting on with the day while getting extra mileage out of your shared time.

On the Right Track

By five books should be very much a part of your child's life. Being read to or poring over the illustrations of favorite books, the experienced five-year-old knows how a book "works." If he's been read to, he knows that the story book goes from left to right, that the story has a beginning, middle, and an end. He's beginning to understand that those dark and white marks under the pictures are words that tell the story. He's proud to show you letters he knows and maybe even a word here and there. He likes to pretend he can read and does a fairly good job of telling a familiar story from the illustrations in favorite books. All and all he's on the right track.

Booklist for Fives

Independence and Interdependence

The Story About Ping by Marjorie Flack. Penguin, 1977. In many ways *Ping* is a perfect developmental match for five-year-olds. The story begins when Ping, a small duck, does not want to get spanked for being the last duck home. Of course, it wasn't Ping's fault that he didn't hear anyone calling. He was wrong side up trying to catch a little fish in the Yangtze River. So Ping hides and soon finds himself separated from his mother, father, two sisters, three brothers, eleven aunts, seven uncles, and forty-two cousins.

What follows is an adventure full of danger, fear, and friendship. Young Ping is captured and comes frightfully close to becoming duck dinner. But the same boy who caught Ping is also the one to free him. Ultimately, Ping finds his way back home. He is late again but willingly takes the inevitable spank for being last but happily reunited with his family. Like Ping, your five-year-old wants to be boss of himself. Much as he wants to please others, he often finds it hard to leave the toy or game he has plunged into. He is too busy to hear someone calling, "Dinner," "Bathtime . . ." Each day he goes off on his own, away from the familiar security of home and family. Although he may be eager for independence, his small daily ventures out into the world of school and playground are tinged with moments of doubt, fear, and loneliness. For fives, *The Story About Ping* is a reassuring adventure. It confirms the fact that there are people out there who are more friendly than unfriendly. From start to finish Ping speaks to the ambivalent feelings children have about dependence and independence. While the young schoolchild is ready for limited journeys into the bigger world, a safe return to home and family remains the centerpost of security.

Corduroy by Don Freeman. Viking, 1968. A tender little fantasy about a less than perfect toy bear who finds a friend and a home.

Curious George by H. A. Rey. Houghton Mifflin, 1941. George's curiosity has a way of getting him in some tight spots. Fortunately for this little monkey there's always a way out with a little help from his big friend in the Yellow Hat. This is the first of an excellent series.

Frederick by Leo Lionni. Pantheon, 1967. Here's a new twist to the old tale. Frederick, a mouse not unlike the fabled Ant and Grasshopper, does not prepare for winter by gathering food. Yet he brings something equally valuable to nourish his mice brothers.

The Little Engine That Could by Watty Piper. Bucaneer Books,

1981. A classic tale of determination and belief in oneself with lots of rhythmic refrains, "I think I can, I think I can," speaks to the hearts of small children who relate to the small engine that does what the big powerful engine couldn't and wouldn't do.

Pelle's New Suit by Elsa Beskow. Harper & Row, 1929. An old favorite that's partly about the step-by-step way clothes used to be made. But in a larger sense it's a story about interdependence and mutuality—a big task fives are working at.

Nutshell Library by Maurice Sendak. Harper & Row, 1962. Four tiny gems: *Chicken Soup and Rice, One Was Johnny, Pierre, Alligators All Around* packed together in a small case that can go everyplace—from long trips to short hops into bed. You'll find an alphabet, a counting book, a moral tale, and a romp through the seasons.

Pig-Pig Rides by David McPhail. Dutton, 1982. Fun loving Pig-Pig has a wild day of adventure planned and a loving Mama. What else could a pig need?

The Runaway Bunny by Margaret Wise Brown; illustrated by Clement Hurd. Harper & Row, 1942. A tender loving tale of a little bunny who dreams of runaway adventures and a loving mom who reassures her runaway that she'll never be far away.

Ferdinand the Bull by Munro Leaf; illustrated by Robert Lawson. Viking, 1977. A classic tale of a rugged individualist, in this case the beloved Ferdinand, a bull who did not choose to be like everyone else.

Swimmy by Leo Lionni. Pantheon, 1968. An exquisitely illustrated story of a little fish who not only looks different from other little fish, but thinks differently, too. It's that difference that saves the day for Swimmy and his friends.

The Tale of Peter Rabbit by Beatrix Potter. Warne, 1902. A classic tale about the adventures of a mis-

Page from *El cuento de Fernando,* Spanish language version of *Ferdinand the Bull.*

chievous bunny who gets his comeuppance and returns
home weary but wiser.

Three Rounds with Rabbit by William H. Hooks. Lothrop, Lee and
Shepard, 1984. In a series of humorous encounters, Little
Rabbit learns that his new found independence needs to be
tempered with some sage advice such as, "Look before you
hop!"

Two Little Bears by Ylla. Harper & Row, 1954. Two bear cubs
forget Mother Bear's warning and wander deeper and
deeper into the woods until they are lost. Illustrated with
stunning photos and information told in a story framework.
One of five handsome books for young animal lovers illustrated by Ylla.

When Small Is Tall by Seymour V. Reit, William Hooks, and Betty
Boegehold; illustrated by Lynn Munsinger. Random
House, 1985. Three of Aesop's fables retold with rebuses
and amusing refrains that children will enjoy saying and
"reading" from dialogue balloons.

The Wild Baby Goes to Sea by Barbro Lindgren; illustrated by Eva
Erikson, adapted from the Swedish by Jack Prelutsky.
Greenwillow, 1982. Young Ben has a great adventure at sea
without ever leaving home.

Friendship and Other Growing Pains

While most kids relate readily to both animal and human characters, some children have decided preferences for one or the
other. Although many issues are easier to deal with cast in fantasy, some children tune them out. *Best Friends for Frances,* cast
as an animal story, deals with the same feelings of jealousy and
resentment that the realistic *Katharine's Doll* deals with. Which
should you choose? Again, you really need to know your child
to know what will appeal most.

Until the 1960s few books were published that included
minority group children. Today some of the best loved picture
books have Hispanic and black children as the central characters. For the minority child such books provide a visual link that
was long missing in picture books. For the white child who sees
few minority children in her immediate and narrow world, such
books provide a first link with the real world with its rich and

wonderful diversity. So books such as *The Snowy Day, Rosa Too Little,* or *Sam* are not intended for a limited audience. Although they feature minority children and families, they have at their heart a story with universal appeal to all children.

Here's a mixed book bag of "realities" and child-in-fur animal stories that can help you find your way.

Are We Still Best Friends? by Carol Barkin and Elizabeth James; photos by Heins Kluetmeier. Raintree Editions, 1975. A photoessay featuring two schoolgirls and their friendship.

Best Friends for Frances by Russell Hoban; illustrated by Lillian Hoban. Harper and Row, 1969. Part of the Frances Series about a loveable badger and her growing-up problems. Frances teaches her friend Albert about friendship and learns to appreciate her little sister Gloria at the same time.

George and Martha by James Marshall. Houghton Mifflin, 1972. Five warm and amusing stories about the ups and downs of friendship between a loveable pair of hippos.

George and Martha Rise and Shine by James Marshall. Houghton Mifflin, 1976. Stories about telling fibs, curiosity, scary movies, a secret club, and those two close friends, George and Martha.

Guinea Pigs Don't Read Books by Colleen S. Bare. Dodd, Mead, 1985. This charming photoessay points out that although guinea pigs don't read, they do make good friends.

Katharine's Doll by Elizabeth Winthrop; illustrated by Marilyn Hafner. Dutton, 1983. When Katharine gets a new doll from her grandmother, her best friend Molly gets left out until Kate discovers how limited her doll is compared to a real live friend.

Let's Be Enemies by Janice May Udry; illustrated by Maurice Sendak. Harper & Row, 1961. A near-classic tale about friendship and inevitable squabbles.

Lizzie and Harold by Elizabeth Winthrop; illustrated by Martha Weston. Lothrop, Lee and Shepard. Lizzie wants a best friend and tries all sorts of ways, overlooking entirely her good friend Harold. A familiar scenario for fives.

Meet M and M by Pat Ross; illustrated by Marilyn Hafner. Pantheon, 1980. Two girls face both joys and problems in becoming real friends.

One Monday Morning by Uri Shulevitz. Scribner's, 1967. A cumulative tale, a friendly fantasy, in which the King, Queen, Prince, and ever-expanding cast come to visit, but the hero's not there. Told through the days of a week. Winds up to a happy ending.

The Pearl by Helen Heine. Atheneum, 1985. Beaver has terrible dreams about the jealousy of his friends over the pearl mussel he has found. He finally decides it is better to throw it back into the water and be happy with his friends.

We Are Best Friends by Aliki. Greenwillow, 1982. Robert and Peter, best friends, are unhappy when Peter moves away. But all ends well with new friends and old.

Where Are You, Ernest and Celestine? by Gabrielle Vinvent. Greenwillow, 1985. Children will love the little mouse-child and her big bear friend. Celestine, the mouse, gets separated from Ernest, the bear, in a museum, but after a frantic search the two of them are united and all ends happily.

Won't Somebody Play with Me? by Steven Kellogg. Dial, 1972. It's Kim's birthday but she can't find anyone to play with her. She's got a great imagination for games but is totally shocked to find all her friends at Tony's house for a surprise birthday party for Kim.

Going to School

First Grade Jitters by Robert Quackenbush. Lippincott, 1982. A small boy rabbit wonders about going to first grade and worries that his teacher will say, "Oogley boogley" and expect him to understand things he hasn't learned yet. A reassuring little tale for end of summer.

I'd Rather Stay Home by Carol Barkin and Elizabeth James; photos by Heins Kluetmeier. Raintree Editions, 1975. A photoessay that walks the child through the doubts and pleasures of that first day in school.

Is It Hard? Is It Easy? by Mary M. Green; illustrated by Len Gettleman. Young Scott/Addison-Wesley, 1960. A photoessay that shows four children and the differences between them. This one talks right to the heart of the child's feelings of competence. A reassuring book that says we're not all good at the same things.

Leo the Late Bloomer by Robert Kraus; illustrated by Jose Aruego. Windmill Books, 1980. A reassuring story of a small tiger who couldn't read, write, or do many things other small tigers could do, until "in his own good time" he bloomed.

Petunia by Roger Duvoisin. Knopf, 1950. Silly Goose Petunia thinks that just owning a book makes her wise. Thinking herself wise, she begins to look and act wise. In the end she discovers it's what's inside a book that counts, and Petunia resolves to learn how to read.

Rosa-Too-Little by Sue Fett. Doubleday, 1950. Here's an oldie but goodie about a girl who was too little to do many things she wished to do, but not too little to learn how to write her name so she could get her own library card and borrow books.

Will I Have a Friend? by Miriam Cohen; illustrated by Lillian Hoban. Macmillan, 1967. A reassuring story of a small boy's fears of going to school and having friends.

Family

Although Mother tends to remain the expert and all-knowing person fives still want to please, fives are about to reach that moment when some doubt about their parents' perfection creeps in. Now there are new experts to be compared with and quoted, such as "My teacher says," or "Laurie's mommy does." It's sometimes hard for parents to step down from the pedestal, but it's inevitable. It's one of the ways children learn that nobody's perfect.

Ebbie by Eve Rice. Greenwillow, 1975. Sometimes families hold on to baby talk longer than they should. When Eddie loses his first teeth (by accident) he calls himself Ebbie and so does everyone else—until Eddie gets big and wants to be called by his real name.

Even If I Did Something Awful by Barbara Shook Hazen; illustrated by Nancy Kincade. Atheneum, 1982. A warmly reassuring affirmation of parental love, even if a child "does something awful." At the same time, Mom is able to show her negative feelings. A great book for both child and parent! Excellent pictures and a text that captures the essence of children's imaginative speech.

My Mama Says There Aren't Any Zombies, Ghosts, Vampires, Creatures, Demons, Monsters, Fiends, Goblins or Things by Judith Viorst; illustrated by Kay Chorao. Atheneum, 1977. Use your judgment on this one. It may be scary to some, but funny to kids who feel pretty sure about real and make believe.

My Mom Travels a Lot by Caroline F. Bauer; illustrated by Nancy W. Parker. Warne, 1981. The good and bad things about having a working mom who travels a lot.

The Quarreling Book by Charlotte Zolotow; illustrated by Anita Lobel. Harper & Row, 1963. Some days just start off badly and this is one of those grim, gray days when everyone gets off to a bad start—but gets turned around before day is done.

The Terrible Thing that Happened at Our House by Marge Blaine; illustrated by John C. Wallner. Four Winds, 1975. Everything seems to go wrong when Mom goes to work. But never fear, they get the whole thing ironed out without Mom giving up her career.

Grandparents

I Dance in My Red Pajamas by Edith Thacher Hurd; illustrated by Emily Arnold McCully. Harper & Row, 1982. Jenny's visit to her grandparents' house is a fun-filled time of joy, noise, and love.

Grandmother and I by Helen Buckley; illustrated by Paul Galdone. Lothrop, Lee and Shepard, 1961. A cozy book about the comforts of Grandmother's lap. Also see *Grandfather and I.*

A Little at a Time by David A. Adler. Random House, 1976. A gentle day shared with Grandpa who patiently explains how, what, and why—"a little at a time."

Now One Foot, Now the Other by Tomie de Paola. Putnam, 1981. When his grandfather has a stroke, Bobby teaches him to walk just as his grandfather had once taught him.

Through Grandpa's Eyes by Patricia MacLachlan; illustrated by Deborah K. Ray. Harper & Row, 1980. A young boy learns a different way of seeing the world from his blind grandfather.

New Babies

A Baby for Max by Kathryn Lasky; photos by Christopher Knight. Scribner's, 1984. Told by five-year-old Maxwell Knight, this is the story of a family awaiting and welcoming a new baby.

A Baby Sister for Frances by Russell Hoban; illustrated by Lillian Hoban. Harper & Row, 1964. When Frances's baby sister Gloria arrives, Frances has a terrible time sharing her parents' affection and attention. A situation handled with warmth, humor, and love.

Nobody Asked Me If I Wanted a Baby Sister by Martha Alexander. Dial, 1971. A funny little book that goes from angry feelings of sibling rivalry to warm feelings of sibling love.

101 Things to Do with a Baby by Jan Ormerod. Lothrop, Lee and Shepard, 1984. A big sister tells 101 things to do with a baby with as many amusing illustrations. Everyone in the family will enjoy this one.

Peek-a-Boo by Janet and Alan Ahlberg. Viking, 1981. Invites talk and comparing what baby can see through peek-a-boo cut-out and all the things on the fully exposed page turn.

Peter's Chair by Ezra Jack Keats. Harper & Row, 1967. Peter deals with his mixed feelings about growing up and becoming a "big brother."

When the New Baby Comes, I'm Moving Out by Martha Alexander. Dial, 1979. Oliver is going to be a big brother and he doesn't like the idea at all.

Siblings

Big Sisters Are Bad Witches by Morse Hamilton; illustrated by Marylin Hafner. Greenwillow, 1981. Little sisters will certainly identify with Kate, who is about to become a better big sister than her mean old sister Emily.

A Birthday for Frances by Russell Hoban; illustrated by Lillian Hoban. Harper & Row, 1968. When her little sister Gloria's birthday rolls around, Frances has a typically tough time dealing with her jealousy. But, generosity and sibling affection win out in the end.

Good Lemonade by Frank Asch; illustrated by Marie Zimmerman. Watts, 1976. Hank's attempt to get rich quick are unrewarded until he discovers the secret of success is a good product. Underlying theme here of a young brother's loyalty.

If It Weren't for You by Charlotte Zolotow; illustrated by Ben Schecter. Harper & Row, 1966. A slightly bittersweet soliloquy of an older brother's view of all the pleasures he'd have if it weren't for his little brother.

I Hate My Brother Harry by Crescent Dragonwagon. Harper & Row, 1983. Does anyone ever learn to love the way big brothers tease little sisters? Of course not, but the teasing hurts less as kids understand themselves and others, especially brothers.

My Brother Never Feeds the Cat by Reynold Ruffins. Scribner's, 1979. Anna's brother never feeds the cat, takes out the garbage, rakes the leaves, picks up his toys, and there's good reason. Big sisters and brothers will see the humor and enjoy the surprise ending.

Sam by Ann H. Scott; illustrated by Symeon Shimin. McGraw-Hill, 1967. A slice of life about a small boy, a busy family, and the need we all have for love and attention.

Why Couldn't I Be an Only Kid Like You, Wigger by B. S. Hazen; illustrated by Leigh Grant. Atheneum, 1975. Lucky Wigger never has to share or get blamed for messes he didn't make; but, being an only child has its bad side too.

Divorce

Breakfast with My Father by Ron Roy. Clarion, 1980. A touching story about a boy and his continuing relationship with his dad after a divorce separates them.

Daddy by Jeannette Caines. Harper & Row, 1977. A small girl with divorced parents looks forward to her Saturday visits with Dad.

Daddy Doesn't Live Here Anymore by Betty Boegehold; illustrated by Deborah Borgo. Golden, 1985. All children will empathize with Casey as she comes to understand that her mother and father still love her, despite the fact that they can no longer live together.

Emily and the Klunky Baby and the Next Door Dog by Joan Lexau; illustrated by Martha Alexander. Dial, 1972. Emily has more problems than she can deal with a new baby, divorced parents, and not enough attention. When she trys to run away, her mom gets the message.

I Wish I Had My Father by Norma Simon; illustrated by Arieh Zeldich. Whitman, 1983. This is a special book to fill a special need. The story of a boy who finds Father's Day tough to deal with because his father left him years ago and never calls or writes.

Feelings and Fears—Real and Imagined

Bedtime for Frances by Russell Hoban; illustrated by Garth Williams. Harper & Row, 1960. Frances is in bed singing the alphabet until she gets to T for tiger and begins wondering if there are any tigers in her room. Kids will easily identify with the little badger's problem.

Come to the Doctor, Harry by Mary Chalmers. Harper & Row, 1981. When Harry the cat catches his tail in the screen door, he has to go to the doctor. Harry doesn't like going but ends up a wiser and braver cat in the end.

Curious George Goes to the Hospital by Margaret and H. A. Rey. Houghton-Mifflin, 1966. George swallows a piece of a jigsaw puzzle and so begins his adventures in the hospital.

Gila Monsters Meet You at the Airport by Marjorie W. Sharmat; illustrated by Byron Barton. Macmillan, 1980. When a boy from New York is faced with moving out west, he's not sure of what to expect and therefore expects the very worst things . . . including gila monsters.

Go Away, Bad Dreams! by Susan Hill; illustrated by Vanessa Julian-Ottie. Random House, 1985. An understanding and imaginative mother helps Tom gradually get rid of bad dreams in this warm and attractively illustrated book about family living.

Ira Sleeps Over by Bernard Waber. Houghton Mifflin, 1972. Ira's got mixed feelings about his first night away from home and bringing his security doll along.

I Was So Mad! by Norma Simon; illustrated by Dora Leder. Whitman, 1974. Kids will relate to the angry feelings here and also discover they're not the only ones who "get mad." Also see *I Know What I Like* and *How Do I Feel?* by the same author.

Little Rabbit's Loose Tooth by Lucy Bate; illustrated by Diane De Groat. Crown, 1975. When Little Rabbit's first baby tooth starts wiggling, the problems begin. What can she eat? Will it get lost? Will the tooth fairy come? Good fun with tender moments that ring true.

Pig-Pig Goes to Camp by David McPhail. Dutton, 1982. Though fives don't generally go to sleep-away camp, Pig-Pig's camp experience is so happy in a silly way, it may change some reluctant day campers' views or at the very least amuse them.

Spectacles by Ellen Raskin. Atheneum, 1976. Iris Fogel didn't always wear glasses, so sometimes she saw things other people didn't—until she gets spectacles and can see two ways! A humorous approach to the troublesome business of having to wear glasses.

What's the Matter, Sylvia, Can't You Ride? by Karen Born Andersen. Dial, 1981. Sylvia's problems with learning to ride a bike are a real (but humorous) lesson in the old adage, "Try, try again."

William's Doll by Charlotte Zolotow; illustrated by William Pene Du Bois. Harper & Row, 1972. Nobody seems to understand William's great desire for a doll—nobody, that is, until Grandmother steps in and sets things right.

Big World of Things that Go

Airport by Byron Barton. Crowell, 1982. Clear and handsome illustrations and sparse text tell the step-by-step adventure of an airborne journey from arriving at the airport to take-off.

Fire! Fire! by Gail Gibbons. Crowell, 1984. After a trip to the firehouse, here's a good follow-up book that explains how firefighters deal with fire in the city, country, the forest, and the waterfront.

Harbor by Donald Crews. Greenwillow, 1982. True color illustrations of a busy harbor and the various boats and ships that are found in port. Little text. Also by the same author: *Trucks, Freight Train, School Bus.*

Katy and the Big Snow by Virginia Lee Burton. Houghton Mifflin, 1943. If it weren't for Katy, the city of Geoppolis would be covered with a blanket of snow. But, this strong little plow does the job.

Little Toot by Hardie Gramatky. Putnam, 1939. Like many a five-year-old, Little Toot, the tugboat, loved to play. Work, he thought, was for other boats. Besides he was frightened of going too far out to sea. Until, one day, Little Toot finds himself face to face with a terrible storm and an ocean liner in distress. The rest is history. *Little Toot* is a classic.

Mike Mulligan and His Steam Shovel by Virginia Lee Burton. Houghton Mifflin, 1939. Mike Mulligan and his steam shovel Mary Ann still have a meaningful story to tell about faithful friends, and about "new" not necessarily being best.

Planes by Anne Rockwell. Dutton, 1985. Two rabbit children learn about planes, visit an airport, and even make a model airplane. Rockwell's bright pictures complete the pleasant package. Also: *Cars.* Dutton, 1984. This one, in the same format, features dogs—dogs riding, picnicking, playing golf, and filling cars with gasoline.

Round Trip by Ann Jonas. Greenwillow, 1983. This stark black-and-white book really does take the suburban child "round trip" to the city and home again. Kids will love the business of turning the book upside down for the return trip.

Truck Song by Diane Siebert; illustrated by Byron Barton. Harper & Row, 1984. A rhythmic tone poem to trucks of all kinds and to the truckers. The graphics are stunning and the whole package seems to have been completed by an author and illustrator who share children's love of trucks.

Old and New Folktales

Ask Mr. Bear by Marjorie Flack. Macmillan, 1932, '58, '65. This modern classic has the repetitive charm and cumulative rhythm of a folktale. It's about a small boy looking for a gift for his mother's birthday.

Caps for Sale by Esphyr Slobodkina. Addison-Wesley, 1947. A small gem of a mystery that kids solve before the grownup peddler does. They'll love the repetition and power of telling those monkey-see-monkey-do thieves to "give me back my caps!"

The Foolish King by Lisl Weil. Macmillan, 1982. A new version of an old favorite—*The Emperor's New Clothes*.

Hans in Luck by Paul Galdone; retold from Grimm. Parents Magazine Press, 1979. Kids enjoy feeling ever so much smarter than Young Hans who has a rather upside-down cockeyed view of "luck."

Henny Penny by Paul Galdone. Houghton Mifflin, 1968. It all begins when an acorn falls and Henny Penny spreads the news, "The sky is falling."

It Could Be Worse Margot Zemach. Farrar, Straus and Giroux, 1976. An amusing Yiddish folktale about a foolish man who learns the hard way that things could always be worse.

Jack and the Beanstalk adapted and illustrated by Tony Ross. Delacorte, 1980. A slightly modernized telling of Jack, with a giant who says "Fe Fi Fo Fum . . . I smell the blood of a little one." Lots of amusing details in the relatively benign illustrations.

The Little Red Hen by Paul Galdone. Seabury, 1973. Everyone should know the story of the industrious Little Red Hen and her lazy friends who get their comeuppence in the end. Galdone's lively illustrations add new dimensions to story and characterization. Also by the same artist see: *The Three Billy Goats Gruff, The Three Bears, The Three Little Pigs.*

Millions of Cats by Wanda Gag. Coward, McCann, 1928. Now a classic, this "modern" folktale is the story of a very old man who set out to look for one sweet fluffy cat and returned with "hundreds of cats, thousands of cats, millions and billions and trillions of cats." Fives will readily understand the old man's problem with choosing just one cat and the humor of his bringing them all home. They most especially love the rhythm and rhyme of the repeated refrain.

Old Lars adapted and illustrated by Erica Magnus. Carolrhoda, 1984. A simple old Norwegian tale of Old Lars and his faithful horse Blakken who go up to the woods for firewood and return without any.

Six Foolish Fishermen by Benjamin Elkin; illustrated by Katherine Evans. Children's Press, 1957. This is a retelling of a famous old tale about six foolish brothers who think one brother has drowned because each time one counts he forgets to count himself—a problem fives can identify with. In the end a small but wise boy comes to the rescue.

Stone Soup retold and illustrated by Marcia Brown. Scribner's, 1947. A delicious tale about three hungry soldiers and how they made soup with three stones plus a dash of cunning and humor for spice. An old favorite. Afterwards why not make some stone soup for dinner? Get the ingredients from the book.

The Story of the Three Little Pigs by Joseph Jacob; illustrated by Lorinda Bryan Cauley. Putnam, 1980. Old telling of the tale —new, wonderful full-color illustrations, especially that crafty gentlemanly wolf.

The Three Billy Goats Gruff retold and illustrated by Marcia Brown. Harcourt, 1957. Fives love chiming in on the repetitive refrains and the triumph of those clever little goats who outsmart the mean old troll.

Anthologies

Don't overlook the abundance of good stories bound together in anthologies.

The Child's First Book of Nursery Tales selected and adapted by Selma G. Lanes; illustrated by Cyndy Szekeres. Golden, 1983. You may want to save a few of these for a year or two, but here's a beautifully illustrated book that includes *The Little Red Hen, Chicken Little, The Three Pigs,* and *The Three Bears,* among others.

The Fairy Tale Treasury selected by Virginia Haviland; illustrated by Raymond Briggs. Coward, McCann, 1972. Most of the famous folktales you'll want to share are in this handsome volume. Some will be more appropriate for six to eights, so this is one to grow into.

Helen Oxenbury Nursery Story Book retold and illustrated by Helen Oxenbury. Knopf, 1985. A delightful collection of nursery tales just right for now, illustrated by one of the best.

My First Book of Nursery Tales retold by M. Mayer; illustrated by W. Joyce. Random House, 1983. Five old favorites—*The Three Bears, The Three Pigs, The Little Red Hen, The Three Billy Goats Gruff,* and *The Gingerbread Boy*—all in one slim volume.

A Treasury of Little Golden Books. Golden, 1982. This really is a treasury of some of the best-loved Golden Books, including several by Margaret Wise Brown.

Alphabet Books

Typically parents and grandparents zoom in on alphabet and counting books for prereaders. To most of the Sesame Street generation, the ABCs and 1-2-3 are old hat. Fives may enjoy some of the alphabets that go beyond naming objects and letters. Here are a few notables.

A Apple Pie by Kate Greenaway. Warne, 1886. A true classic—no less delicious today than one hundred years ago.

A Is for Annabelle by Tasha Tudor. Random House, 1954. An illustrator whose appeal has captivated children for many years presents the alphabet in an engaging manner.

A-B-C-ing: An Action Alphabet by Janet Beller. Crown, 1984. For those who know their ABCs here's a new look with action words from A to Z and kids in photographs doing the dancing, eating, jumping, and more.

Alfred's Alphabet Walk by Victoria Chess. Greenwillow, 1979. Alfred's mom tells him to stay in the front yard until he knows his ABCs, but Alfred goes for a walk that does the trick from A to Z.

Alphabears by Kathleen Hague; illustrated by Michael Hague. Holt, 1984. If you've got a teddy bear lover, he or she will love this alphabet book with bears and rhymed couplets for each letter. The illustrations are the beary best part of the book.

Applebet on ABC by Clyde Watson; illustrated by Wendy Watson. Farrar, Straus and Giroux, 1982. This one has a story with a lady farmer and her daughter on the way to the county fair. There's a continuous puzzle built in as the Apple continues on every page.

The Guinea Pig ABC by Kate Duke. Dutton, 1983. A cast of lively guinea pigs Awake, Bounce, Clean, get Dirty, etc. on each page. This is a vocabulary stretcher with humorous illustrations.

On Market Street by Arnold Lobel; illustrated by Anita Lobel. Greenwillow, 1981. This is a Caldecott honor book. A stunning ABC shopping trip.

Richard Scarry's ABC Word Book by Richard Scarry. Random House, 1971. Teaches all the letters of the alphabet and shows how they're used in everyday words. Featured letters are highlighted in red as they appear in beginning, middle, or end of words. Also: *Scarry's Find Your ABCs.*

Counting Books

Anno's Counting Book by M. Anno. Crowell, 1977. Here's one for looking at again and again for details and changes as the same pastoral scene grows busier and busier.

Chicken Little Count to Ten by M. Friskey and K. Evans. Children's Press, 1946. A classic counting book for little children.

Count and See by Tana Hoban. Macmillan, 1972. Another handsome photoessay with plenty of familiar things to count. Gives one to fifteen then skips to tens and jumps from fifty to one hundred, which may be confusing.

Helen Oxenbury's Numbers of Things by Helen Oxenbury. Delacorte, 1967. Bright, clear, and amusing illustrations for
counting from one to ten and then on to twenty, thirty,
forty, fifty, and infinity.

Roll Over illustrated by Mordicai Gerstein. Crown, 1984. Here's
a wonderful old counting chant illustrated with charm and
wit that introduces subtraction in a concrete way children
can understand.

Two Lonely Ducks by Roger Duvoisin. Knopf, 1955. A counting
story of two little ducks who won't be lonely when one, two,
three, four, five, six, seven, eight, nine, ten little ducklings
hatch. Introduces cardinal and ordinal numbers in a story
frame.

Wordless Books

A step beyond ABC, and well on the road to reading comprehension, are the wordless picture books that preliterate kids can
"read." Here the teller must follow the pictures in sequence or
the story makes little sense. Wordless books also demand that
the child interpret the story from the illustration. "Reading" the
story pictures helps kids focus on details, just as they will eventually need to focus on the differences between hit, hat, and hot.
At this stage, reading pictures is appropriate and can help develop a sense of story that kids will need to bring to "real"
reading. Unlike toddler books with isolated pictures of objects,
these books have a real thread—a beginning, middle, and end.
As the small drama unfolds, the child is a partner in the telling.
So the book becomes the child's story, told in his own words.

While some are far too sophisticated for the very young,
several are right on target for fives. Take turns being the listener
and the teller.

Ah-choo by Mercer Mayer. Dial, 1976. When Elephant sneezes,
he sets off a whole sequence of laughable events that lead
to a happy ending.

Bobo's Dream by Martha Alexander. Dial, 1970. Bobo the dachs-
hund's bone is almost lost to a big shaggy dog. When
Bobo's small master saves the day, Bobo dreams big dreams
of returning the favor. This is a story of "right over might."

Deep in the Forest by Brinton Turkle. Dutton, 1976. Here's the

Three Bears turned around when a small bear wanders into a human house and gets into the porridge, chairs, and beds. Obviously, the amusing twist of an old favorite tale will be enjoyed by those who know the original.

Each Peach, Pear, Plum by Janet and Allan Ahlberg. Viking, 1984. This is a peek-a-boo game that presupposes a certain amount of literary background. You'll see Mother Hubbard down in the cellar and have to find Cinderella. This is a fun-filled book for looking at details.

Hiccup by Mercer Mayer. Dial, 1978. Two hippos in a rowboat would be funny enough, but when one gets the hiccups, it gets hilarious.

What's Inside? by Duanne Daughtry. Knopf, 1984. Presents pairs of photos, the first showing the outside of an object and inviting the reader to guess what's inside . . . before turning the page to find out. Good fun for talking and maybe thinking of other examples.

Concept and Information Books

People, places, and things are becoming more and more important to five-year-olds. They are ready for simple, straightforward information that relates to their expanded experiences in the real world. If your child likes this kind of book, don't hesitate to dip into the list of concept books in the previous chapter; most of them are still appropriate for five-year-olds.

Busiest People Ever by Richard Scarry. Random House, 1976. Several small stories with people to find within the big busy scenario packed with action and humor. Kids will love poring over this one alone after the read-aloud time is over.

The Color Kittens included in *A Treasury of Little Golden Books* by Margaret Wise Brown. Golden, 1982. Not just about naming colors, this concept book on mixing colors is told in a playful story format.

Crash! Bang! Boom! by Peter Spier. Doubleday, 1972. Here's a catalogue of the multitude of sounds made by people and things. Fives will love poring over it.

Elephant Bathes by Derek Hall; illustrated by John Butler. Sierra

Club/Knopf, 1985. When Elephant Baby is stung by hornets, his mother takes him to the river for a soothing bath. One of a series of handsome books with straightforward information in a small story frame. Also: *Polar Bear Leaps* and *Gorilla Builds*.

Faces by Barbara Brenner; photos by George Ancona. Dutton, 1970. Clear, charming photos and delightful text emphasize the features of the face and explore their use in four of the five senses by showing things that a child may see, hear, smell, or taste. Although the face of one child often reappears, the point is made that each face is unique by showing a wide variety of faces of many races and ages.

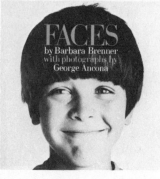

Fast-Slow, High-Low by Peter Spier. Doubleday, 1972. This wordless book of opposites has no real text but the watercolor catalogue of illustrations provides plenty to talk about and some chuckles as well.

Follow Me by Mordicai Gerstein. Harper & Row, 1983. These colorful Chinese ducks want to get home for dinner, but they don't know the way, until a small boy leads them happily home.

Gobble, Growl, Grunt by Peter Spier. Doubleday, 1971. Animals grouped by night, barn, jungle, pond, you name it, all illustrated with the sounds they make.

The Great Blueness by Arnold Lobel. Harper & Row, 1968. "Long ago there were no colors in the world . . ." the story begins. So a kind wizard uses his magic and stirs up blue, yellow, and red, and the rest is history. A good one for pure fun and mixing colors.

Have You Seen Trees? by Joanne Oppenheim; illustrated by Irwin Rosenhouse. Addison-Wesley, 1967. Written in verse, this first in a series of concept books explores the sizes, colors, names, and things we get from trees. Also: *Have You Seen Birds?* Scholastic, 1986.

A House Is a House for Me by Mary Ann Hoberman; illustrated by Betty Fraser. Viking, 1978. In lilting verse, here's a concept book that expands on the idea of houses for people, animals, and things.

I Know a Lady by Charlotte Zolotow; illustrated by James Stevenson. Greenwillow, 1984. Here the seasons are explored by following the relationship between an old woman and two children who live down the street and enjoy her flowers in summer, her treats in winter, and her love all year long.

The Important Book by Margaret Wise Brown; illustrated by Leonard Weisgard. Harper & Row, 1949. One of the best of its kind, this catalogue of familiar objects examines each item, listing its attributes and then caps each with "the important thing" to remember.

Jump Frog Jump by Robert Kalan; illustrated by Byron Barton. Greenwillow, 1981. This is a cumulative tale like *The House That Jack Built,* but here Frog stays one jump away from disaster with each turn of the page.

The Little House by Virginia Lee Burton. Houghton Mifflin, 1942. Here's a gem that takes a little house through changes of seasons and years. As time passes so does the changing scene that features new houses and transportation. The house is ultimately removed from the city and taken to a new grassy hill in the country. A classic.

The Little Rabbit by Judy Dunn; photos by Phoebe Dunn. Random House, 1980. A realistic story about an Easter Bunny that becomes a child's pet and the mother of seven bunnies. Also: *The Little Lamb.*

Noisy Book by Margaret Wise Brown; illustrated by Leonard Weisgard. Harper & Row, 1939. If you haven't met Muffin yet, you've got a great treat waiting. Lots of interaction in this and all the sequels. See: *Country Noisy Book* and *Seashore Noisy Book.*

Only the Cat Saw by Ashley Wolff. Dodd Mead, 1985. A poetic little story that captures the sights of night not ordinarily seen by a child. Text and illustrations of the child's world alternate with glorious full-color views of what the cat saw.

The Philharmonic Gets Dressed by Karla Kuskin; illustrated by Marc Simont. Harper & Row, 1982. With wit and charm 105 people get showered, dressed, and ready to go to work. Here's a backstage eyeful of musicians getting ready to make music.

Push-Pull, Empty-Full: A Book of Opposites by Tana Hoban. Macmillan, 1972. Using lush black and white photos, Hoban zooms in for close-up views of the familiar. With little or no text these photo essays can generate lots of talk and thinking about opposites. Also see: *Over, Under, and Through and Other Spacial Concepts,* Macmillan, 1973, and *Circles, Triangles, and Squares,* Macmillan, 1974.

Rosie's Walk by Pat Hutchins. Macmillan, 1968. The concepts of across, around, over, and under are eased into an amusing story featuring a dumb chicken called Rosie who evades a fox in spite of her stupidity. Kids love it!

Summer Is by Charlotte Zolotow; illustrated by Ruth L. Bornstein. Harper & Row, 1983. Poetic text and lovely illustrations. Good for talk about changing seasons.

A Visit To the Library by Deborah Hautzig; illustrated by Joe Mathieu. Random House/Children's Television Workshop, 1986. Big Bird introduces young readers to the riches contained in libraries. Not only is there a goldmine of books for information and fun, but also lots of activities such as story reading, listening to records and tapes, and doing arts and crafts.

A Year of Birds by Ashley Wolff. Dodd Mead, 1984. With little text and handsome block prints the seasons unfold, month by month, with notable changes as the child and the family grow and creatures, leaves, bugs, and birds come and go.

Poetry and Song

Many children's books are written in verse. At their worst they're doggerel, at their best they sparkle. Here are a few picture books based on songs and collections of poetry for the young.

An Arkful of Animals: Poems for the Very Young selected by William Cole. Houghton Mifflin, 1978. Short, humorous poems about a great variety of animals, insects, and birds. Fun for reading aloud.

I Think I Saw a Snail selected by Lee Bennett Hopkins; illustrated by Harold James. Crown, 1969. Exceptionally attractive picture book of poems about the seasons. Large, lively charcoal drawings of children of various racial backgrounds.

Lavender's Blue compiled by K. Lines; illustrated by H. Jones. Oxford University Press, 1983. A classic collection of well-loved nursery rhymes.

Father Fox's Pennyrhymes by Clyde Watson; illustrated by Wendy Watson. Macmillan, 1971. Children who have loved Mother Goose will take to these catchy rhymes and miniature pictures crammed with country sights.

Listen, Children, Listen: An Anthology of Poems for the Very Young by Myra Cohn Livingston (Ed.); illustrated by Trina Schart Hyman. Harcourt, 1972. Poems especially loved for sound and rhythmic quality are collected here in a small book the right size for small hands.

Nibble, Nibble by Margaret Wise Brown. Addison-Wesley, 1959. Charming poems about small creatures.

Over in the Meadow by Olive A. Wadsworth; illustrated by Ezra Jack Keats. Scholastic, 1971. Here'a a counting poem you can sing together and let your child pore over the pictures for solo song time.

A Pocketful of Rhymes by Katherine Love (ed.); illustrated by Henrietta Jones. Crowell, 1946. This collection has been around a long time, because its short poems about plants, animals, stars, and moon never go out of date.

Poems to Read to the Very Young collected by Josette Frank; illustrated by Eloise Wilkin. Random House, 1982. This is a reissue of a book you may have enjoyed as a child.

The Rebus Treasury by Jean Marzollo; illustrated by Carol Devine Carson. Dial, 1986. A delightful collection of familiar nursery rhymes and folk songs told in words and rebuses. Fun for "reading" together with young children, where the child reads the pictures and the adult reads the words.

Just for the Fun of It

Sometimes we get so carried away with the more serious side of life we forget the value of humor and entertainment for its own sake. While many of the books already reviewed have their light side, don't overlook some of the characters and storybooks that can tickle the funnybone. This is the age when Dr. Seuss's delicious nonsense verse and zany storylines have an enormous appeal. Indeed, such books may often be a better tonic for low spirits than a book that addresses a real problem at hand. It's like switching the channel and getting away from the real world for a while. Humor can offer more than escape. It can refresh the spirits and add another dimension to the pleasures found in books.

Cloudy with a Chance of Meatballs by Judi Barrett; illustrated by Ron Barrett. Atheneum, 1984. Imagine living in a town like Chewandswallow where breakfast, lunch, and dinner fall from the sky—things like hot dogs, mustard clouds, baked beans, and a drizzle of soda. Here's a silly story fives and ups will find delicious.

Giant John by Arnold Lobel. Harper & Row, 1964. Giant John, a benevolent giant, just can't help dancing when the fairies make music. But, one day the music and dancing become too much of a good thing.

If You Give a Mouse a Cookie by Laura Joffe Numeroff; illustrated by Felicia Bond. Harper & Row, 1985. A very funny story about the chain of events that follows when you "give a mouse a cookie." Just the right kind of humor for this age.

Mr. Gumpy's Outing by John Burningham. Puffin, 1970. When Mr. Gumpy takes too many riders aboard his boat, you can predict what happens in the end. See also: *Mr. Gumpy's Motor Car.*

The Shopping Basket by John Burningham. Crowell, 1980. Steven's little shopping expedition lends itself to some counting and some strange encounters.

The Stupids Step Out by Harry Allard. Houghton Mifflin, 1974. The Stupid family and their dog Kitty spend a ridiculously funny day together. Just the kind of upside-down humor young listeners love.

And To Think I Saw It on Mulberry Street by Dr. Seuss. Vanguard, 1937. Fives, masters of the art of exaggeration, will be tickled when they meet another tall teller of tales who spins a whopper.

What Do You Say, Dear? by Sesyle Joslin. Scholastic, 1980. A first book of manners that conveys the message about pleases and thank-yous with humor instead of preaching.

Yertle the Turtle and Other Stories by Dr. Seuss. Random House, 1950. When power goes to Yertle's head, another turtle proves that even the smallest can affect the mightiest. In the same volume enjoy the woeful tale of Gertrude McFuzz, who envies others but comes to appreciate herself, and The Big Brag, a story about a boastful rabbit. Also see: *Horton Hears a Who* and *Will You Please Go, Now, Marvin K. Mooney?*

REMINDERS FOR CHOOSING BOOKS FOR FIVES

- Introduce a variety of books, from fantasy to fact. Reread old favorites and add new ones to your storytime.
- Encourage children to tell original stories or retell old favorites. Provide puppets, paper, and crayons to extend the verbal experience to a visual one.
- Introduce some classic folktales but steer clear of overly complex or gory ones.
- Borrow books from the library and build a small library of the child's own books, special favorites they can read and reread.
- Draw attention to printed words but don't push for learning to read—loving books and stories is where reading begins!

TEN BOOKS EVERY FIVE-YEAR-OLD SHOULD KNOW

Bedtime for Frances by Russell Hoban
The Best Word Book Ever by Richard Scarry
Caps for Sale by Esphyr Slobodkina
The Little Engine that Could by Watty Piper
Mike Mulligan by Virginia Lee Burton
Millions of Cats by Wanda Gag
Nutshell Library by Maurice Sendak
The Runaway Bunny by Margaret Wise Brown
Stone Soup by Marcia Brown
The Story About Ping by Marjorie Flack

Frederick by Leo Lionni
George and Martha by James Marshall
An Arkful of Animals: Poems for the Very Young by William Cole
Cloudy with a Chance of Meatballs by Judi Barrett
Ira Sleeps Over by Bernard Waber
Yertle the Turtle (et al) by Dr. Seuss

C H A P T E R   V I

Books for Sixes and Sevens

THE NEED TO KEEP READING ALOUD

For sixes and sevens, books take on a new dimension. These are the years when children get started with the formal business of learning to read. It's also the time when all too often reading to kids stops. Eager as you may be to encourage your reader to practice, this isn't the time to switch roles totally. Sure, kids take pride in showing off their new skills and parents can do a lot to encourage them. However, kids who are limited to a diet of easy-to-read books may begin to lose their appetite for books at just the time they need it most.

WOLF'S FAVOR

FULVIO TESTA

For the next year or two (or three) children and books tend to be out of sync. Their ability to understand and enjoy complex stories goes well beyond their word-attack skill. In fact, the process of laboriously sounding out words can sap the joy and meaning out of the best story. There is a great difference between what they can read independently and what they can listen to, understand, and enjoy. Rather than sticking to the controlled vocabulary of beginner books, sixes and sevens really stretch their language skills when we share stories and books rich with language. How else could they enter *The House at Pooh Corner* or journey to meet *The Wonderful Wizard of Oz?*

Like young pianists children need to hear a tune as well as practice scales. For many kids the task of learning to read is rough going. After the first flush of newness and excitement fades, kids often lose that initial enthusiasm. Perhaps the best tonic for keeping motivation alive comes from parents and teachers who take the time to share good books with children in the listening mode. From such pleasurable experiences, kids get recharged with the reason to work at the task of learning to read. Reading aloud also gives parent and child a place to meet that's removed from the usual nitty gritty exchanges about taking baths, picking up toys, and tying shoelaces. It's a place touched with humor, suspense, drama, adventure and feelings parent and child can share simply by opening the covers of a variety of books. Together you can laugh at *Mr. Popper's Penguins*, worry over Wilbur's fate in *Charlotte's Web*, take delight in the fall of that braggart, *Rumpelstiltskin.*

THE DEVELOPMENTAL CONNECTION

While many of the books enjoyed earlier will be of continued interest, sixes and sevens are a bit further along on the road to independence from home and family. At the same time, they are developing a new kind of dependence on their peers. Each day is a kind of adventure out into the bigger world with friendly (and not-so-friendly) people.

One of the major developmental tasks of this age group is to find some acceptance among one's agemates—to be able to hold one's own in the classroom and on the playground. It's not a question of being first or best, but more a matter of fitting in. There are few things the school age child wants more than to make friends. But making and keeping friends isn't always easy. Like Beverly Cleary's *Ramona the Pest* and *Ramona the Brave* sixes and sevens are still pretty rigid in their thinking. They see things as all good or all bad; fair or not fair; all right or all wrong. Of course, such judgments are made on the basis of the child's own point of view. From where he sits there's no problem in calling someone else a "crybaby," but don't call him any names! It's still tough for sixes and sevens to see the other guy's side of an issue.

EASY TO READ

A great many of the books published for six- and seven-year-olds to read independently fall into the category of "Easy to Read" books. Several publishers do series of books designed for beginning readers. However, it is important to understand that within such series the level of difficulty varies immensely. So, you can't judge a book by its cover or label. It may say it's easy to read, but the question is, easy for whom? Some are easy enough for early first grade, while others are challenging to average third graders. What makes choosing even tougher is the fact that kids' reading skills within each grade vary tremendously. There are first-graders who are reading *Charlotte's Web* independently by spring and others who are just getting started with *Go Dog Go*. Keep in mind, too, that many picture books, although not part of an easy-to-read series, are nonetheless easy enough for independent reading.

So, how can you know which books to choose? Your best solution is to let the child participate in choosing. If that's not possible, the next best option is to pick easier rather than harder books for solo times. Why? Isn't it better to buy something challenging for them to grow into? Not necessarily. What beginning readers need more than challenge is a growing sense of competence that comes from reading with ease and fluency. Although parents and teachers are often eager to see kids move ahead to the next grade level, children seem to need plenty of time to consolidate what they have learned. The second grader gets a real sense of satisfaction from picking up a first grade book and being able to zip through it without stumbling. That "can do" pleasure may be of more value in the long run than pressing for the next step up. At every stage along the way, kids need time to stay at a plateau for a while before climbing up to the next level. They themselves generally begin looking for new and more challenging books when they are ready.

BOOKS ARE BRIDGES

For six- and seven-year-olds, books are more than vehicles for practicing reading skills. In a sense, books can offer a bridge to understanding that other people have problems, feelings, and experiences like their own. A picture book offers kids an opportunity to do a little "decentering" from their usual egocentric stance. A good story invites them to step outside themselves and into someone else's shoes for a while. It's a lot like pretend play and the wide range of feelings kids can experience vicariously.

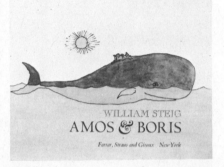

Perhaps that's what makes William Steig's *Amos and Boris* such a meaningful book for sixes and sevens. Like Amos, the mouse who builds his own ship and sails off to sea, sixes and sevens set off each day on unknown adventures of their own. They too are "full of wonder, full of enterprise and full of love for life." But, when small Amos rolls overboard and into the immense sea and begins to wonder about ever getting home again, Boris the whale bursts through the water and begins one of the most memorable friendships found in picture books. "They became the closest possible friends. They told each other about their lives, their ambitions. They shared their deepest secrets." There's a wonderful mutuality in that friendship that grows as Boris takes Amos back to shore and a sad farewell. Neither Boris nor Amos can foresee a time when Little Amos could ever hope to return the favor. But the story leaps forward several years and we find poor Boris caught in a storm that ultimately tosses him out of the sea. Enter small but wise Amos who rescues Boris with a bit of help from some friends.

Unlike *The Story About Ping* which centers on one small duck's adventure, *Amos and Boris* gives us two more fully developed characters who are dependent on one another. We actually get inside the hearts and heads of both Big Boris and Little Amos. We get both sides of the story. We're privy to their thoughts and feelings, to their reactions as well as their actions.

While sixes and sevens still tend to view the world from their own self-interest, they are beginning to grasp the idea of "you scratch my back and I'll scratch yours." Although friendships at six and seven are rarely deep and long lasting, the mutual needs of Boris and Amos parallel the child's own experience with friendship and mutuality.

However, *Amos and Boris* is more than a story about friendship. It also speaks to the still small and relatively powerless child and says size is not the only measure that counts. Faced with what seems like impossible odds, Amos uses his brain to find the necessary brawn to save Boris. He enlists the aid of two jumbo elephants, so it is a cooperative group effort that saves the day—another big idea for sixes and sevens.

On yet another level, *Amos and Boris* confronts issues of life and death, powerful thoughts young children are just beginning to grapple with in terms of themselves and others. As Boris disappears into the waves, the book ends with these words: "They knew they might never meet again. They knew they would never forget each other."

The story told through animal characters provides the young listener with food for thought. Cast in reality the same incidents with real people might be too painful to consider. Here, there is just enough distance for the child to identify and empathize with Amos or Boris from a safe vantage point outside the story. True, there are books that deal directly with death and separation. But unlike a story specifically about a grandparent who dies or a friend who moves away, *Amos and Boris* speaks in more universal terms that are meaningful in more contexts than one.

In contrast to the limited vocabulary of easy-to-read books, Steig's images are painted with words that stretch rather than put a lid on language. Although in isolation words like "phosphorescent," "luminous," "akin to" might be beyond children this age, in context the meaning comes through. It doesn't condense but rather enlarges the child's ever-expanding vocabulary. Just as they learned to speak before they could read simple sentences, now they can understand many more words than they can read or are likely to use. Buried in the text itself is a great deal of colorful information about the tools used by sailors and

a solid fact or two about mammals—"the highest form of life."
With their great appetite for information, sixes and sevens are
fascinated by such asides. While they also enjoy some straightforward books that explain how things work, often information
gathered in the context of a story holds their interest more and
therefore has greater meaning and staying power.

BOOKLIST FOR SIXES AND SEVENS

Independence and Interdependence

Unlike books for the younger child that center close to home
and family, the adventure in tales for this age almost always
begins with parents left behind or offstage. We never see that
mother who sends Max to his room before he takes off to *Where
the Wild Things Are* by Maurice Sendak. It's on his own that Max
faces the unknown and grows both literally and figuratively as
he takes charge of the Wild Things and commands them to
dance as he wills.

Amos and Boris by William Steig. Penguin, 1977. Amos the mouse
and Boris the whale become the closest of friends in a
wonderful adventure that speaks to the hearts and minds of
six- and seven-year-olds. An almost perfect match between
child and book for this age group.
Anatole by Eve Titus; illustrated by Paul Galdone. McGraw-Hill,
1956. Who's the best cheese taster in all France? Again
small triumphs over tall and brains beat brawn. The first of
an amusing series with a word or two of French tucked in
for extra flavor. For further adventures: *Anatole and the Cat*
and *Anatole over Paris*.
Arnold of the Ducks by Mordicai Gerstein. Harper & Row, 1983.
A touching reversal of the "ugly duckling" theme, full of
adventure, imagination, and humor.
Bear's Picture by Manus Pinkwater. Holt, 1972. A young bear
paints a "masterpiece" to please his own sense of beauty,
despite some well-intentioned critics.

Benji by Joan M. Lexau; illustrated by Don Bolognese. Dial, 1964. About a shy little boy who overcomes his bashfulness when his Granny loses an earring Grandpa had given her years ago. Set in Harlem, the story of Benji has universal appeal and speaks to the heart.

Benji on His Own by Joan M. Lexau; illustrated by Don Bolognese. Dial, 1964. When Benji's Grandma doesn't show up after school, Benji, who wants more independence, feels pleased, but his pleasure soon runs downhill as he discovers he doesn't really know the way home or what has happened to Granny. When he finds his Grandmother sick, he must on his own find help and he discovers he's not alone.

The Biggest Bear by Lynd Ward. Houghton Mifflin, 1952. Johnny's pet bear cub spoils everything by outgrowing the cute stage and becoming a real problem. How do they solve it, short of shooting him?

Garth Pig and the Ice Cream Lady by Mary Rayner. Atheneum, 1977. Here's the big bad wolf dressed up as the Ice Cream Lady who doesn't outfox the wise piglets.

Gorky Rises by William Steig. Farrar, Straus and Giroux, 1980. As soon as his parents leave, young Gorky the frog brews up a magic potion that lets him fly. But, after the novelty wears off there's still the problem of how to get home. It's the wise and competent Gorky who manages to solve the situation by himself.

Hurray for Pippa by Betty D. Boegehold; illustrated by Cyndy Szekeres. Dell, 1980. The adventures of a feisty girl mouse, Pippa, who not only cleans her room, but ventures into hang gliding.

In My Treehouse by Alice Schertle; illustrated by Meredith Dunham. Lothrop, Lee & Shepard, 1983. A first-person account by a child who enjoys adventures real and imagined by playing alone. This really does describe the delights of solitude.

In the Castle of Cats by Betty D. Boegehold; illustrated by Jan Brett. Dutton, 1981. A gentle, charming story of a young cat who is curious about the outside world but has scary dreams about it. A wise old cat helps to dispel the nightmare, and the young cat takes her first steps toward independence. A touching story with magical illustrations. It will strike a responsive chord in young readers and listeners.

Jennie's Hat by Ezra Jack Keats. Harper & Row, 1966. Jennie's new spring hat is a gorgeous creation, a gift from her feathered friends.

Lentil by Robert McCloskey. Viking, 1940. An old-fashioned yarn about a boy who can't sing but develops his musical talent on a harmonica and ends up a hero in his small town.

Little Tim and the Brave Sea Captain by Edward Ardizzone. Penguin, 1983. Young Tim lives in a house by the sea and wants to be a sailor. In this first adventure, Tim gets his wish. He stows away aboard a steamer, lives the life of a sailor complete with a shipwreck and happy return home. Fans of Tim will also enjoy further adventures in *Tim All Alone, Tim and Ginger,* and *Tim to the Rescue.*

Max by Rachel Isadora. Macmillan, 1976. When Max takes his sister to dance class, he discovers a new way to warm up for the baseball game.

The Mysterious Tadpole by Steven Kellogg. Dial, 1977. Louis receives a small tadpole that grows into an enormous but funny problem.

Old Mother Witch by Carol Carrick; illustrated by Donald Carrick. Seabury, 1975. While trick and treating on Halloween night, David discovers his next door neighbor, the crabby old Mrs. Oliver, has had a heart attack and needs help.

The Polar Express by Chris Van Allsburg. Houghton Mifflin, 1985. A little boy is invited to ride the Polar Express to the North Pole on Christmas Eve, and there Santa gives him his chosen gift, a silver bell from the reindeer's harness. Next morning his parents can't hear the bell's sweet tinkling sound, but the little boy can, and continues to hear it over the years. The book has wonderful pictures full of mystery and magic.

Sleep Out by Carol and Donald Carrick. Clarion, 1973. Dad is too
  tired to go camping, so Christopher and his dog go off on
  their own and share a memorable adventure.
Three Big Hogs by Manus Pinkwater. Scholastic, 1975. This frac-
  tured fairy tale is a combination Three Pigs and Goldilocks
  tale with plenty of laughs and an underlying theme about
  growing self-sufficient.
Where the Wild Things Are by Maurice Sendak. Harper & Row,
  1963. When Max, who's been acting like a "wild thing," is
  sent to bed without supper, he takes off on an adventure
  that leads to a special place where he becomes king and
  commands his wild subjects to do as he bids them.

Family

While many books focus more on adventures in independence,
the family is not entirely cast off and forgotten either in real life
or fiction. Home and family continue to provide the firm anchor
kids depend upon. Books that reflect that delicate mix of separation and attachment may be cast in fantasy as in *Sylvester and the
Magic Pebble,* or in realistic fiction as in *Like Jake and Me.* Just like
real-life parents, the adults in such stories are somewhat less
than perfect.

Alexander and the Terrible, Horrible, No Good, Very Bad Day by Judith
  Viorst; illustrated by Ray Cruz. Atheneum, 1972. Everyone
  has days when nothing goes right, when you wish you'd
  stayed in bed or left for Australia. Alexander's complaints
  are both recognizable and (at another level) laughable.
Archer Armadillo's Secret Room by Marilyn Singer; illustrated by
  Beth Lee Weiner. Macmillan, 1985. Archer's heart is broken when his father announces the family must move. It's
  Old Paw, his grandfather, who helps Archer take leave of
  the old comforts of home and move on to the new.
A Chair for My Mother by Vera B. Williams. Greenwillow, 1983.
  When the family's possessions are lost in a fire, a small girl
  helps save money to buy her mother a new chair.
Daddy Doesn't Live Here Anymore by Betty D. Boegehold. Golden,
  1985. A wonderful book to help parents and children deal
  with the sensitive topic of divorce. This warm reassuring

story, told from a child's point of view, will be helpful for the entire family.

Daddy Is a Monster . . . Sometimes by John Steptoe. Lippincott, 1950. A warm story about a Daddy who is anything but a monster.

Gregory, the Terrible Eater by Mitchell Sharmat; illustrated by Jose Aruego and Ariane Dewey. Four Winds, 1950. An upside down story about Gregory, a goat who upsets his parents because he prefers healthy food to their usual diet of newspapers, ties, barber poles, and other "junk" food.

Like Jake and Me by Mavis Jukes; illustrated by Lloyd Bloom. Knopf, 1984. Alex's new stepfather seems stronger and braver than anyone. Alex is sure nothing could scare Jake until a wolf spider crawls into the picture and Alex saves the day. A warm, loving family story.

The Patchwork Quilt by Valery Flournoy; illustrated by Jerry Pinkney. Dial, 1985. Tanya's grandmother begins piecing together a patchwork quilt. When grandmother becomes ill, Tanya continues and discovers the joys of stitching love and memories into a "masterpiece." A warm family story.

Pop's Secret by Maryann Townsend and Ronnie Stern. Addison-Wesley, 1981. A warm relationship between a grandfather and child. The text features old and new photos that show Pop growing up.

Lyle, Lyle, Crocodile by Bernard Waber. Houghton Mifflin, 1965. Mr. and Mrs. Primm and their son Joshua just happen to have an unusual pet, a lovable crocodile named Lyle. One of a series, this one is about a neighbor who hates Lyle until he comes to the rescue. Also: *The House on East 88th Street* and *Lyle and the Birthday Party.*

The Relatives Came by Cynthia Rylant; illustrated by Stephen Gammell. Bradbury, 1985. What a visit! All those relatives from Virginia have piled into their car and driven north to visit. Such hugging, eating, working and playing—and everybody happy all the time. Vivid words and pictures explode with life.

The Stories Julian Tells by Ann Cameron. Pantheon, 1981. Six warm stories about everyday family events with plenty of humor and natural loving affection. Also: *More Stories Julian Tells.*

The Story of Babar, The Little Elephant by Jean de Brunhoff. Random House, 1933, 1961. The old favorite and its many sequels has enchanted generations of children. Readers no doubt forget that Babar is an elephant. He is loved because he is seen as a person growing through familiar life situations such as death of mother, schooling, homesickness, marriage. The pictures in this elephant-human land are very endearing.

Tell Me a Trudy by Lore Segal; illustrated by Rosemary Wells. Farrar, Straus and Giroux, 1977. Three funny stories that deal with going to bed, sharing, and getting some outer-space creatures out of the bathroom. A warm, loving, playful family sitcom.

Sylvester and the Magic Pebble by William Steig. Simon & Schuster, 1969. When Sylvester finds a magic pebble that grants wishes, little does he know his troubles have just begun. It is his faithful and loving parents who ultimately help to unlock him from the spell.

Watch Out for the Chicken Feet in Your Soup by Tomie de Paola. Prentice-Hall, 1974. When he brings his friend along for a visit, Joey is embarrassed by his old-fashioned, foreign-style grandma. But it's Grandma's uniqueness that charms Joey's friend the most.

When I Have a Little Girl by Charlotte Zolotow; illustrated by Hilary Knight. Harper & Row, 1965. A small book with big appeal to that faraway in the future time when they'll allow their little girl to eat snow, stay out past dark, wear party dresses to school, and other mischievous wishes. Also see *When I Have a Son.*

White Dynamite and Curly Kidd by Bill Martin, Jr., and John Archambault; illustrated by Ted Rand. Holt, 1986. Dad is a bull rider and daughter is the cheering section in this language-rich picture story about a rodeo. Vigorous illustrations augment the dialogue between father and kid.

Separation and Death

The Accident by Carol Carrick; illustrated by Donald Carrick. Clarion, 1976. When his dog Bodger is hit by a truck, Christopher must deal with his grief and anger with the help of his caring and sensitive parents.

Annie and the Old One by Miska Miles; illustrated by Peter Parnall. Little, Brown, 1971. Annie, a Navajo girl, refuses to accept the idea that the Old One, her grandmother, will die when the rug on the loom is finished. So, Annie waits for night to unravel the day's weaving and hold back time. It is the Old One who helps Annie accept the inevitable cycle of time.

Blackberries in the Dark by Mavis Jukes; illustrated by Thomas B. Allen. Knopf, 1985. Austin's summer visit to his grandparents' home can't be the same since Grandpa died. A tender story about remembering old traditions and discovering new ones.

Dear Daddy by Phillippe Dupasquier. Bradbury, 1985. Sophie is separated from her daddy by a long sea voyage. The letters she writes to him provide the narrative that tells what is happening at home as the seasons change. At the top of each page we see the wordless story of Daddy's voyage.

My Grandson Lew by Charlotte Zolotow; illustrated by William Pene Du Bois. Harper & Row, 1974. A poetic, touching book. A boy and his mother share memories of Grandpa, who has died but is remembered with love.

Mama One, Mama Two by Patricia MacLachlan; illustrated by R. L. Bornstein. Harper & Row, 1982. This isn't for everyone, but for the child who's uprooted and put in foster care or who has a playmate going through it, this book may be meaningful.

Nana Upstairs and Nana Downstairs by Tomie de Paola. Putnam, 1973. A bittersweet story about a small boy's relationship with his grandmother and greatgrandmother. Here's a gentle story about love and death through the eyes of a child.

Now One Foot, Now the Other by Tomie de Paola. Putnam, 1981. When Bobby's grandfather has a stroke, Bobby teaches him to walk, just as his grandfather had once taught him.

The Tenth Good Thing About Barney by Judith Viorst; illustrated by Erik Blegvad. Atheneum, 1971. With some help from his parents a boy recalls all the good things about his cat Barney who has died.

The Two of Them by Aliki. Greenwillow, 1979. Love between
   grandfather and granddaughter grows into a beautiful rela-
   tionship that remains cherished memories when he dies.
Uncle Elephant by Arnold Lobel. Harper & Row, 1981. When
   Mother and Father Elephant are lost at sea, Old Uncle
   Elephant cares for their elephant child with great affection.
   Some second graders may be able to read this alone, but
   more will enjoy hearing this gentle story about a loving old
   gent and his nephew.
When Grandpa Came to Stay by Judith Casely. Greenwillow, 1986.
   Grandpa comes to stay because Grandma has died. Little
   Bunny learns that grownups cry sometimes, and he also
   learns what a cemetery is. But life is as important as death
   in this family story, illustrated in cheerful pastel colors.

Siblings

Brothers by Florence B. Freedman; illustrated by Robert Andrew
   Parker. Harper & Row, 1985. A retelling of the Biblical
   legend of Dan and Joel that manages to be both simple and
   moving. "How good it is for brothers to live in friendship"
   is one message, lovingly illustrated.
The Day I Was Born by Marjorie and Mitchell Sharmat; illustrated
   by Diane Dawson. Dutton, 1980. On facing pages two
   brothers give their own accounts of the same event, a kind
   of junior version of Roshomon, with the accent of brotherly
   love.
Do You Have the Time, Lydia? by Evaline Ness. Dutton, 1971.
   Lydia, the big sister, is always starting new things and never
   finishing, telling her little brother she has no time. Until one
   day she discovers that her father is right when he says, "If
   you take time you can have time."
The Half-Birthday Party by Charlotte Pomerantz; illustrated by D.
   DiSalvo-Ryan. Houghton Mifflin, 1984. A charming story
   about a party Daniel gives for his sister's half-year birthday.
I'll Fix Anthony by Judith Viorst; illustrated by Arnold Lobel.
   Harper & Row, 1969. "When I'm six," a little brother
   dreams of dozens of ways to get even with his big brother
   Anthony. Humor with a biting edge.
James Will Never Die by Joanne Oppenheim; illustrated by True

Kelley. Dodd, Mead, 1983. Everyone (especially younger brothers and sisters) knows someone like James, who always has to win or be the boss. In a series of pretend games, Anthony, the younger brother, finally outmaneuvers James.

Tell Me a Mitzi by Lore Segal; illustrated by Harriet Pincus. Farrar, Straus and Giroux, 1970. Three tongue-in-cheek tales about a big sister and her little brother who get around the city with a flair.

She Come Bringing Me That Little Baby Girl by Eloise Greenfield; illustrated by John Steptoe. Lippincott, 1974. Kevin wanted a brother but what did he get? Here's a loving family and an uncle who puts baby sisters in a new perspective.

Stevie by John Steptoe. Harper & Row, 1969. When little Stevie comes to live with the family, Robert, an only child, is bothered with Stevie and "his old spoiled self." But, pesty as Stevie may be, the bond between the two grows. A touching story.

Worse Than Willy by James Stevenson. Greenwillow, 1984. When Mary Ann and Louis complain to Grandpa about their new baby brother, Grandpa spins them a wild tale about his own brother who just happened to save his life.

Friends—on Two Feet and Four

The Checker Players by Alan Venable; illustrated by Byron Barton. Lippincott, 1973. Two friends, very different by nature, put their best ideas together and solve a problem.

The Costume Party by W. B. Park. Little, Brown, 1983. At a costume party a mystery guest appears who almost ruins the party because he's so pushy, rude, and bearish!

A Dog I Know by Barbara Brenner; illustrated by Fred Brenner. Harper & Row, 1983. A touching, humorous, but realistic picture of a child and his dog.

Feelings by Aliki. Greenwillow, 1984. With tons of tiny illustrations, dialogues, poems, and short short stories, *Feelings* looks at jealousy, fear, anger, joy, and love with just enough humor to give you a lift.

Friends by Helen Heine. Atheneum, 1983. A simple, straightforward book about a rooster, a mouse, and a pig who discover some basic things about being friends.

Frog and Toad Are Friends by Arnold Lobel. Harper & Row, 1970. Although written in an easy-to-read format, these five short stories about two loyal friends can be enjoyed as read-alouds. They're right on target in feelings. Also: *Frog and Toad Together, Frog and Toad All Year,* and *Days with Frog and Toad.*

I Know a Lady by Charlotte Zolotow; illustrated by James Stevenson. Greenwillow, 1984. A child's-eye view of an old lady who lives next door, someone she'll long remember.

The Island of the Skog by Steven Kellogg. Dial, 1973. A fantasy about some young and adventurous mice and a lonely "skog" they befriend.

Ira Sleeps Over by Bernard Waber. Houghton Mifflin, 1972. When Ira is invited to sleep over at his friend Reggie's, the question is, should he bring his bedtime bear or will Reggie laugh at him? A really satisfying solution handled with humor and feelings kids will recognize.

It's Not Fair by Charlotte Zolotow; illustrated by William Pene Du Bois. Harper & Row,1976. Martha has everything—long black hair, a better teacher, a nicer mother, nearer Grandma. Talks right to the heart of jealousy.

A Letter to Amy by Ezra Jack Keats. Harper & Row, 1968. Peter is having a birthday but the invitation to his friend Amy almost spoils everything.

Lizard's Song by George Shannon; illustrated by Jose Aruego and Ariane Dewey. Greenwillow, 1981. Bear tries to learn Lizard's song, but it's not until Lizard helps Bear find his own song that Bear can remember.

M and M and the Haunted House Game by Pat Ross; illustrated by Marylin Hafner. Pantheon, 1980. Mini and Marty, neighbors and friends, play a game that backfires.

More Alex and the Cat by Helen V. Griffith; illustrated by Donald Carrick. Greenwillow, 1983. Three warm and witty stories in which Alex, a somewhat young dog, learns about life with some help from his friend the cat.

My Friend Jacob by Lucille Clifton; illustrated by Thomas Di Grazia. Dutton, 1980. The friendship between eight-year-old Sam and a teenage retarded boy is based on genuine caring and appreciation of what each boy can do rather than what they can't do.

Old Mother Witch by Carol and Donald Carrick. Seabury, 1975. A sensitive story about some trick-or-treaters who set out to tease a nasty old neighbor and end up facing a life-and-death situation.

Oliver Button Is a Sissy by Tomie de Paola. Harcourt, 1979. Everyone calls Oliver a sissy because he doesn't like to do just what everyone else expects. He does like to tap dance and doesn't let his friends' teasing stop him. Not exactly a happy ending. He loses a talent show but becomes "a star" to his friends, family, and himself.

Rotten Ralph by Jack Gantos; illustrated by Nicole Rubel. Houghton Mifflin, 1976. A rather tall tale about an outrageous cat friend called Ralph who is rotten but trying to reform.

Sam Bangs and Moonshine by Evaline Ness. Holt, 1966. It takes a near tragedy for Sam (short for Samantha) to understand the difference between telling the truth or talking "Moonshine." A gem!

Take It or Leave It by Osmond Molarsky; illustrated by Trina Schart Hyman. Scholastic, 1980. A tale about sixes' and sevens' typical sport of swapping possessions and not always coming out even.

Thy Friend, Obadiah by Brinton Turkle. Viking, 1969. Set in old Nantucket, the little Quaker boy Obadiah finds the meaning of friendship and being needed. Also: *Obadiah, the Bold.*

Ty's One-man Band by Mildred Pitts Walter; illustrated by Margot Tomes. Four Winds, 1980. Here's a lyrical story about a stranger who comes into Ty's hum-drum nothing-to-do day and sets the whole town to dancing.

You Ought to See Herbert's House by Doris Lund; illustrated by Stephen Kellogg. Watts, 1973. Herbert visits his friend Roger and tells a lot of tall tales that catch up with him in the end.

Tales Out of School

Crow Boy by Taro Yashima. Viking, 1955. A touching story about a boy who is "different" but discovers, as do his classmates, that everyone has something special to offer to be appreciated for.

The Day Jimmy's Boa Ate the Wash by Trinka Noble; illustrated by

Steven Kellogg. Dial, 1980. Here's a school field trip to end all field trips. When Jimmy secretly brings his pet snake along, the silly tale unfolds.

Lost in the Museum by Miriam Cohen; illustrated by Lillian Hoban. Greenwillow, 1979. In his eagerness to see the dinosaurs Danny gets half of his first grade class lost, but manages to get found again, too.

Miss Nelson Is Missing by Harry Allard; illustrated by James Marshall. Houghton Mifflin, 1977. Miss Nelson's mischievous class gets its comeuppance when a witchy substitute arrives with a no-nonsense approach. This is a bit of a mystery with a surprise ending listeners love.

Mrs. Peloki's Snake by Joanne Oppenheim; illustrated by Joyce Audy dos Santos. Dodd Mead, 1980. Bedlam breaks out in the second grade when Kevin thinks he's discovered a snake in the boys' room. Also: *Mrs. Peloki's Class Play.*

Teach Us, Amelia Bedelia by Peggy Parrish; illustrated by Lynn Sweat. Greenwillow, 1977. Here's good old Amelia Bedelia getting things all mixed up as a substitute teacher.

That Dreadful Day by James Stevenson. Greenwillow, 1985. When Mary Ann and Louie complain about their first day at school, Grandpa, a fabulous storyteller, spins them a yarn about his bad old days. Really funny.

Veronica, the Show Off by Nancy Robinson; illustrated by Sheila Greenwald. Scholastic, 1983. Veronica thinks showing off is the way to make friends.

When Will I Read? by Miriam Cohen; illustrated by Lillian Hoban. Greenwillow, 1977. A reassuring little book about a first-grader who's been waiting "all his life" to learn how to read.

Humor

What sixes and sevens find laughable is a lot subtler than the obvious upside-down humor that tickles fours and fives. By six or seven, most kids have a firm fix on fantasy and reality. So they can deal with the suspense of two green monsters tiptoeing into a bedroom and enjoy the last laugh when the occupant in *Pleasant Dreams* turns out to be a little green monster herself. For younger kids the same story might be more frightening than funny. At any age humor plays on our notions of the expected and unexpected. As children get older they have a broader frame of reference, so there are more facets to play on. This is the time when riddles like "What's black and white and read all over?" produce a howl. Indeed, the ability to play with multiple meanings of words and see the humor marks a new level of sophistication. Often the most pleasing sort of humor involves the young hero outsmarting the older, wiser, or supposedly stronger character, and winning the day. For the young school child such conquests are a notch in the belt, further proof of gaining independence.

Alexander, Who Used to Be Rich Last Sunday by Judith Viorst; illustrated by Ray Cruz. Atheneum, 1978. Alexander had a dollar on Sunday, but one misfortune after another empties his pocket.

The Bear's Toothache by David McPhail. Little, Brown, 1972. Sixes who frequently suffer from a painful tooth will see the humor of this tall tale of a boy and a great big baby of a bear.

Bored—Nothing to Do by Peter Spier. Doubleday, 1978. Almost wordless book about two boys and their imaginative way of handling an otherwise boring day. A zany adventure.

Chloe and Maude by Sandra Boynton. Little, Brown, 1985. A rare find, a truly funny and insightful book for children. Kids of all ages will delight in the quirky friendship of Maude, the imaginative, temperamental cat, and her friend, Chloe, who is sensible and patient. The humorous drawings are a perfect match to the text.

Come Away from the Water, Shirley by John Burningham. Crowell, 1977. While Shirley's Mom and Dad sit in their beach chairs telling her to stay away from the water, Shirley has a wonderful adventure on board a private ship.

Dr. DeSoto by William Steig. Farrar, Straus and Giroux, 1982. The kind-hearted dentist, Dr. DeSoto, and his able assistant, Mrs. DeSoto (both mice), never treat cats or other dangerous animals. However, when a jaunty fox with a toothache pleads for mercy, the DeSotos take him on and outfox the fellow with a humorous but fitting ending. Another triumph of small over big, of brain over brawn.

Gorilla by Anthony Browne. Knopf, 1983. Hannah's toy gorilla is transformed and leads her to a great adventure. A fantasy with fantastic illustrations.

Her Majesty, Aunt Essie by Amy Schwartz. Bradbury, 1984. A tongue-in-cheek tale about a little girl with a great imagination and a boast that almost backfires.

My Uncle by Jenny Thorne. Atheneum, 1982. Here's a tall tale about a rather droll character named Uncle and his misadventures. Highly stylized illustrations, several frames to the page, but not cartoonish.

Pinkerton, Behave! by Steven Kellogg. Dial, 1979. Great big dog Pinkerton may not make the grade in obedience school, but he turns out to be a hero.

Pleasant Dreams by Anna B. Francis. Holt, 1983. An almost wordless book full of suspense as two great green monsters tiptoe into guess whose bedroom. You'll laugh together at the funny ending. Not for the squeamish.

Simple Pictures Are Best by Nancy Willard; illustrated by Tomie de Paola. Harcourt, 1976. Although the photographer tells them "simple pictures are best," the zany husband and wife keep adding one ridiculous thing after another.

Folktales—Old and New

Among the best-loved stories for sixes and sevens are the familiar folktales that have been handed down from generation to generation. Historically, long before books were widely available, such tales were told aloud. They became part of every child's literary heritage. Indeed, stories such as *Cinderella, Sleeping Beauty,* and *Hansel and Gretel* have inspired operas, ballets, symphonies, and some of the most exquisite picture books ever published.

While many of the traditional tales were too complex and even frightening for the preschooler, sixes and sevens are developmentally ready for greater flights of fancy. By now they have a firmer grasp of real and make-believe. So, wicked witches with evil spells now fit into the realm of safe-scare. They belong to "once upon a time and long ago"—a great place to visit for vicarious adventure.

Indeed, some psychologists believe that the underlying themes of folktales are the most soul-satisfying stories for the middle years of childhood.

What are the ingredients that kids find so appealing? Again and again the folktales spin stories of the young, independent adventurer, face to face with danger that demands great courage. They are stories of good triumphing over evil; about young against old; the weak versus the strong. In the end not everyone lives happily ever after. *The Fisherman's Wife* ends up with her tumble down hut because she is too greedy. The Hare loses the race because he's too smug. And all wicked witches, cruel stepmothers, and jealous sisters get their just desserts in the end! Where else can we find such absolute justice? This sense of fair and foul, right and wrong, good and evil all match the child's own rather rigid moral sensibilities.

Since many of the elements of folktales are similar, experienced listeners begin to pick up on the similarities and differences between stories. In fact, parents can encourage such literary comparison by selecting stories that are related. After reading *The Fisherman and His Wife* kids will see obvious common threads in the old favorite *The Three Wishes*. Or read the old Aesop Fable about the Lion and the Mouse followed by *Andy and the Lion*.

Aesop's Fables selected and illustrated by Michael Hague. Holt, 1985. Hague's beautiful paintings illustrate a baker's dozen of the most familiar Aesop Fables.

Alexis and the Golden Ring by Linda Heller. Macmillan, 1980. For his kindness to an old woman, Alexis receives a magical ring that saves his dear Natasha.

Cinderella translated and illustrated by Marcia Brown from Perrault. Scribner's, 1954. This is a slightly longer and richer version of the familiar tale with memorable fairy tale pastel illustrations.

Everyone Knows What a Dragon Looks Like by Jay Williams; illustrated by Mercer Mayer. Four Winds, 1976. In China the City of Wu is saved from the Wild Horsemen of the North because a young boy has enough faith for everyone.

The Fisherman and His Wife by Margot Zemach from the Grimm
Brothers. Norton, 1966. When the Fisherman finds a magic
fish that grants wishes, his greedy wife keeps demanding
more and more until at last they have nothing. Kids love to
chant the magic refrain with the storyteller.

The 500 Hats of Bartholomew Cubbins by Dr. Seuss. Vanguard,
1938. One of Dr. Seuss's earliest and still well-loved stories
about a boy, a king, and 500 magical hats.

Hansel and Gretel translated by Charles Scribner, Jr.; illustrated
by Adrienne Adams. Scribner's, 1975; and *Hansel and Gretel*
retold by Rika Lesser; illustrated by Paul O. Zelinsky. Dodd,
Mead, 1984. Two of the most beautifully illustrated versions of this tale from the Grimm Brothers. Look at both
and choose your favorite.

The Hare and the Tortoise by La Fontaine; illustrated by Brian
Wildsmith. Watts, 1966. A classic tale about an overconfi-
dent hare and a one-step-at-a-time-stick-to-it turtle. Gorgeous illustrations.

The House that Jack Built illustrated by Rodney Peppe. Delacorte,
1985. An old Mother Goose cumulative tale with lively illustrations and plenty of repetition for beginning readers to
relish.

Journey Cake, Ho by Ruth Sawyer; illustrated by Robert McCloskey. Viking, 1953. Those who know *The Gingerbread Boy* will
see the similarities and differences between that old favorite
and this new twist. Here a poor old man and woman pack
young Johnny off to make his way in the world with a Journey Cake that leaps out and leads Johnny plus a barnyard
full of creatures back home. Also: *Johnny-Cake* as told by
Joseph Jacobs.

The North Wind and the Sun, A Fable by La Fontaine; illustrated
by Brian Wildsmith. Watts, 1964. When the Wind and the
Sun vie to see who can make a horseman remove his cloak,
the power of the wind is less strong than the gentle ways of
the sun.

Pancake Pie by Sven Nordquist. Morrow, 1985. Here's a modern-
style cumulative tale in which everything goes wrong for
Farmer Festus and his cat until the inventive duo put their
heads together and the tale unwinds.

Potatoes, Potatoes by Anita Lobel. Harper & Row, 1967. A modern folktale about war and peace between West and East and a mother who put an end to it.

Rapunzel from Grimm retold and illustrated by Bernadette Watts. Crowell, 1975. Here's the beautiful young girl with long, long hair who's imprisoned by a witch until she is found by a young prince.

Red Riding Hood retold by Beatrice Schenk de Regniers; illustrated by Edward Gorey. Atheneum, 1972. The familiar tale of Little Red Riding Hood told in verse.

Rumpelstiltskin by Brothers Grimm; illustrated by Jacqueline Ayer. Harcourt, 1967. When the miller boasted that his daughter could spin straw into gold, the poor girl is forced to make a deal with that nasty fellow Rumpelstiltskin. But good triumphs over evil.

Rumpelstiltskin by Brothers Grimm; retold and illustrated by Paul Galdone. Clarion, 1985. In this faithful retelling of the gripping old tale, large-scale drawings literally fill the large pages. There is enough color, liveliness and characterization here to lure almost any child.

The Shoemaker and the Elves retold and illustrated by Cynthia and William Birrer. Lothrop, Lee and Shepard, 1984. Handsome illustrations capture a simple but well-loved fairy tale about a poor cobbler and his magical helpers.

Sleeping Beauty told and illustrated by Warwick Hutton. Atheneum, 1981. Beautifully illustrated version of a classic tale with a wicked witch, a magic spell, and a happy ending.

Sleeping Ugly by Jane Yolen; illustrated by Diane Stanley. Coward, McCann, 1981. Here's a very new tale about a beautiful (but mean) Princess, a sweet but Plain Jane, and a Fairy who grants wishes. Kids who know their Sleeping Beauty will love the turnabout humor in this one.

Strega Nona retold and illustrated by Tomie de Paola. Prentice-Hall, 1975. If you are looking for a gentle witch tale, Strega Nona and her assistant Big Anthony will provide plenty of pasta and laughter when Anthony learns only one half the magic he needs and can't stop the Pasta Pot.

That Noodle-Head Epaminondas by Eve Merriam. Follett, 1968. A funny tale about a literal-minded boy who always listens but misses the message.

The Three Wishes illustrated by Paul Galdone. McGraw-Hill,

1961. When the woodman spares a tree a fairy grants him three wishes that lead to less happiness than one might expect.

Tikki, Tikki, Tembo retold by Arlene Mosel; illustrated by Blair Lent. Holt, 1968. Young listeners enjoy the repetition of that tongue twisting name, Tikki tikki tembo-no sa rembo-chari bari ruchi-pip peri pembo, and the predicament two mischievous Chinese brothers get into.

Anthologies of Folktales and Fairy Tales

The Big Golden Book of Fairytales retold by L. Leete-Hodge; illustrated by B. Manson. Golden, 1981. Eleven well-known tales, including *Sleeping Beauty, Rumpelstiltskin, The Golden Goose,* and *Snow White.*

The Big Purple Book of Fairy Tales illustrated by Caroline Sharpe. Simon & Schuster, 1984. A handsome collection of most every tale you will want to share and then some you might want to save for next year or the year after.

The Fairy Tale Treasury edited by Virginia Haviland; illustrated by Raymond Briggs. Coward, McCann, 1972. One of the best collections of old favorites for this age group.

Tasha Tudor's Book of Fairy Tales illustrated by Tasha Tudor. Platt & Munk, 1961. This may be the volume you had as a child with Tasha Tudor's beautiful illustrations.

Twelve Tales from Aesop retold and illustrated by Eric Carle. Philomel, 1980. Here's a bright and appealing collection of classic fables retold and illustrated with great style.

The Ugly Duckling by Hans Christian Andersen; illustrated by Monika Liamgruber. Greenwillow, 1985. A great old favorite in a picture book unique for its design and large, handsome, realistic illustrations.

Wordless Books

Among the most humorous books are many storybooks told purely by pictures. Wordless books were introduced in the last chapter and many of the simpler books suggested for fives may be a better departure point for the uninitiated. For sixes and sevens the more complex wordless books demand closer examination, interpreting details and expressions, in order to understand what's happening. Such skills are as basic to reading as decoding letters. They are the basic ingredients of reading comprehension, the meaning underneath the words.

The Adventures of Paddy Pork by John S. Goodall. Harcourt, 1968. Kids with a good sense of story will be able to "read" the pictures of the folk-style tale of a pig who runs away from home to join the circus and meets with adventure, dashed dreams, but returns home to a warm welcome from Mama.

Alligator's Toothache by Diane De Groat. Crown, 1977. Poor Alligator's got a toothache but is scared of going to the dentist. So the dentist comes to Alligator.

The Bear and the Fly by Paula Winter. Crown, 1976. Three bears are having dinner when a pesky fly enters the scene and the rest is mayhem! The paperback comes with stickers so you can add words like "Swat!," "Pow!," and "Where Is He?"

Birds of a Feather by Willi Baum. Addison-Wesley, 1969. A funny wordless tale about a little bird who longs to be different and ends up happy to be like his fellow birds-of-a-feather.

Catch That Cat by Fernando Krahn. Dutton, 1978. Trying to catch that cat leads to a boy's adventure on the high seas with a safe return home.

The City by Douglas Florian. Crowell, 1982. Full of details with a touch of sly humor. Follow the lady with the red bag through the city to discover what she carries.

The Great Ape by Fernando Krahn. Viking/Penguin, 1978. A totally new slant on King Kong and a fair young damsel whom the Ape rescues.

The Grey Lady and the Strawberry Snatcher by Molly Bang. Four Winds, 1980. Sort of a spooky tale. The mysterious strawberry snatcher does his evil best to catch the grey lady, but everyone ends up in the "berries."

The Happy Dog by Hideyuki Tanaka. Atheneum, 1983. Three delightfully childlike stories about a shaggy dog and his misadventures with a ball and bat, a puddle, and a balloon.

Here Comes Alex Pumpernickel by Fernando Krahn. Little, Brown, 1951. A collection of small stories without words about the curious and unpredictable Alex.

The Mystery of the Giant Footprints by Fernando Krahn. Dutton,

1977. Most sixes and sevens love Bigfoot tales and this one will especially tickle them since two kids outsmart the adults and actually capture the elusive beasts.

Paddy Pork's Holiday by John S. Goodall. Atheneum, 1976. Paddy Pork's overnight camping trip is a series of hilarious near .disasters cleverly averted at each turn by the wise and lovable pig.

Paddy Underwater by John S. Goodall. Atheneum, 1981. Here's fearless Paddy in an underwater adventure that leads our hero from danger to monsters, mermaids, and long lost treasure!

The Snowman by Raymond Briggs. Random House, 1978. Probably the most exquisite of its genre, a fantasy about a boy and his snowman who take off on a thrilling adventure—the stuff of which snowflakes and daydreams are made.

Up and Up by Shirley Hughes. Prentice-Hall, 1979. That universal childhood dream of flying takes wing here with a magic egg.

Who's Seen the Scissors? by Fernando Krahn. Dutton, 1975. If scissors could fly then this flight of fancy might explain where a mischievous pair of scissors might go.

More Information, Please

Sixes and sevens have an appetite for information about the real world of animals, people, and things. "Is that really true?" they ask. They have a budding sense of time and are beginning to understand the existence of faraway places. Although few second graders can accept the idea that no people were alive when dinosaurs roamed the earth, they are fascinated by what they ate, where they lived, how they looked, the music of the names stegasaurus, tyrannosaurus, and brontosaurus.

Although the books that follow are especially designed for young readers and listeners, don't overlook more complex books and magazines. You may not want to read such volumes word for word, but they can enjoy the captions of pictures and capsule versions of texts from adult books and field guides.

An Apartment House Close Up by Peter Schaaf. Four Winds, 1980. An almost wordless text gives inside views of how water, heat, elevators, and such work.

The Big Dipper by Franklyn Branley; illustrated by Ed Emberly. Crowell, 1962. For young stargazers, an easy-to-read-and-understand book about the Big Dipper and how it got its name. One of Branley's many excellent books for the *Let's Read and Find Out Series*.

The Bionic Bunny Show by Marc Brown and Laurence K. Brown. Little, Brown, 1984. An amusing and informative book that takes kids behind the scenes of a superhero TV show. There are two stories running here: a TV cartoon show interrupted every few pages by off-screen business when Bionic Bunny goofs and proves he is anything but a superhero.

Color Kittens by Margaret Wise Brown (included in *Treasury of Little Golden Books*). Golden, 1982. Two kittens, Hush and Brush, mix up all the colors in the world. A perfect choice for young artists discovering the magic of mixing paints.

The Day the Sun Danced by Edith Thacher Hurd; illustrated by Clement Hurd. Harper & Row, 1966. A poetic book about the animals in the forest who gather to welcome spring.

Department Store by Gail Gibbons. Crowell, 1984. From start of the day to closing this tells about all the behind-the-scenes jobs that go on in a big department store. Wonderful illustrations.

Dinosaur Time by Peggy Parish; illustrated by Arnold Lobel. Harper & Row, 1974. Handsome illustrations in this catalogue of familiar and not-so-familiar dinosaurs in an easy-to-read format.

A First Look at Dinosaurs by Millicent E. Selsam and Joyce Hunt; illustrated by Harriett Springer. Walker, 1982. Solid information without an overload for young readers.

A House Is a House for Me by Mary Ann Hoberman; illustrated by Betty Fraser. Viking, 1978. A catalogue of animals and their homes told in sprightly verse.

Houses from the Sea by Alice E. Goudey; illustrated by Adrienne Adams. Scribner's, 1959. For young shell collectors a picture book with lyrical text, beautiful illustrations, and information to identify shells.

How Puppies Grow by Millicent Selsam; illustrated by Esther Bubley. Four Winds, 1971. Appealing photos and simple text tell the story of six new puppies and how they grow.

Jemima Remembers by Crescent Dragonwagon; illustrated by Troy

Howell. Macmillan, 1984. Jemima has spent the summer with her aunt at the lake and now it is time to leave. A lovely mood piece about saying good-bye to summer.

Large As Life—Nighttime Animals by Joanna Cole; illustrated by Kenneth Lilly. Knopf, 1985. Stunning illustrations of creatures in their habitats portrayed in true life size. The straightforward information on each double page spread is further amplified with nature notes at the end of the book for those who want to know more. Also: *Large As Life—Daytime Animals.*

The Life of a Dog by Jan Feder; illustrated by Tilman Michalski. Children's Press, 1982. A story of a year in the life of a farm watchdog, followed by an illustrated catalogue and text presenting more detailed information. Also in the Animal Lives Series: *The Life of a Cat, The Life of a Rabbit,* and *The Life of a Hamster.*

Lavinia Bat by Russell Hoban; illustrated by Martin Baynton. Holt, 1984. More than a science book, this is a poetic and moving story about the cycle of life. "Pass it on," as Lavinia says.

The Lion by Margaret Lane; illustrated by David Nockels. Random House, 1985. One of the *Early Bird Animal World* series that describes the day-to-day life of one particular animal in a small but informative volume. Also: *The Elephant, The Giraffe,* and *The Chimpanzee.*

Moon, Sun, and Stars by John Lewellan. Children's Press, 1981. An introduction to astronomy with emphasis on the relationship between the moon, earth, and the sun. Part of *A New True Book* series.

My Visit to the Dinosaurs by Aliki. Crowell, 1969. A child's visit to the museum with solid information in a story frame.

Once There Was a Tree by Natalia Romanova; illustrated by Gennady Spirin. Dial, 1985. This extraordinarily beautiful book tells in simple language who "owns" a tree from the time it is cut down to the time when it finally sends out new branches and takes its place as a tree once again. How all life is interrelated is the clear message in this book originally published in the Soviet Union.

Panda by Susan Bonners. Delacorte, 1978. A beautiful book about the life of a giant panda from birth until at six years she has her own cub.

Sails, Rails, and Wings by Seymour Reit; illustrated by Roberto Innocenti. Golden, 1978. Busy pages with brief text lends itself to lots of independent looking. Transportation from early history to futuristic looks ahead.

Sharks by Ann McGovern; illustrated by Murray Tinkelman. Four Winds, 1976. Using a question format, McGovern answers basic questions kids have about sharks.

Some Busy Hospital by Seymour Reit; illustrated by Carolyn Bracken. Western, 1985. This big book gives kids a look at the many workers and jobs they do in a busy hospital. Goes beyond doctors, nurses, and sick people and takes some of the mystery out of the child's-eye view of a big impersonal building.

Trucks by Gail Gibbons. Harper & Row, 1981. A busy book chockfull of transporting, building, and service trucks all shown in action. Great for solo looking. Very little text.

Truck Song by Diane Siebert; illustrated by Byron Barton. Crowell, 1984. A lilting journey in verse that follows a trucker in his rig cross country. Stunning illustrations.

Up Goes the Skyscraper by Gail Gibbons. Four Winds, 1986. Every step from the first surveying to the final installation of fixtures is shown, as page by page the skyscraper rises.

What Do People Do All Day? by Richard Scarry. Random House, 1968. Fewer labels but tons of pictorial information about work, workers, and the tools they use all set in short-story format. Scarry breaks down complex processes into child-size bites of information.

What Makes a Bird a Bird? by May Garelick; illustrated by Leonard

Weisgard. Follett, 1969. Is a bird a bird because it can fly, has wings, can sing, builds nests, lays eggs? Here's an informative book bound to stimulate talk and thought.

What Makes It Go? Work? Fly? Float? by Joe Kaufman. Golden, 1971. For all those questions about how things work, here are child-size answers.

Alphabet, Counting, and Concept Books

As children master letters and numbers, they enjoy books that go beyond simply matching objects with symbols. Now they are ready to play with letters, words, and numbers. Many alphabet books take on a riddlelike quality that is more challenging than "A is for Apple." This is also the time when kids actually enjoy reading a dictionary if it's well illustrated with colorful pictures.

A, B, See! by Tana Hoban. Greenwillow, 1982. The whole alphabet is strung out on each page with each letter featured in large size, and objects to be named beginning with that letter in striking black and white.

Brown Cow Farm by Dahlov Ipcar. Doubleday, 1959. It's wintertime on Brown Cow Farm and all the animals are in the barn. All the better for counting! Here's a near classic counting book that goes from one to ten then on to one hundred by tens.

CDB by William Steig. Simon and Schuster, 1968. Once kids firmly know the letters and names of the alphabet, they'll have a good laugh over the cartoons captioned with playful messages written in "code."

Easy As Pie by Marcia and Michael Folsom; illustrated by Jack Kent. Houghton Mifflin, 1985. Here's an alphabetical guessing game. "A . . . Straight as an ?"; "B . . . Snug as a ?" The clue is on one page and the answer is on the flip side. All based on familiar sayings.

Harold's ABC by Crockett Johnson. Harper & Row, 1963. A playful adventure with the alphabet with that whimsical Harold.

I Found Them in the Yellow Pages by Norma Farber; illustrated by Marc Brown. Little, Brown, 1973. A catalogue of working people found in the Yellow Pages from A to Z. Zany illustrations.

Lentil Soup by Joe Lasker. Whitman, 1977. Set in pioneer days, this is an amusing story about a farmer's wife who couldn't make great lentil soup. Built in are concepts about days of the week and cardinal/ordinal numbers.

The Most Amazing Hide and Seek Alphabet Books by Robert Crowther. Viking, 1977. These are flip books that are fun to manipulate with some help from a grown-up.

One Old Oxford Ox by Nicola Bayley. Atheneum, 1977. Tongue twisters to tickle the ear and count by.

One, Two, Three—An Animal Counting Book by Marc Brown. Little, Brown, 1976. For young animal lovers an interesting menagerie of creatures quietly but exquisitely drawn. Clear counting from one to twenty, but each spread invites a closer look, especially the feline pages.

Q Is for Duck by Mary Elting and Michael Folsom; illustrated by Jack Kent. Clarion, 1980. Not your basic alphabet book, here's a playful alphabet guessing game that is more like a riddle book than an ABC. "A is for zoo." Why? Because animals live in the zoo. Can you guess why I is for mosquito?

Richard Scarry's Best Word Book Ever by Richard Scarry. Golden, 1963. Oversized pages chock-full of action-packed pictures to pore over for details and all labeled for reading solo or with a little help from a friend. Beginning readers prove how smart they are when they half read/half deduce the printed words from context. Also see: *Richard Scarry's Best Counting Book Ever.*

Seven Little Rabbits by John Becker; illustrated by Barbara Cooney. Scholastic, 1973. A subtraction story about seven bunnies who go to sleep one at a time.

Trucks You Can Count on by Doug Magee. Dodd Mead, 1985. Here's a double concept book. On one level it explores how people count on trucks to bring us things. On another level there are close-ups of trucks to count from one to eighteen.

What's Inside? by Satoshi Kitamura. Farrar, Straus and Giroux, 1985. Part alphabet, part guessing game as letters are introduced on objects such as boxes, cans, and cars. You must turn the page to see if you guessed right, and then find the next little mystery.

Dictionaries

The New Golden Dictionary by Bertha Morris Parker; illustrated by
Aurelius Battaglia. Golden, 1972. Words used in sentences
with illustrations.

New Illustrated Grosset Dictionary. Delair, 1977. Each entry is used
in a sentence and then followed by a sentence using a syno-
nym. Each entry illustrated.

Richard Scarry's Storybook Dictionary. Golden, 1966. Each word
entry in small story frame. Words used in sentences and
illustrations tell story.

Very First Dictionary. Macmillan, 1983. Has a somewhat older
look and not all words are illustrated.

Easy-to-Read Books

The books that follow range from very easy to moderately difficult. A few of the harder books, such as *Little Bear* and *Frog and
Toad,* make perfectly fine storybooks for you to read aloud.
Eventually kids will enjoy switching roles or rereading those
books on their own. However, for the most part, easy-to-read
books should not replace or displace the read-aloud books suggested. Indeed, since there are relatively few truly easy-to-read
books for beginners, they should be saved for that magic time
when a child can open them and say, "I really can read this!"

Are You My Mother? by P. D. Eastman. Random House, 1960. A
small bird falls out of its nest and goes looking for his
mother.

Bennett Cerf's Book of Riddles by Bennett Cerf; illustrated by Roy
McKie. Random House, 1960. Just right for six- and seven-
year-old riddle lovers. Also *Bennett Cerf's Book of Animal Riddles.*

Cars and Trucks and Things That Go by Richard Scarry. Golden,
1974. An oversized book full of action, little dramas, and
tons of details. Labels are extra fun for sight reading and
putting new reading skills in action.

The Cat in the Hat by Dr. Seuss. Beginner Books, 1958. Almost
qualifies as a classic for beginners. Also: *The Cat in the Hat
Comes Back.*

Cinderella told by Fran Hunia; illustrated by Brian Price Thomas. Ladybird Books, 1978. One of a series of easy-to-read adaptations of fairy tales. Shouldn't replace a read-aloud version but may be of interest for independent reading. Also: *Red Riding Hood,* and *The Princess and the Pea.*

Danny and the Dinosaur by Syd Hoff. Harper & Row, 1958. A zany adventure as Danny spends the day with a dinosaur from the museum. Also: *Sammy the Seal.*

Fee, Fi, Fo, Fum by Allan Ahlberg; illustrated by Colin McNaughton. Random House, 1985. One of the very easy Rednose Reader series. Few words, lots of action and humor that will tickle the beginning reader. Also: *Help!, Happy Worm,* and *Big Bad Pig.*

Go, Dog, Go! by P. D. Eastman. Random House, 1961. Action-packed dogs with plenty of zany humor to add story to limited text.

Hattie Be Quiet, Hattie Be Good by Dick Gackenbach. Harper & Row, 1977. One of a series featuring young Hattie Rabbit and her family and friends. Also: *Hattie Rabbit.*

Little Bear by Else H. Minarik; illustrated by Maurice Sendak. Harper & Row, 1957. One of a series of five lovable books about Little Bear, his friends, and family. *A Kiss for Little Bear* is the easiest to read. Don't miss the others: *Father Bear Comes Back, Little Bear's Friend,* and *Little Bear's Visit.*

Mine's the Best by Crosby Bonsall. Harper & Row, 1973. An *Early I Can Read* book about two boys who argue over whose beach toy is best. A funny one! Also: *The Day I Had to Play with My Sister,* and *And I Mean It, Stanley.*

Mouse Tales by Arnold Lobel. Harper & Row, 1972. Papa Mouse tells some funny bedtime stories for his little mouse children. Full of humor and charm. Also: *Frog and Toad Together, Frog and Toad Are Friends,* and *Frog and Toad All Year.*

Nobody Listens to Andrew by Elizabeth Guilfoile; illustrated by

Mary Stevens. Follett, 1957. Andrew has something important to tell, but nobody will listen. Kids love the surprise
ending.

One Fish, Two Fish, Red Fish, Blue Fish by Dr. Seuss. Random
House, 1960. Wonderfully easy and rhythmic. Also: *Green
Eggs and Ham.*

Red Fox and His Canoe by Nathaniel Benchley; illustrated by Arnold Lobel. Harper & Row, 1964. There's more humor than
history in this tall tale about an Indian boy and some animal
friends in a canoe.

Ten Apples up on Top by Theodore Le Sieg; illustrated by Roy
McKie. Random House, 1961. Here's a zany counting book
in rhyme with only seventy-five words for beginning readers.

Three to Get Ready by Betty Boegehold; illustrated by Mary
Chalmers. Harper & Row, 1965. Four charming stories
about a wise mother cat and her three kittens. Also: *Pippa
Mouse* series. Knopf.

Series Books

Some second-graders begin looking down their noses at "easy-
to-read" books with few words and a picture on every page. The
idea of reading longer books, often with chapters, seems to fit
their grown-up sense of themselves as readers. For such kids,
there are some slightly longer, wordier, but still relatively easy-
to-read books available. The books listed here are part of a
series, featuring the cast of characters in different situations.
Knowing the characters and format gives kids an edge and eases
the way to another level of reading independence. For fluent
readers some of the mystery series in the next chapter may also
be good choices.

Big Max by Kin Platt; illustrated by Robert Lopshire. Harper &
Row, 1965. When the King of Pooka Pooka's prize elephant
was stolen, who did he call? Big Max, of course! Here's a
mystery and a detective young readers have loved for years.
Also: *Big Max in the Mystery of the Missing Moose.*

The Case of the Hungry Stranger by Crosby Bonsall. Harper & Row,

1963. One of a series for mystery lovers. In this one the Private Eyes Club gets involved with the disappearance of a blueberry pie. Plenty of humor and suspense in this and other Private Eye adventures: *The Case of the Dumb Bells, The Case of the Double Cross, The Case of the Cat's Meow,* and others.

Nate the Great and the Phony Clue by Marjorie Weinman Sharmat; illustrated by Marc Simont. Coward, McCann, 1977. Nate the Great, a pint-size Sherlock Holmes, finds the missing pieces of a special invitation that proves how great a sleuth Nate can be. Also: *Nate the Great, Nate the Great Goes Undercover,* and *Nate the Great and the Lost List.*

Poetry

Most sixes and sevens are still listening to rather than reading poetry on their own. They enjoy the rhythmic sounds they hear and with a little encouragement they'll chime right in and chant all or parts of particular favorites. This is the age when nonsense verse seems to have great appeal since children themselves are ready to enjoy the fun of playing with words and other people's playful ideas.

An Arkful of Animals selected by William Cole; illustrated by Lynn Munsinger. Houghton Mifflin, 1978. All sorts of creatures here by many well-known poets, including Aiken, Silverstein, Jarrell, and Coatsworth.

A Child's Garden of Verses by Robert Louis Stevenson; illustrated by Brian Wildsmith. Watts, 1966. First published in 1885, these poems have spoken to the hearts of children for more than a century. In this lavish full-color edition Wildsmith brings his own special talents to make a good thing even better.

Complete Nonsense Book by Edward Lear. Dodd, Mead, 1962. Here's the master of nonsense, with his original pictures and verse, originally published in 1912.

Dinosaurs and Beasts of Yore selected by W. Cole; illustrated by S. Natti. Collins, 1979. When dinosaur fever strikes, here's a wonderful book to stir in with big factual books. This collection has humor and charm.

Father Fox's Pennyrhymes by Clyde Watson; illustrated by Wendy Watson. Crowell, 1971. With a lilt and a laugh you'll find yourself enchanted with the sad and silly songs Father Fox sings. Kids will need to hold this close up to enjoy the playfully detailed illustrations that tell little stories of their own. A gem.

Gregory Griggs selected and illustrated by Arnold Lobel. Greenwillow, 1978. This is no ho-hum ordinary collection of old nursery rhymes. Old, yes, but full of humor and new life, thanks to Lobel's wit and charm.

Hailstones and Halibut Bones by Mary O'Neill; illustrated by Leonard Weisgard. Doubleday, 1961. A collection of poems that explores the touch, sound, smell, and sight of colors.

Honey, I Love by Eloise Greenfield; illustrated by Diane and Leo Dillon. Crowell, 1972. Sixteen tender poems about love from the child's-eye view. Illustrations featuring a black child are charming, and the themes are universal.

Jamboree: Rhymes for All Seasons by Eve Merriam; illustrated by Walter Gaffney-Kassell. Dell, 1985. A splendid collection, including many cherished poems from Merriam's out-of-print book *There Is No Rhyme for Silver.*

One at a Time by David McCord; illustrated by H. B. Kane. Little, Brown, 1977. They'll return again and again to this collection of McCord's poems. If you can't find this big volume, look for some of the small collections such as *Take Sky, Every Time I Climb a Tree,* and others.

The Queen of Eene by Jack Prelutsky; illustrated by Victoria Chess. Greenwillow, 1978. Wonderful nonsense sixes and sevens will relish.

This Little Pig-A-Wig and Other Rhymes collected by Leonore Blegvad; illustrated by Erik Blegvad. Atheneum, 1978. Twenty-two old English and American rhymes with loveable pigs pictured in all sorts of moods.

Tirra Lirra by Laura Richards. Little, Brown, 1935. An old but well-loved collection of humorous verse perfect for reading aloud.

When We Were Very Young by A. A. Milne; illustrated by E. H. Shepard. Dutton, 1924. A classic collection of poems by the author of *Winnie the Pooh.* Also: *Now We Are Six.*

Whiskers and Rhymes by Arnold Lobel. Greenwillow, 1985. A rollicking collection of rhymes that both tickle and touch. Though they echo old nursery rhymes, these are fresh, original, and sprightly with delicious illustrations to match.

Longer Books for Read-Aloud Sharing

While picture books are the mainstay for story time, sixes and sevens also enjoy listening to longer books in chapters. Unlike the thirty-two page self-contained story that's read in one sitting, older children can now hold onto the story thread of a book read over a period of many days. Sharing books with more fully developed characters and plots builds a new level of sophistication. It stretches the young listener's comprehension skills. Unlike the picture book with illustrations on every page, these novels have limited line drawings. So, the child must make pictures in his mind's eye from the words he hears. This ability to spin one's own images is no small task, especially for children who have grown up with TV. Yet, such an intellectual task is basic to reading beyond the most simplistic level.

Here are some safe bets that you'll probably enjoy as much as your appreciative listener:

The Bears on Hemlock Mountain by Alice Dalgliesh; illustrated by Helen Sewell. Scribner's, 1952. A young boy's adventure when he is sent over the mountain to borrow a big pot, stays too long, and must then face his worst fear, the bears on Hemlock Mountain. Another favorite by the same author: *The Courage of Sarah Noble.*

The Cat Club by Esther Averill. Harper & Row, 1944. Jenny Linsky, a shy black cat, longs to join the Cat Club but feels she has no special talent, the ticket to belonging. With some help from Captain Tinker, she finds the key and joins the club. Also: *The School for Cats, Jenny's First Party,* and others.

Charlotte's Web by E. B. White; illustrated by Garth Williams. Harper & Row, 1952. A story about friendship, love, life, and death. Young Wilbur, the pig, is saved from certain death by Charlotte, a spider you'll never forget. Also: *Stuart Little.*

The House at Pooh Corner by A. A. Milne; illustrated by E. H. Shepard. Dutton, 1961. The stories about Pooh Bear, Eeyore, Piglet, and Kanga are just right for reading aloud. Some adapted versions have bigger, brighter pictures, but sixes and sevens are ready for the rich language of the original text and the delicate charm of Shepard's pen and ink drawings. Sit close and enjoy.

James and the Giant Peach by Roald Dahl; illustrated by Nancy Ekholm Burkett. Knopf, 1961. An orphan boy named James left with his mean relatives finds a fascinating route of escape inside a Giant Peach. Too hard for independent reading, but just right for listening.

The Littles by John Peterson. Scholastic, 1970. This is the first of a series about a little family that secretly lives in the walls of the Bigg's house and deals with all the problems one might imagine six-inch-small people would have. While the idea here is clearly "borrowed" from the famous *Borrowers,* the Littles are a livelier family for reading aloud to this age group.

Mary Poppins by P. L. Travers; illustrated by Mary Shepard. Harcourt, 1981 (revised edition). Disney's *Mary Poppins* is much sweeter than the original, so even if they know her film persona, don't skip over that peppery-rich character P. L. Travers created more than half a century ago. Great fun for family read-aloud time.

Misty of Chincoteague by Marguerite Henry; illustrated by Wesley Dennis. Rand McNally, 1947. A touching story about two children and their love for a wild pony from Chincoteague Island. A good choice for reading aloud. If they like this, they'll want to go on to *Sea Star.*

The Monster in the Third Dresser Drawer by Janice Lee Smith; illustrated by Dick Gackenbach. Harper & Row, 1981. Poor Adam Joshua has to move to a new town, share his life with a new baby, and lose a tooth all in a few short months. With humor and affection the author has captured the ups and downs of real life.

My Father's Dragon by Ruth S. Gannett. Random House, 1948. The first in a series of fantasy adventures with plenty of action, suspense, and good triumphing over evil. Some sevens may be able to read this and the sequels on their own.

Mr. Popper's Penguins by Richard and Florence Atwater; illustrated by Robert Lawson. Little, Brown, 1938. A funny fantasy about a dozen penguins who take over Mr. Popper's house. A jolly read-aloud for fantasy lovers.

Ramona the Pest by Beverly Cleary; illustrated by Louis Darling. Morrow, 1968. Ramona is a kindergartener in this one and is having plenty of trouble with the teacher, a classmate, and her own idea of how things are " 'sposed to be." Things are not all smooth at home either with Beezus, her big sister, and mother's part-time job. Cleary rings true and touches sixes' and sevens' feelings and funny bone. They'll also enjoy *Ramona the Brave* and others in the series, but leave some for independent reading pleasure.

The Wonderful Wizard of Oz by L. Frank Baum. Ballantine, 1980. Even if they have seen the film, the story of Dorothy and her friends makes great reading as do the many sequels: *Dorothy and the Wizard of Oz, The Emerald City of Oz,* etc.

REMINDERS FOR CHOOSING BOOKS FOR SIXES AND SEVENS

- Offer a variety of books with more complex plots and characters.
- Take your cues from their interests and expand on those interests.
- Provide plenty of easy-to-read books.
- Continue reading aloud, especially books that may be a little difficult for sixes and sevens to read independently.
- Involve children in selecting books to borrow from the library and/or purchase for their personal library.

• • •

Ten Books Every Six- and Seven-Year-Old Should Know

Alexander and the Terrible, Horrible, No Good, Very Bad Day by Judith Viorst
Amos and Boris by William Steig
The Fairy Tale Treasury by Virginia Haviland
Frog and Toad Are Friends by Arnold Lobel
Go, Dog, Go by P. D. Eastman
The House at Pooh Corner by A. A. Milne
Ramona the Pest by Beverly Cleary
The Snowman by Raymond Briggs
Stevie by John Steptoe
Where the Wild Things Are by Maurice Sendak

James and the Giant Peach by Roald Dahl

The Monster in the Third Dresser Drawer by Janice Lee Smith

Mr. Popper's Penguins by Richard and Florence Atwater

The Wonderful Wizard of Oz by L. Frank Baum

Misty of Chincoteague by Marguerite Henry

Mary Poppins by P. L. Travers

CHAPTER VII

Books for Eights and Nines

Selecting books for eights and nines calls for more individual attention than ever, since the range of their reading abilities and interests is now more varied. Some eights, who may well become avid readers, are still breaking the reading code. Others are able to read almost everything, from the fine print on cereal boxes to the novel on your bedside table. Some kids this age can tackle a classic like *The Borrowers,* where they can live vicariously in a world of miniature people. Others may be more comfortable reading *The Littles,* a simpler version of the same kind of story. Both still enjoy being read to.

WHAT EIGHTS AND NINES ARE LIKE

Among both groups, the skilled and less skilled, the reading habit may be a sometime thing. There are distractions that compete with books. Kids of this age group are preoccupied with more physical and social pursuits. Bikes, baseball, clubs, lessons, school, and friends are the high priority tickets to becoming accepted members of their peer group. Eights and nines have a great appetite for trying out new experiences and trying themselves out in new situations. There are other distractions too. Television is not just easier to switch on, it has social content as well. Last night's sitcom or shoot-'em-up is this morning's shared topic of conversation at the pencil sharpener or in the lunchroom. It may also lead to faddish book jags with Ewoks and Droids or other licensed literary lightweights.

By now the world of school has become familiar. Compared to his former self, the eight- or nine-year-old is a relatively independent and skillful doer. Much as he wants to please parents and teachers and win their praise, he takes a new measure of himself against his agemates.

The Triple Bind

The child at this stage is in something of a triple bind. He wants to live up to his own expectations, the group's expectations, and what he believes adults expect of him. Whether they are in the classroom or on the playground, eights and nines tend to be judgmental about themselves and others. They can be particularly critical of their own failings. Although they may knock their own efforts and call themselves stupid, they have trouble accepting criticism from others. Often their self-deprecating remarks are a veiled invitation for praise or at least assurance that they are doing all right. For kids who are late bloomers the going is

Illustration by Maurice Sendak from *Higglety, Pigglety, Pop!*

tougher than for the more average middle-of-the-road child. Parents may need to give more support and assurance that no one is good at everything. They may also need to help kids adjust their expectations of themselves and others. Book choices are sometimes most difficult for such kids, who find the big print and format of easy-to-read books beneath their dignity. They may need a little help in finding short but simple books that they can handle on their own. Books with short chapters, action, and lively dialogue such as Patricia Giff's *Polk Street School Series* and Elizabeth Levy's *Something Queer Books* are good transition books kids can dive into on their own.

Relationships with the teacher are shifting. The tattletale of six and seven has grown into a child with more allegiance to his agemates. He'd rather plead ignorance than tell on a classmate. Still, the teacher remains the authority and her opinion is important because it is often so public among those who really count —the other kids.

Separation of the Sexes

During these years, one-to-one friendships tend to last longer and have more substance. Mutual interests are often the glue that holds such relationships together. By now kids can better predict and understand the way other people feel and think. Although some earlier formed boy-girl friendships may continue, now is the time when most best friends tend to be of the same gender. In fact, continuing a boy-girl friendship of long standing is difficult at best. Kids are drawn between old loyalty to a friend and opposing loyalties to the new group.

This two-way tug is wonderfully drawn in Bette Greene's *Philip Hall Likes Me, I Reckon Maybe.* Here the long-standing friendship between Beth Lambert and her near neighbor Philip Hall starts coming unhinged. When Philip doesn't invite Beth to his birthday party, Beth insists on knowing why. " 'Cause . . ." he explains, " 'cause I was afraid they'd call me sissy. Then they'd go 'round saying I liked you and that you was my girlfriend . . ."

The separation between the sexes is true of most teams and the ever-blooming clubs that come and go so quickly. Philip Hall has his *Tiger Hunters Club* and Beth her *Pretty Pennies.* These little self-formed groups reflect the child's way of creating instant membership and satisfies the need to belong. Such clubs are a kind of mutual admiration society whose chief function is to include some and exclude others. Some groups may include both boys and girls; more usually they are divided by sex as in Beverly Cleary's *Henry and the Clubhouse.* It's as if the only way they can affirm their gender identity as "one of the boys" or "one of the girls" is to band together. In the clubhouse or on the ball field there is often more talk than action. There are endless debates about who will be president, who can be captain, and what are the rules.

Their new interest in forging rules comes along with a

newly emerging ethical sense and a greater concern for fairness. Indeed, the group ethic can act as a positive force, a spur to mastering social as well as academic skills.

WHERE DO BOOKS FIT?

Where do books fit into this busy expansive lifestyle? It really depends on what's offered. For some eights and nines the business of learning to read has been such a struggle that books may be regarded as more "required" than "desired." This is also true of kids who are pushed (or push themselves) to the level of their own incompetence. Librarians report that parents at this stage often urge their young readers to select something longer, more challenging, and "less babyish." While many kids themselves take pride in their growing skill and select "real books with chapters," such selections often end up going home and back to the library unread. Others keep returning to the scene of their earliest triumphs. They select books they have read and reread, books that are obviously "below their reading level."

Yet parents and teachers can take some of the reading roadblocks out of the way with a variety of approaches. For the child who seems stuck on reading simple books, try to relax rather than push. Children need time to consolidate new skills, to grow a heady sense of competence. A sense of success, ease, and pleasure with books will have bigger payoffs in the long run than pressure for new achievements. After a period of plateauing, kids themselves will move on to more challenging material. In the meantime, give them some latitude in selecting books independently, but continue to read aloud to them from the rich repertoire of books suggested for this age group. Sometimes young listeners get a foothold in a book that they might never have attempted on their own. Once launched they may take the book and go on independently. Even if they don't, the pleasures of sharing a great book like *Charlotte's Web* or *The Cricket in Times Square* has real value in building the connections between kids and books. Indeed, whether they read extremely well or not, the family storytime should not be abandoned. As with earlier stages, the child's listening ability still outreaches his independent reading abilities.

On their own they may be plugged into comic books. This too shall pass. Keep reading out loud. The young reader may be an avid mystery reader, but with a little assist you can open the doors to other genres.

THE ELECTRONIC CONNECTION

While a great deal has been said about TV robbing time from reading, it's also true that television can act as a catalyst and stimulate interest in books. It was the TV series of *Little House on the Prairie* that gave Laura Ingalls Wilder's books a new generation of readership. The same is true of *The Littles* series published almost twenty years ago but going strong again, thanks to their animated adventures on network TV. PBS's *Reading Rainbow* is doing the same thing for the picture book set. TV weekend and holiday specials often dramatize young people's novels and inspire viewers to go seek the real thing in a library. In a sense the electronic runthrough may whet the appetite or serve as a "pony" for getting into the world of print. It provides the pictures young readers may need to bring as background for the more demanding task of reading and making pictures in the mind's eye from words alone. Via TV kids may make their first acquaintance with fact as well as fiction. Special events, documentaries, and docudramas bring facts to life on the screen and may light up new interests that can be extended through related books and magazines. So, the possibilities offer a two-way street.

If you know something worthwhile is coming on the tube, take the time to watch it together and talk about it.

If you've watched something that catches their interest or imagination and there's a link, help them make the book connection. It may be something on your family bookshelf or it may involve a trip to the library.

With the growing supply of videocassettes available through library and rental, families now have access to many more choices than the networks present. Used selectively the electronic connection need not be seen as a threat to literacy, but rather as another route to the printed page.

. . .

BOOKS THEY ENJOY

A look at the most popular books among eights and nines reveals that young readers and listeners are still sampling from many genres, rather than digging in with one type of book. While individuals may have decided preferences for fantasy, mystery, or informational books, most children enjoy switching gears and exploring a variety of books.

Among the many books for eights and nines few are more popular than Beverly Cleary's books about Ramona Quimby and Henry Huggins. Cleary's characters, situations, and dialogue ring true and deal with recognizable problems eights and nines have in school and at home. In *Ramona Quimby, Age 8,* third-grader Ramona is coping with her parents' busy schedule, a new school, classmates who tease, and a misunderstanding about her teacher's feelings toward her. Stir those ingredients together and you get a story that touches the schoolchild's heart. Eager for independence, Ramona tries at every turn to handle her problems and, as always, Cleary gives her plenty of solo success while also providing warm and supportive adults who are there when the going gets tough. This is also true in *Henry and the Clubhouse* with Mrs. Huggins, his mom, pinchhitting on Henry's paper route. Typical of boys this age, Henry and his buddies get involved in building an overly ambitious clubhouse and it is Mr. Huggins who has to step in and set firm limits on priority chores. The "boys only" rule holds until Henry gets into a jam that Ramona and her sister Beezus have to help him out of.

Like Henry and Ramona, eights and nines tend to believe they can do almost anything. They are more optimistic than realistic about grand schemes for building clubhouses, cooking dinner, or going into business. Through such realistic fiction kids see a reflection of their own lives. They find comfort in knowing they are not the only person in the world to have felt awkward, overly ambitious, foolish, or shy. Through sympathetically drawn characters they may also begin to see the humor of some sticky predicaments and perhaps learn to laugh a little at themselves as they identify with Ramona and Henry.

For eights and nines books in series such as Ramona and Henry have great appeal that goes beyond plot. Using a familiar world with a continuing cast of characters, books in series are easier to enter. The characters are predictable and so is their neighborhood. Each chapter has some roundness of its own so the book can be put down and returned to without losing the thread. These books are more complex than a picture book, but quite straightforward and clear. For many eights and nines books in series are also another route to the collector's bug that hits at this age. Lined up on the bookshelf, the series represents solid proof of being an avid reader—a newly found skill with status to take pride in. Many of the books listed in this chapter have one or more sequels.

BOOKLIST FOR EIGHTS AND NINES

Group Life

Unlike books for slightly older kids where home and family are quickly disposed of or are incidental to the plot, in most books for eights and nines, adults still play supporting roles. Of course, the thrust of the story centers on the child's strong need to find a place in that sometimes difficult world of the group. One of the best books that deals with this struggle is Eleanor Estes's *The Hundred Dresses.* Here is the story of a child who doesn't fit in and is ostrasized by others. Wanda, the poor girl who wears the same faded dress everyday, is the butt of the "group's" putdowns. In the end it is the others who must deal with what they have done. On the lighter side, Judy Blume's *Freckle Juice* gives the reader another look at the ridiculously high price of trying to look like everyone else.

Aldo Applesauce by Johanna Hurwitz. Morrow, 1979. When Aldo moves from the city to the suburbs, he has a hard time feeling at home. To make matters worse, on his first day in a new school he spills applesauce all over the lunchroom floor and is dubbed Aldo Applesauce. It's his friendship with De De, a girl who just happens to wear a fake moustache, that helps him put his new life together.

"B" Is for Betsy by Carolyn Haywood. Harcourt, 1939. Although

the heroine is only six and the neighborhood is a little dated, Betsy and her experiences in school continue to charm young girl readers. Part of a series of relatively easy-to-read chapter books.

The Beast in Ms. Rooney's Room by Patricia Reilly Giff; illustrated by Blanche Sims. Dell, 1984. One of a series about the Kids of the Polk Street School. This small chapter book features Richard "Beast" Best who was left back in second grade because he had a slow start in reading. With time and a little help from the teacher, Richard does some growing up and discovers he actually enjoys reading and school. Also: *Fish Face, The Candy Corn Contest,* and others.

Betsy-Tacy by Maud Hart Lovelace; illustrated by Lois Lenski. Harper & Row, 1940. First of a series of easy-to-read chapter books about friendship between two schoolage girls and life in a small town at the turn of the century. Also: *Betsy-Tacy and T.6, Betsy and Tacy Go Downtown,* and many others.

Crow Boy by Taro Yashima. Penguin, 1976. Told in a picture-book format, this is a subtle but moving story about a boy who is different and misunderstood by his peers. Plenty of food for thought here.

The 18th Emergency by Betsy Byars; illustrated by Robert Grossman. Viking, 1973. Benjie, otherwise known as "Mouse," makes the mistake of taking on Maru Hammerman, one of the biggest and strongest kids in school. Mouse's buddy, Ezzie, has worked out what to do in all sorts of terrible emergencies, but not this one. Mouse is sure Maru is going to hurt him and tries to avoid the inevitable confrontation. There's plenty of humor, action, and wisdom.

Freckle Juice by Judy Blume; illustrated by Sonia O. Lisker. Four Winds, 1971. More than anything, Andrew wanted freckles like his classmate, Nicky. He's so eager that he pays Sharon fifty cents for a secret recipe. A slim but amusing little book about group life and the sometimes foolish desire to conform.

Friends Are Like That! selected by Child Study Children's Book Committee; illustrated by Leigh Grant. Crowell, 1979. Subtitled "Stories to Read to Yourself," here are nine easy-to-read, excellent stories by well-known authors in a gaily illustrated book for young readers.

The Hateful Plateful Trick by Scott Corbett; illustrated by Galdone. Little, Brown, 1971. Kerby and Fenton get into another jam with the Feats o' Magic Chemistry Set while babysitting Kerby's cousin Gay. When they end up smelling like cornbeef and cabbage, hotdogs and sauerkraut, and tomato soup, they turn to their oddball friend, Mrs. Graymalkin, who helps them find a distasteful hateful solution. One of a series for independent reading. Also: *The Lemonade Trick, The Mailbox Trick, The Baseball Trick,* and others.

Henry and the Clubhouse by Beverly Cleary; illustrated by Louis Darling. Morrow, 1962. One of several books about Henry Huggins, a neighbor of Cleary's popular characters Ramona and Beezus. In this one Henry and his buddies are building a clubhouse with no girls allowed, but when Henry gets locked in, guess who gets him out! Also: *Henry Huggins and the Paper Route, Henry and Beezus,* and others.

How to Eat Fried Worms by Thomas Rockwell; illustrated by Emily McCully. Watts, 1973. Billy makes a bet that he can and will eat fifteen worms. What follows is a fast-paced, humorous story that's not for those with squeamish stomachs.

The Hundred Dresses by Eleanor Estes; illustrated by Louis Slobodkin. Harcourt, 1944. Life in the group isn't always easy, especially for someone who is "different." Wanda, a Polish girl who wears the same faded dress every day is the butt of the "group's" putdowns. No one believes the boast that she has a hundred dresses. Worse, Maddie does nothing to stop others from teasing and making fun of Wanda. Everyone is shocked when Wanda moves away before winning a prize for her hundred dresses—all drawn to perfection. This is a gem that may stimulate some talk and thought about differences and relating to others who are not just like us.

Left Handed Shortstop by Patricia Reilly Giff; illustrated by Leslie Morrill. Delacorte, 1980. Walter Moles knows he's no shortstop, so when the honor and homework load of the fourth grade falls on his shoulders, Walter and his friend Casey come up with a creative solution. One of a series of amusing books featuring Casey Valentine and her friends. Also: *Fourth Grade Celebrity, The Girl Who Knew It All,* and others.

Philip Hall Likes Me, I Reckon Maybe by Bette Greene; illustrated by Charles Lilly. Dial, 1974. You can't help loving spunky Beth Lambert, her warm and loving family, and the troubles she has with her friend Philip Hall. Told in the first person, eleven-year-old Beth gives us a lively, humorous, and moving portrait of growing up in rural Arkansas. Each chapter is a complete story unto itself with a touch of mystery, a rescue, a competition. This is the story of a black child that resonates with the real and universal world of the middle years of childhood.

Ramona Quimby, Age 8 by Beverly Cleary; illustrated by Alan Tiegreen. Morrow, 1981. Independent Ramona runs into a lot of problems trying to cope with a new school, her parents' busy schedule, and a misunderstanding with her teacher. Cleary paints a real world kids can readily relate to. Also: *Ramona the Pest, Ramona and Her Father,* and *Henry and the Clubhouse.*

Skinnybones by Barbara Park. Knopf, 1982. Skinnybones will touch the funny bone of those who have struck out and fouled up on their Little League team. With his wonderful sense of humor, Alex provides some good laughs and gets the last laugh on the boastful T. J. Stoner, the best player in school.

Soup and Me by Robert Newton Peck; illustrated by Charles Lilly. Knopf, 1975. Soup and his buddy Rob, two mischievous boys, and their shenanigans are bound to tickle the funny bone. Kids will laugh out loud when the boys' stolen pumpkin rolls right into the Baptist Church Halloween Party and when Soup sells Rob on the idea of using haircut money for bubble gum and gives Rob a "free" scalping. Based on the author's childhood in Vermont, these somewhat nostalgic stories manage to ring true and have a timeless quality. This is the sequel to *Soup,* which features the same lively friends.

Family

Much as life centers on friends and school, the child's relationships in the family is also reflected in realistic fiction. Indeed, all the newest (as well as the most traditional) family arrangements can be found in books for this age group. What with new babies, aging grandparents, divorce, and stepparents, such books offer kids a glimpse into other lifestyles. Vicariously, the child reader can step into Peter's shoes and deal with a little brother like Fudge in *Tales of a Fourth Grade Nothing* or spend the weekend with Sonia, her stepmother and father in *No One Is Going to Nashville*. Whether the situation is familiar or strangely unlike their own, such books can help children understand themselves and others. Some of the best family-centered stories are listed here and you will find more under the heading *Historic Fact and Fiction*.

Be a Perfect Person in Just Three Days by Stephen Manes; illustrated by Tom Huffman. Clarion, 1982. Milo thinks he's found the perfect solution to all his problems—a how-to book that promises to tell how to become a perfect person! Following Dr. K. Pinkerton Silverfish's advice leads Milo to some interesting discoveries about himself and perfection.

Busybody Nora by Johanna Hurwitz; illustrated by Susan Jeschke. Morrow, 1976. A short but sweet chapter book about a middle-class urban family and their neighbors. Nora and her little brother, Teddy, are both storybook lovers and manage to stir up some Stone Soup, throw a big party, and enjoy the grandparents' version of *Jack and the Beanstalk*. Easy to read; part of a series. Also: *Nora and Mrs. Mind Your Own Business, New Neighbors for Nora,* and others.

The Carp in the Bathtub by Barbara Cohen; illustrated by Joan Halpern. Lothrop, Lee and Shepard, 1972. Leah and her little brother Harry attempt to rescue a live carp their mother has bought to make gefilte fish for the family's Passover feast. A touchy situation is handled with humor, sympathetic understanding, and supportive adults.

Confessions of an Only Child by Norma Klein; illustrated by Richard Cuffari. Pantheon, 1974. Third-grader Toe, that's short for Antonia, has some mixed feelings about the arrival of a baby brother or sister. In fact, most of her feelings are pretty negative. She likes being an only child and when the baby is born prematurely and dies, Toe has to deal with the guilt. A tender story about a family.

Grandpa, Me, and Our House in the Tree by Barbara Kirk. Macmillan, 1978. A photoessay and simple text tell a moving story of love between a young boy and his ailing grandpa, who can no longer climb into the treehouse they built together. Done in a picture-book format, but clearly for older readers.

The Hundred Penny Box by Sharon Bell Mathis; illustrated by Leo and Diane Dillon. Viking, 1975. "When I lose my hundred penny box, I lose me," Michael's Great-Great Aunt Dew tells him. But, Michael's mother wants to throw out the beaten up, always underfoot box that holds a penny for every year of Aunt Dew's life. This is a warm and moving story about the love between old and young.

Learning to Say Good-bye: When A Parent Dies by Eda LeShan; illustrated by Paul Giovonopoulos. Macmillan, 1975. A supportive book in language children can understand by an eminent psychologist. There are many real-life anecdotes that beautifully illustrate how to deal with the death of a parent.

Mustard by Charlotte Graeber; illustrated by Donna Diamond. Macmillan, 1983. The experience of coping with an old beloved pet cat's illness and having to decide on euthanasia is traumatic and one that many readers face. Beautifully but simply written, and sensitively illustrated, this book offers solace.

My Mother Is the Smartest Woman in the World by Eleanor Clymer; illustrated by Nancy Kincade. Atheneum, 1982. Here's a short but snappy novel about a girl who inspires her mom to run for mayor. Told in the first person, this is a portrait of a warm and supportive family caught up in the work of a political campaign. Solid information along with a nice story.

My War with Mrs. Galloway by Doris Orgel; illustrated by Carol Newsom. Viking, 1985. Told in the first person, this is eight-year-old Rebecca's story about her war with Mrs. Galloway, the take-charge babysitter her doctor/mom depends upon. Mrs. G. starts out hateful but evolves as Rebecca does a little growing up. A relatively easy-to-read chapter book that children of working parents will identify with easily.

No One Is Going to Nashville by Mavis Jukes; illustrated by Lloyd Bloom. Knopf, 1983. Sonia's relationship with her father and stepmother is so warmly real that all three characters seem to leap into life in a story that is a refreshing tonic to mean old stepmother stories. But, at its heart the book is about a girl who desperately wants to hold on to a stray dog that her father insists she can't keep. A humorous, poignant story.

Ramona and Her Father by Beverly Cleary; illustrated by Alan Tiegreen. Morrow, 1975. This time Ramona's father has lost his job and everyone in the family is down. Ramona has a scheme, a dream of how to make a million dollars so that everyone will be happy again. Also: *Ramona and Her Mother* and *Ramona Forever*.

The Secret Moose by Jean Rogers; illustrated by Jim Fowler. Greenwillow, 1985. Gerald tells no one in his family about the moose who lies wounded not far from their home. Daily he cuts willow branches to feed the wild creature. His efforts are rewarded when the moose gives birth to a calf and is well enough to move on.

Shoe Shine Girl by Clyde Robert Bulla; illustrated by Leigh Grant. Crowell, 1975. Ten-year-old Sarah Ida is angry when her parents send her to Aunt Claudia's. Having borrowed all her allowance for the summer and spent it, Sarah is broke. When Aunt Claudia won't give her pocket money, Sarah is fortunate enough to find work at Al's Shoeshine Stand and learns a great deal about herself by working with Al.

Stay Away From Simon! by Carol Carrick; illustrated by Donald Carrick. Clarion, 1985. Many people in the neighborhood are afraid of Simon, a retarded boy, who turns out to be a hero to Lucy and her brother.

Tales of a Fourth Grade Nothing by Judy Blume; illustrated by Roy Doty. Dutton, 1972. Life with Fudge, Peter's little brother, is hard to take. No one in the family seems to understand how difficult until Fudge gets hold of Peter's turtle. For further adventures of this duo, try *Superfudge*.

Historic Fact and Fiction

History as a body of facts, dates, names, and places is still too abstract and dry for most eights and nines. However, children at this stage do have a growing interest in the past when the focus is on people and how they lived. It is the everyday details of how people (especially children) worked, played, dressed, and lived that sets the scene and provides the backdrop for a compelling story. When history is presented in this way, embedded in the framework of a good story, then kids can connect with the past in meaningful ways. Perhaps that's what makes Wilder's *Little House* books such favorites among third- and fourth-graders. It's not the big historic events or famous heroes and their exploits, but rather the very human everyday experiences that link the child of today with Laura, her friends, and family on the frontier. By way of stories set in faraway and long ago, children are ready to journey beyond the here and now. From the child's point of view, there are universal connections, a kind of kinship with common childhood feelings that link past and present.

All-of-a-Kind Family by Sydney Taylor; illustrated by Helen John. Dell, 1966. First in a longtime favorite series about a Jewish family on New York's Lower East Side at the turn of the century. Also: *All-of-a-Kind Family Downtown,* and *All-of-a-Kind Family Uptown.*

Anna, Grandpa, and the Big Storm by Carla Stevens; illustrated by Margot Tomes. Clarion, 1982. Eight-year-old Anna draws closer to her "ornery" grandpa when they are stranded on an El train in the Great Blizzard of '88. This gently exciting, easy reading story makes the people of "olden days" come alive for today's youngsters. Warm illustrations of an icy scene.

The Bell Ringer and the Pirates by Eleanor Coerr; illustrated by Joan Sandin. Harper & Row, 1983. An *I Can Read* book. An Indian boy waits for pirates to come to the old Spanish mission; he wants to ring the big bell to warn his people hiking in the hills. An exciting story, vividly illustrated, for new readers. Though some may object to the hints of violence, Pio's bravery and ingenuity provide a good model for children.

Ben and Me by Robert Lawson. Little, Brown, 1939. Here's history through the eyes and pen of a mouse named Amos who claimed to be an intimate friend and technical advisor to none other than Ben Franklin.

The Bicycle Man by Allen Say. Parnassus Press, 1982. A gentle story of a group of Japanese meeting two American soldiers a year after World War II. How fear changes to human warmth and understanding is told and pictured in a very special book.

Caddie Woodlawn by Carol Ryrie Brink. Macmillan, 1935. Based on the true adventures of a pioneer family in Wisconsin in 1864, the novel offers a child's-eye view of frontier life. Caddie, an eleven-year-old tomboy, is a spunky character with a generous nature and an appetite for independence.

The Drinking Gourd by F. N. Monjo; illustrated by Fred Brenner. Harper & Row, 1969. An easy-to-read and fascinating story of the underground railroad as a boy comes face to face with racial prejudice for the first time.

If You Sailed on the Mayflower by Ann McGovern; illustrated by J. B. Handelsman. Scholastic, 1969. One of an excellent series of books done in a question/answer format that zooms in on information reflecting the kinds of questions kids have. Gives young readers a picture of how people worked, played, and felt. Also: *If You Lived in Colonial Times, If You lived with the Sioux Indians,* and *Wanted Dead or Alive: The True Story of Harriet Tubman.*

In the Year of the Boar and Jackie Robinson by Bette Bao Lord; illustrated by Marc Simont. Harper & Row, 1984. This year of the Boar happens to be 1947 and recounts the experiences of a child who leaves her homeland in China to begin a new life with her parents in Brooklyn. Making friends and finding her place as a member of the group makes this a memorable story for kids who know what it's like to be the "new kid" or know someone who's new. Based on the author's own immigrant experience, the story is touched with humor and warmth.

Little House on the Prairie by Laura Ingalls Wilder; illustrated by Garth Williams. Harper & Row, 1935. One of a series that chronicles the Ingalls family move West and life on the frontier with its dangers, hard work, hardships, and adventure. Fans of the Little House TV show will recognize this title, but the series of books actually begins with *Little House In the Big Woods* and is followed by seven other volumes.

Roller Skates by Ruth Sawyer; illustrated by Valenti Angelo. Viking, 1964. When Lucinda's parents go off to Europe, she stays behind. Set in New York City in the 1890s, here's a delightful journey back as seen through the eyes of a ten-year-old who befriends a wonderful cast of characters as she wheels down city streets on roller skates.

Sarah, Plain and Tall by Patricia MacLachlan. Harper & Row, 1985. Two motherless children and their father advertise for a wife/mother. What they get is Sarah, who is plain and tall but possessed of a beauty all her own. A wonderful, moving book set in the last century.

Wagon Wheels by Barbara Brenner; illustrated by Don Bolognese. Harper & Row, 1978. A beginning reading book full of interest and suspense. An unusual but true story of black pioneers in the old West.

What's the Big Idea, Ben Franklin? by Jean Fritz; illustrated by Margot Tomes. Coward, McCann, 1982. One of several lighthearted biographies written with refreshing style and humor. Plenty of facts in a story frame. Also: *Will You Sign Here, John Hancock?* and *And Then What Happened, Paul Revere?*

PAUL REVERE, PATRIOT

Illustration by Margaret Tomes from *And Then What Happened Paul Revere?*

Wheel on the School by Meindert De Jong; illustrated by Maurice Sendak. Harper & Row, 1954. It's Lira, the only schoolgirl in a small Dutch village, who stirs her friends, teacher, and eventually the whole community to bring storks back to the rooftops of their town. A story of adventure and action that brings young and old together. Probably best read aloud.

Mysteries

Among eights and nines, mysteries have special appeal. Even the simplest kind of mystery with its "what next?" plot grabs the young reader and keeps the pages turning. Light on character development and descriptive prose, these are books built on action and suspense. Popular mystery series, such as *Nancy Drew* and *The Hardy Boys* seem to match this transition stage, just a step beyond beginning reading. They provide a simple plot, familiar characters, welcome support to independent reading.

As children read for clues, they are also learning to read for details, a skill they can take to more complex reading.

For many kids these are the first chapter books and they gobble them up, one after another, like peanuts. To the child the long row of matched books on the shelf may represent a kind of status symbol, proof of their new competence and standing as a reader and collector of books. Although librarians and schools have traditionally ignored the popular series on the basis of their limited literary value, many adult readers acknowledge that this is where their love affair with books began. So, parents need not worry that kids will never get beyond this stage. Once the reading habit takes hold, kids themselves begin to look for new horizons.

Fortunately, publishers have recognized the popularity of the mystery genre and have produced a great wealth of new choices. Sleuths come in all genders and species. There's the Great McGoniggle and his sidekick Ken or Rebecca and her Robot. Don't overlook Freddie, a pig who styles himself after Sherlock Holmes, or George, a dog who stalks the mysterious Bunnicula, the vampire bunny. There are young detectives who operate out of a clubhouse and others, like Encyclopedia Brown, who involve the reader in deducing the solution and becoming sleuths themselves.

Essentially, these are books for entertainment, a valuable and lasting link that children need to bring to books and reading.

Bunnicula by Deborah and James Howe; illustrated by Alan Daniel. Atheneum, 1979. Told by Harold, "a dog by profession," this is a mystery-comedy about Bunnicula, a bunny found in a movie theater where *Dracula* was playing. Chester, the family cat, discovers Bunnicula's fangs and weird markings. It's when veggies are found drained white and dry that Chester tries to warn them that Bunnicula is a vampire bunny. Enough suspense and humor for family read-a-loud time. Also: *The Further Adventures of Bunnicula, The Celery Stalks at Midnight.*

Encyclopedia Brown Saves the Day by Donald J. Sobol; illustrated by Leanord Shortall. Nelson, 1970. Mr. Brown may be the chief of police in Idaville, but it's his ten-year-old son, Encyclopedia, who is the real brain, the one who solves every crime. One of a series, this little book has ten cases the reader can try to solve before turning to Encyclopedia Brown's explanation of the solution. Also: *Encyclopedia Brown, Boy Detective, Encyclopedia Brown Gets His Man, Encyclopedia Brown Finds the Clues,* and many others.

Frankenstein Moved in on the Fourth Floor by Elizabeth Levy; illustrated by Mordicai Gerstein. Harper & Row, 1979. Sam and his younger brother Robert are convinced that Mr. Frank, the strange new neighbor on the fourth floor, is none other than the real Frankenstein. Plenty of suspense and humor with an ending that leaves you wondering! Also: *Dracula Is a Pain in the Neck.*

Freddie the Detective by Walter R. Brooks; illustrated by Kurt Wiese. Knopf, 1932. Freddie, a pig who styles himself after Sherlock Holmes, solves one mystery after another on the Bean Farm. An old but well-loved series in chapters that are easy to read. You may want to read aloud the first chapter or two to get them launched. Also: *Freddie Goes to Florida, Freddie Goes to the North Pole,* and others.

The Ghost-Eye Tree by Bill Martin, Jr., and John Archambault; illustrated by Ted Rand. Holt, 1985. A young boy and his older sister must pass the Ghost-Eye Tree on their way home at night. The adventure makes for a wonderful, shivery story that should be read aloud to be fully enjoyed. The eerie illustrations add just the right touch to a deliciously scary tale.

The Great McGonniggle's Key Play by Scott Corbett; illustrated by Bill Ogden. Atlantic Monthly, 1976. When McGonniggle and his friend Ken go out collecting for charity, they get much more than small change. Police sirens whine through the shopping mall and an action-packed adventure begins. Short and lively with plenty of humor. Part of a series. Also: *The Great McGoniggle's Gray Ghost.*

Jed's Junior Space Patrol by Jean and Claudio Marzollo. Dial, 1982. Here's easy-to-read science fiction with robots and telepathic creatures in an intergalactic adventure.

The Muffin Fiend written and illustrated by Daniel Pinkwater. Lothrop, Lee and Shepard, 1986. In this perfectly delicious mystery Wolfgang Amadeus Mozart (as detective), Don Pastrami, and Inspector Le Chat find a muffin fiend. This one will be gobbled up by any youngster looking for a good read.

My Robot Buddy by Alfred Slote; illustrated by Joel Schick. Lippincott, 1975. Jack wants a robot for his tenth birthday because he's lonely. His robot, Danny One, looks so much like a boy that a "robotnapper" (one who kidnaps robots) is after the wrong boy. Set in the future, short, fast-paced, and easy reading. Also: *Omega Station* and others.

Mystery of the Plumed Serpent by Barbara Brenner; illustrated by Blanche Sims. Knopf, 1980. Elena and Michael Garcia are twins who have keen noses for mystery. The clues they discover lead them to ancient Mexican treasure. Children will be caught up in this fast-paced mystery that is well researched and well written. Also: *Mystery of the Disappearing Dogs.*

The Mystery on Bleeker Street by William H. Hooks; illustrated by Susanna Natti. Knopf, 1980. Ten-year-old Chase's best friend is a seventy-eight-year-old eccentric French lady named Babette. Together they solve mysteries that baffle the local police. The rapid, action-packed, short chapters will keep readers holding their breath; but there is also insightful interaction between the young boy and a senior citizen. Also: *The Mystery on Liberty Street.*

The Robot and Rebecca by Jane Yolen; illustrated by Lady McCrady. Knopf, 1980. Lighthearted, fantastic adventures about a girl who wants to be a detective and her robot Watson. Also: *The Robot, Rebecca, and the Missing Owser.*

Something Queer at the Lemonade Stand by Elizabeth Levy; illustrated by Mordicai Gerstein. Delacorte, 1982. Gwen and Jill have a successful lemonade stand until something queer begins to find its way into the lemonade. A short, relatively easy-to-read mystery. Part of a series: *Something Queer on Vacation* and *Something Queer at the Haunted School.*

Something Suspicious by Kathryn O. Galbraith. Atheneum, 1985. A fun-to-read mystery featuring Lizzie and Ivy in pursuit of a mysterious bank bandit and a secret.

The Spook Birds by Eve Bunting; illustrated by Blanche Sims. Whitman, 1981. A fascinating mystery for those just beyond easy reading, with unexpected turns, an eerie atmosphere,

and a down-to-earth boy. Youngsters will be gripped by this
unusual short novel.

Super Sleuth: Twelve Solve-It-Yourself Mysteries by Jackie Vivelo. Putnam, 1985. Plenty of wit and humor in these solve-it-yourself mysteries.

Fantasy

Despite their great appetite for facts and information, you might
assume that your eight- or nine-year-old "realists" have no interest in make-believe. Yet a look at their favorite books indi-
cates a continuing delight in fantasy with a strong footing in
reality. Take Pippi Longstocking, that mischevious, zany girl
who lives on her own with no one to tell her when to wash, go
to school, do her chores, or go to bed. Her independence is a
child's dream come true. The fact that she can only exist in a
storybook world is understood but doesn't diminish the refreshing, powerful, often amusing joy of it all.

This preference for fantasy with plenty of humor and reality
mixed in matches the child's own way of pretending and trying
on new roles. Games of pretend often spring from comics, TV,
and movies rather than the child's own imaginings. Games with
rules and skills are more possible and popular, although the
uniforms and seriousness attached to such play demand a new
kind of role-playing. Now, it's not a question of who's going to
be the Daddy, but who's going to be the Captain. It's not who
will be the Mommy, but who will be the President. The young
entrepreneur runs a lemonade stand; the organizer forms a
club; the theatrical type stages magic shows, circuses, and other
extravaganzas. In other words, the pretend has much more reality to it than make-believe.

In the world of fantasy the child listener is at safe enough
distance to examine some issues that might be too heavy to
handle in the real world. E. B. White's classic *Charlotte's Web*
opens with the grim reality of Fern's father going out with an ax
to do in the runt of a litter, the piglet that becomes Wilbur, one
of the most endearing young characters in literature for children. While Fern and her family are laced through the book, the
"true" story revolves around the friendship and caring devotion
that grows between Wilbur and the lovable spider, Charlotte.

This is a story that has everything—humor, suspense, "magic," loyalty, friendship, and the roundness of life's cycle.

Though few books touch as many places in the heart as *Charlotte's Web,* the books in this section will be enjoyed by the whole family. Most are probably better read aloud. That doesn't preclude the child's possibility of rereading on her own, but taking off into fantasy may be easier with a companion. Here are some of the best.

A Bear Called Paddington by Michael Bond; illustrated by Peggy Fortnum. Houghton Mifflin, 1962. Young Paddington, a bear from Deepest Peru, arrives in London on his own and has the good fortune to be found and adopted by the Brown family. Each chapter is a complete adventure with innocent, curious, and spunky Paddington getting into sticky situations. First of a series.

Charlotte's Web by E. B. White; illustrated by Garth Williams. Harper & Row, 1952. A beloved treasure about a spider and a pig. It has everything children of this age relish—suspense, humor, friendship, and adventure. The entire family will love this one. A book to share.

Chocolate Fever by Robert K. Smith. Dell, 1978. A funny story with a real message about the consequences of "too much of a good thing." Henry Green, a chocoholic, eats chocolate for breakfast, lunch, and dinner until he comes down with a terrible case of chocolate fever that leads to a cure.

The Cricket in Times Square by George Selden; illustrated by Garth Williams. Farrar, Straus and Giroux, 1960. You've heard of a boy and his dog, but, what about a boy and a cricket who can sing the sextet from *Lucia*? It all begins when Chester, a cricket from Connecticut, gets whisked off in a picnic basket and finds himself in the Times Square Subway Station. What follows is a story of friendship, cooperation, adventure, and a taste of fame. A treat for all ages.

Dominic by William Steig. Farrar, Straus and Giroux, 1972. Along life's highway, the ever-present danger of the Doomsday Robbers awaits. But, Dominic, the young hero, is armed with a "magic spear" that helps him to carve out his own identity. On his journey Dominic learns something from each of the friends and foes along the way. He is a model hero—generous, courageous, imaginative, and just. A wonderfully romantic book for sharing.

The Enormous Egg by Oliver Butterworth; illustrated by Louis Darling. Little, Brown, 1956. For dinosaur lovers here's a dream come true. It all begins when a dinosaur hatches from an enormous hen's egg in the small town of Freedom. Here's a wonderful yarn about a boy, his pet, and the excitement they stirred among scientists, schemers, and senators.

My Father's Dragon by Ruth S. Gannett. Random House, 1948. Young Elmer Elevator, an adventuresome boy, sets out to rescue a baby dragon and manages to outwit the lions, tigers, and other creatures on Wild Island. This is the first of several well-loved and relatively easy-to-read books in a series. Also: *Elmer and the Dragon* and *Dragons of Blueland.*

Half Magic by Edward Eager; illustrated by N. M. Bodecker. Harcourt, 1954. It all begins when Jane finds what looks like a nickel but turns out to be a magic coin that grants wishes —at least halves of wishes. So when Mark wishes to go to a desert island, he finds himself not on an island but in the Sahara. Each chapter transports them on some thrilling adventure through time and space, including a trip to King Arthur's court with Sir Lancelot and Merlin. A lighthearted yarn touched with humor and suspense. Also: *Magic by the Lake* and *Knight's Castle.*

James and the Giant Peach by Roald Dahl; illustrated by Nancy E. Burkert. Knopf, 1961. A classic. Orphaned, mistreated by cruel aunts, and then gifted with a magic sack, James, the bumbler, trips, spills his bag, and accidentally creates a vehicle, a giant peach, that takes him to adventure. Aboard the fantastic peach James becomes the clever leader of an industrious group of inhabitants. Although they are faced with one near calamity after another, the journey ends as it should, happily ever after.

The Littles by John Peterson; illustrated by Roberta Carter Clark. Scholastic, 1967. Adventures of a family of tiny people who live in the walls of a house owned by George W. Bigg. Much like the classic family of *The Borrowers,* but much simpler to read. Also: *The Littles to the Rescue, The Littles Take a Trip,* and others.

Lizard Music by D. Manus Pinkwater. Dodd, Mead, 1976. Victor's parents go off for a two-week vacation leaving his hippie sister, Leslie, in charge. But Leslie takes off and that leaves eleven-year-old Victor on his own to stay up late, eat junk food, watch TV, and ultimately take off on a fantastic journey of his own to Thunderbolt City. His mentor, an oddball named Chicken-Man, because he has a chicken in his hat, takes him to an invisible island inhabited by lizards. A little dated now but full of suspense, humor, and imagination.

The Mouse and the Motorcycle by Beverly Cleary; illustrated by Louis Darling. Dell, 1980. Friendship and adventure begin when a boy named Keith arrives in Room 215 at the Mountain View Inn and meets a young resident mouse named Ralph. There's plenty of action, close calls, and quick rescues as Ralph, a mouse with a taste for derring-do, revs up Keith's toy motorcycle and runs into danger.

Pippi Longstocking by Astrid Lindgren; illustrated by Louis S. Glanzman. Viking, 1950. Talk about independence: Pippi heads the list. With her horse and monkey and no grownups to say when, what, or how to do things, Pippi is her own boss. Her next-door neighbors, Tommy and Annika, are fascinated by Pippi's inventive and outrageous approach to life. Also: *Pippi Goes on Board.*

The Real Thief by William Steig. Farrar, Straus and Giroux, 1973. Gawain, the Chief Guard of the Royal Treasury, is the most trustworthy and important goose in the kingdom until rubies start disappearing from the treasury room. Suddenly, Gawain's world turns upside down. He is accused, tried, convicted, and banished by King Basil the Bear. Meanwhile, the real thief suffers pangs of guilt but is afraid to confess. A gem of a story about justice and injustice, issues eights and nines are beginning to grapple with in their relationships with friends and family. A wonderful read-aloud.

Ruthie's Rude Friends by Jean and Claudio Marzolla; illustrated by Susan Meddaugh. Dial, 1985. Ruthie, the only Earthling child type on Planet X10, has problems making friends with the space kids. Plenty of fun, suspense, and action in a science fiction book for beginning readers.

The Sword in the Tree by Clyde R. Bulla; illustrated by Paul Galdone. Crowell, 1956. Set in the days of King Arthur and Camelot, young Shan, a boy who dreams of becoming a knight, is forced to become courageous and protect his mother when his wicked uncle takes over his father's castle. Short but well told and relatively easy to read.

Tales from the Jungle Book by Rudyard Kipling; adapted by Robin McKinley; illustrated by Joseph A. Smith. Random House, 1985. A collection of thrilling stories about the wild and Mowgli, the orphan boy, and his love for the animals of the Indian jungle. Specially adapted for young readers, these three classic tales are a wonderful introduction to one of the best storytellers ever.

Folktales and Fairy Tales

Folktales and fairy tales offer another route to fantasy and adventure. Now that eights and nines are secure in their understanding of real and make-believe, the world of once-upon-a-time provides a splendid realm where one can find safe thrills with witches, dragons, and the unknown. Indeed, fantasy offers a wonderful release from the earthbound world, where life is pretty proscribed with rules and limits. It is through such stories that children can get outside themselves and take off on far-flung fantasy where anything can happen and often does.

These are the years when tall tales with humorous exaggeration, fairy tales, and myths are most appealing. It's not that kids believe in such larger-than-life characters, but rather that such heros and heroines invite kids to suspend belief and journey beyond the rule-ridden world of reality. Through such characters the child can encounter danger, overcome fear, taste courage, and triumph over all odds. The wonderful predictability makes the most frightening journey palatable. Where else can we be so sure that good will triumph over evil?

Like children, the heroes of these stories are usually cast out into the world and forced to overcome their long standing dependence on others. Though he may be frightened, lonely, and somewhat powerless, in the course of events the young hero takes charge and controls his own destiny. While children themselves may lack such powers, the vicarious joy of such triumphs is what makes these stories so appealing to eights and nines.

Anna and the Seven Swans by Maida Silverman; illustrated by David Small. Morrow, 1984. A Russian tale about how Anna rescues her little brother from the witch Baba Yaga.

The Devil's Storybook by Natalie Babbitt. Farrar, Straus and Giroux, 1974. A collection of ten lively tales that are devilishly amusing and also thought-provoking. Stories are short and just right for a brief but pleasing sharing time.

The Good-Hearted Youngest Brother, An Hungarian Folktale translated by Emoke de Papp Severo; illustrated by Diane Goode. Bradbury, 1981. The age-old theme of the youngest son befriending creatures who in return help him fulfill his quest is stunningly illustrated here. The clarity of the jewel-tone pictures illuminates the familiar well-loved fairy tale patterns.

Little Sister and the Month Brothers retold by Beatrice Schenk de Regniers; illustrated by Margot Tomes. Houghton Mifflin, 1976. A retelling of the Slavic fairy tale in which the magical Month Brothers help Little Sister provide the things her mean and greedy stepsisters demand.

The Maid of the North: Feminist Folktales from Around the World collected by Ethel J. Phelps; illustrated by Lloyd Bloom. Holt, 1983. Feminist folktales these may be, but they are not permeated with propaganda. Based on old tales of enchantment and adventure, they are illustrated with drawings full of mystery and power.

The Man Who Could Call Down Owls by Eve Bunting; illustrated by Charles Mikolaycak. Macmillan, 1984. A haunting story of good and evil. Striking illustrations.

Mean Jake and the Devils by William H. Hooks; illustrated by Dirk Zimmer. Dial, 1981. Mean Jake was so-o-o mean that Mister Big Daddy Devil, D. J. (short for Devil Junior) and Baby Deviline came up from down  below to teach Jake a lesson. Young listeners will laugh out loud at these devilish tales that come from old Southern folktales the author heard as a child.

Paul Bunyan retold and illustrated by Steven Kellogg. Morrow, 1984. A lively retelling of the tallest tall tale about that legendary hero, Paul Bunyan, who dug out the Great Lakes, shaped the slopes of the Rocky Mountains, and gouged out the trench we call the Grand Canyon.

Pie Biter by Ruthanne Lum McCunn; illustrated by You-Shen Tang. Design Enterprises, 1983. He ate pies with one hand and swung his axe with the other, so says the legend of the young man from China who worked on the railroad. This large, glowing picture book tells the story succinctly and reflects both Chinese and American motifs.

Saint George and the Dragon retold by Margaret Hodges; illustrated by Trina Schart Hyman. Little, Brown, 1984. Exquisite illustrations illuminate the tale of courage in which George slays the dreadful dragon that has been plaguing the countryside for years.

The Snow Queen by Hans Christian Andersen, retold by Amy Ehrlich; illustrated by Susan Jeffers. Dial, 1983. This old tale doesn't spare the dark side of life or the grandeur, as reflected in its splendid art. Also: *The Wild Swans.*

Snow White and the Seven Dwarfs, translated by Randall Jarrell; illustrated by Nancy E. Burkert. Farrar, Straus and Giroux, 1972. One of the best-loved tales from the brothers Grimm, rendered with great beauty by a poet and artist.

Snow-White and the Seven Dwarfs

The Swineherd by Hans Christian Andersen, translated by Anthea Bell; illustrated by Lisbeth Zwerger. Morrow, 1982. A lively new translation of the story of the foolish princess, with beautifully detailed pictures.

Picture Books for Older Children

Although eights and nines consider most picture books "babyish" and beneath their dignity, there are a number of gems they shouldn't miss. These illustrated storybooks tend to be longer than most picture books but shorter than a novel. But it's not just length that separates these books; it's much more a matter of content. Essentially, these are more complex stories with an assumed kind of literary sophistication that is beyond younger children. Most of Chris Van Allsburg's books fall into this category. True, you could share *The Mysteries of Harris Burdick* with younger children, but the stories they can spin from the provocative illustrations would be quite different from the imaginings of eights and nines. His *The Garden of Abdul Gasazi* might be food for thought for older children and merely confusing (or frightening) to younger listeners.

Come Again in the Spring by Richard Kennedy; illustrated by Marcia Sewall. Harper & Row, 1976. When Death came by, Old Hark refused to go along. The birds needed him to feed them through the winter. "Come again in the spring," he told Death. So Old Hark made a series of wagers with Death and won. A haunting tale told with wit and style.

The Country Bunny and the Little Golden Shoes by DuBose Heyward; illustrated by Marjorie Flack. Houghton Mifflin, 1939. While eights and nines may have given up the Easter Bunny, they will love this near classic about a girl bunny who dreams of growing up to be an Easter Bunny. Here's a heroine that is kind, smart, and brave. Gorgeous illustrations.

Fair's Fair by Leon Garfield; illustrated by S. D. Schindler. Doubleday, 1981. Jackson, a London street urchin, shares his precious food with a huge hungry black dog. The dog has a key under his collar, and Jackson sets out to find the door that fits the key. This is the beginning of a marvelous adventure that changes Jackson's whole life.

The Garden of Abdul Gasazi written and illustrated by Chris Van Allsburg. Houghton Mifflin, 1979. Alan is left to care for Miss Hester's bad-mannered dog, Fritz. His troubles begin when Fritz bolts at the entrance to the forbidden

garden of the magician Abdul Gasazi. This is a tale of mystery and enchantment that lingers on after the story is told.

Hawk, I'm Your Brother by Byrd Baylor; illustrated by Peter Parnall. Scribner's, 1976. A poetic story of a boy, his desire to fly, and the understanding he gathers when he captures a hawk and ultimately sets it free.

How I Hunted the Little Fellows by Boris Zhitkov; translated by Djemma Bider; illustrated by Paul Zelinsky. Dodd, Mead, 1979. Boris has a moral dilemma when he's promised never to touch the delicate ship model on his grandmother's shelf —but can't keep the promise!

Jumanji written and illustrated by Chris Van Allsburg. Houghton Mifflin, 1981. Imagine a game coming to life—a jungle game with roaring lions, chimps, snakes and hippos. Here is an adventure full of danger and suspense with lush oversized illustrations.

The Marzipan Moon by Nancy Willard; illustrated by Marcia Sewall. Harcourt, 1981. It all begins when a poor woman brings an old mended crock to her poor parish priest. Magically the old crock turns out marzipan moon cakes each day until the rich bishop arrives on the scene and values the end product instead of the source.

The Mysteries of Harris Burdick by Chris Van Allsburg. Houghton Mifflin, 1984. This isn't one story but rather an open sesame to fourteen stories! In an introductory note Van Allsburg sets up Burdick as a mystery writer and illustrator who brings a publisher one illustrated page from each of fourteen stories. Burdick promises to return the next day but instead vanishes, never to be heard from again. Those fourteen pages then become the body of a book brimming with possibilities. Each page has a single line of text and an image that will feed the imagination of readers who can spin their own stories. Also see *The Wreck of the Zephyr* and *The Polar Express*.

Ox-Cart Man by Donald Hall; illustrated by Barbara Cooney. Viking, 1979. A detailed glimpse of life and work in early New England. Wonderfully compressed in terse, lucid prose and beautifully illustrated in full-color primitive folk style. The Caldecott Award winner for 1979.

The Shrinking of Treehorn by Florence Parry Heide; illustrated by Edward Gorey. Holiday House, 1971. A surrealistic story about a boy who keeps shrinking, but no one in the adult world seems to care or notice. It is Treehorn who solves his own problem—as everyone must. A psycho-humorous book.

The Whingdingdilly by Bill Peet. Houghton Mifflin, 1970. Scamp, a dog, finds out that wishing to be something else may come true and may also be less grand than imagined. There's plenty of magic and humor—an old-fashioned story about jealousy, friendship, and being yourself. Also: *Buford the Little Bighorn* and many others.

Information Books

School assignments may lead third- and fourth-graders to the encyclopedia, atlas, and other books on the reference shelf. Yet, quite apart from schoolwork, many eights and nines are fascinated with strange-but-true facts. This is the age when kids pour over the *Guiness Book of Records* and sports fans relish *Strange But True Baseball Stories.* Although individual interests vary, some kids gravitate to books about UFOs, witches, ghosts, and mysterious phenomena while others like more practical how-to, and down-to-earth books about stars, planets, baseball, and BMX bikes. While some books are designed especially for young readers, kids may have an appetite for books they can browse through rather than read from cover to cover. So, some books from the adult shelf may be more desirable than simpler volumes on the same subject. What follows is a sampling of some popular informational books for eights and nines.

Beware! These Animals Are Poison! by Barbara Brenner; illustrated by Jim Spanfeller. Coward, McCann, 1980. A fascinating discussion of some hurtful creatures, including scorpions, sting rays, and rattlesnakes. Told in clear, concise prose with lucid, detailed art. Also: *A Snake Lover's Diary.* Harper & Row, 1970.

Billions of Bats by Miriam Schlein; illustrated by Walter Kessell.

Lippincott, 1982. Brief chapters in clear language present a fact-filled book about seventeen different species of bats.

Birds Are Flying: A Let's Read and Find Out Science Book by John Kaufman. Crowell, 1980. A lovely introduction to birds and bird flight, beautifully illustrated, that may awaken children's curiosity to know more about these marvelous creatures. One of a fine series for young readers.

The Fox by Margaret Lane; illustrated by Kenneth Lilly. Dial, 1982. Beautifully illustrated factual information about the fox: how it is born, matures, where it lives, and how it finds food. Also: *The Frog, The Squirrel,* and *The Bear.*

Gobs of Goo by Vicki Cobb; illustrated by Brian Schatell. Lippincott, 1983. "Go on a goo hunt around your house." What child could resist this opening? Then skillfully, one is led through "goo" differences and uses—oil, soap, peanut butter—to a beginning comprehension of body fluids, starch, sugar, etc. An excellent readable introduction to chemistry. Also: *Fuzz Does It!* and *The Monsters Who Died: A Mystery About Dinosaurs.*

The Hospital Book by James Howe; photos by Mal Warshaw. Crown, 1981. A realistic photo essay of what a hospital stay is all about. An informative book for sharing between parent and child.

How the Forest Grew by William Jaspersohn; illustrated by Chuck Eckart. Greenwillow, 1981. A beautifully written science book for that special young naturalist. Easy-to-read format. Fine language, thoughtful information, and magnificent illustrations will attract woods-lovers of all ages.

How You Were Born by Joanna Cole. Morrow, 1984. A clearly written book that answers some of the questions children have about the birthing process. Excellent for parent/child sharing.

I Skate! by Margaret Faulkner. Little, Brown, 1981. The personalized account of a girl skater's arduous training will fascinate would-be Olympic contenders. Although detailed, the text is bright and smooth enough to be easily read by young aficionados. Great photos.

An Insect's Body by Joanna Cole; photos by Jerome Wexler and Raymond Mendez. Morrow, 1984. Handsome black-and-white photos and line drawings zoom in on the exoskeleton, and the muscular, digestive, circulatory, and nervous systems of a common cricket. Also: *A Bird's Body, A Cat's Body,* and *A Frog's Body.*

Kids Computer Capers by Sandra Markle; illustrated by Stella Ormai. Lothrop, Lee and Shepard, 1983. A big book with short but informative sections to plug into. The author presents a bit of history, explores how computers work, and offers activities that can be done with and without a computer.

Little Koala by Suzanne Noguere and Tony Chen; illustrated by Tony Chen. Holt, Rinehart and Winston, 1980. The birth and growth of this fascinating marsupial is told in a straightforward style with Chen's superb illustrations. Also: *Little Raccoon.*

The Scarecrow Book by James Giblin and Dale Ferguson. Crown, 1981. An interesting account of these fascinating figures, including some scarecrow history and how to make one. Plenty of clear photos enrich a concise text.

The Science Book by Sara Stein. Workman, 1979. Why do bedbugs bite? Why do bees dance? How do you talk dog talk? Here's a book brimming with short but clear explanations, simple experiments, and great ideas for observing and understanding the natural world.

Strange Mysteries from Around the World by Seymour Simon. Four Winds, 1980. A fascinating book about ten strange mysteries that really happened. There's the strange case of a ship's crew that vanished without a trace; an atomic explosion that went off forty years before the bomb was invented; the day it rained frogs and fishes and many more unexplained events that have baffled scientists for years. Also: *Exploring Fields and Lots: Easy Science Projects.*

A Very Young Dancer text and photographs by Jill Krementz. Knopf, 1977. An account of a young dancer's experiences from dance classes to the joy of being chosen for the "Nutcracker Suite." The easy text and big clear pictures are fascinating. Also: *A Very Young Gymnast, A Very Young Rider,* and *A Very Young Skater.*

You Can't Eat Peanuts in Church and Other Little-Known Laws by Barbara Seuling. Doubleday, 1975. An amusing collection of little-known but real laws that were written at one time or another in America.

Poetry

Until now the experiences of most eights and nines with poetry have probably been limited to listening and chanting some familiar rhymes. Children of all ages enjoy hearing the rhythm of poetry and at eight or nine they can begin to read it themselves. Indeed, poetry with short phrases lends itself to easy reading. It's at this age that children often begin to write poems, too. Here are some collections that can be enjoyed together, solo, or both.

An Arkful of Animals selected by William Cole; illustrated by Lynn Munsinger. Houghton Mifflin, 1978. A menagerie of creatures romp through this collection of poems about animals. Poems by Jack Prelutsky, Shel Silverstein, Myra Cohn Livingston, David McCord, Conrad Aiken, and others.

A Book of Pigericks by Arnold Lobel. Harper & Row, 1983. Those who love limericks will also love Pigericks. Lobel draws them and tells them as well and as always, Lobel's swell!

If I Were in Charge of the World by Judith Viorst; illustrated by Lynne Cherry. Atheneum, 1982. You know the old saying, "Many a true word is said in jest." Well, here's a collection of true words about life and its little worries told with a dollop of humor to lighten the load.

Knock at a Star: A Child's Introduction to Poetry by X. J. Kennedy and Dorothy M. Kennedy; illustrated by K. A. Weinhaus. Little, Brown, 1983. Here are many appealing short contemporary poems that are not in the usual collections. Children should find them fresh and fun, whether or not they pause to read the author's explanatory sections. Afterword to adults included.

Merry, Merry FIBruary by Doris Orgel; illustrated by Arnold

Lobel. Parents Magazine Press, 1977. Absolute nonsense! That's what this little volume of verse is all about as little fibs grow into great big FIBS. Fun for reading aloud.

Morning, Noon and Nighttime, Too selected by Lee B. Hopkins; illustrated by Nancy Hannans. Harper & Row, 1981. A number of our best contemporary poets are represented in this collection of short poems to take a child all through a day.

The Other Side of a Poem edited by Barbara Abercrombie; illustrated by Harry Bertschmann. Harper & Row, 1977. A collection of poems by many well-known writers selected for reading aloud by an editor who has brought poetry and children together through poetry workshops in elementary schools.

Piping Down the Valleys Wild edited by Nancy Larrick; illustrated by Ellen Raskin. Delacorte, 1968. You'll find over two hundred poems in this handsome anthology that parents and teachers have shared with children for several decades.

Poem Stew selected by William Cole; illustrated by Karen Ann Weinhaus. Lippincott, 1981. Here's a feast of funny poems about food by such popular writers as Ogden Nash, John Ciardi, Shel Silverstein, and William Cole. A tasty mix that's bound to whet kid's appetites for poetry.

The Sheriff of Rottenshot by Jack Prelutsky; illustrated by Victoria Chess. Greenwillow, 1982. Zany illustrations perfectly mated with humorous poems that will tickle young listeners or readers. Also: *The Snopp on the Sidewalk* and *Nightmares*.

Speak Up: More Rhymes of the Never Was and Always Is by David McCord; illustrated by Marc Simont. Little, Brown, 1981. This volume of playful poems should be read aloud for the fun of the sounds. Attractive format and illustrations.

Street Talk by Ann Turner; illustrated by Catherine Stock. Houghton Mifflin, 1986. Twenty-nine poems that catch the cadence of city life and paint word pictures of people and things.

Up and Down the River: Boat Poems by Claudia Lewis; illustrated by Bruce Degen. Harper & Row, 1980. Anyone who reads or listens to these lovely, perceptive poems must forever see the river with new eyes.

Where the Sidewalk Ends by Shel Silverstein. Harper & Row, 1974.

A delicious collection of poems and drawings with a rich blend of warmth and wit. *Where the Sidewalk Ends* is a place colored with playful thoughts, feelings, and words.

Wind Song by Carl Sandburg; illustrated by William A. Smith. Harcourt, 1960. Selected by Sandburg himself, these poems were not written for children but they do speak to children! They especially love "Arithmetic" and "We Must Be Polite." A book they'll enjoy parts of now and return to later.

THINGS TO REMEMBER WHEN SELECTING BOOKS FOR EIGHTS AND NINES

- Books at this stage should be "desired" not "required."
- Give kids options to exercise their own taste, even "poor taste."
- Look for read-aloud stories with more three-dimensional characters and complex plots.
- Select stories you enjoy so that you convey that joy.
- If they find an author they like, encourage them to look for other books by that author.
- Choose books from various genres; but if they seem to favor fantasy or mysteries or fairy tales, build on their enjoyment.
- Avoid pushing them to read at the next level independently. Longer and harder is not necessarily better.

TEN BOOKS FOR EIGHTS AND NINES TOO GOOD TO MISS

Bunnicula by Deborah and James Howe
Charlotte's Web by E. B. White
The Cricket in Times Square by George Selden
Dominic by William Steig
Freckle Juice by Judy Blume

The Garden of Abdul Gasazi by Chris Van Allsburg
Little House Series by Laura Ingalls Wilder
No One Is Going to Nashville by Mavis Jukes
Ramona Quimby, Age 8 by Beverly Cleary
Sarah, Plain and Tall, by Patricia MacLachlan

Chocolate Fever by Robert K. Smith

The Enormous Egg by Oliver Butterworth

The Fallen Spaceman by Lee Harding

Dexter by Clyde Robert Bulla

Warton and Morton by Russell Erickson

The Witch of Fourth Street by Myron Levoy

The Adventures of Pinocchio by Carlo Collodi

Homer Price by Robert McCloskey

CHAPTER VIII

Books for Ten-to Twelve-Year-Olds

ON BEING TEN

Ten-year-olds are noted for their self-acceptance, their easygoing ways. Growing pains may be part and parcel of childhood, but the ten-year-old seems to be relatively free of them. At ten most kids seem happy with themselves and their families. Most tens have mastered certain skills such as reading, and they have acquired considerable social know-how. They usually like their friends and their teachers. If they look ahead into the future, they look with confidence, because they're comfortable in the present. So for many kids, ten is a pleasant plateau.

This tranquility is reflected in their choice of reading material. Tens we talked to said they liked books with happy endings and light nonfiction of the "freaky fact" variety. They also like funny books like *How to Eat Fried Worms: And Other Plays* by Thomas Rockwell or the *Choose Your Own Adventure* books. At this age children often choose their own books and are aware of the author behind the book. In other words, rather than simply picking a subject or depending on the librarian, they are becoming increasingly selective.

Because ten-year-olds are so comfortable with what they know, they may be inclined to stick to familiar books, or at least familiar authors. So the youngster who first met Beverly Cleary through her *Ramona* books at eight or nine, is likely to gravitate at ten to new *Ramona* books and later to Cleary's *Dear Mr. Henshaw.*

Tens may even go back to books they enjoyed at a younger age. You can often find a boy or girl of this age avidly reading *Charlotte's Web* again or even rereading a younger sibling's copy of *Curious George* by H. A. Rey, or Dr. Seuss's *The Cat in the Hat.* This is not a sign of retrogression. It is, in fact, a sign that the book habit is firmly in place and that the youngster is working at incorporating literature into her total life experience. It means that she is beginning to appreciate the fact that a good children's book can be enjoyed in different ways at different ages.

The Great Brain

By John D. Fitzgerald

ILLUSTRATED BY MERCER MAYER

A YEARLING BOOK

Ten can be a high point of the interest in series books. During this time a kid may gorge on *The Hardy Boys* or *Nancy Drew* series, especially now that the characters are also on TV. Some parents worry about the lack of substance in these books. And we know librarians who won't even give them shelf space. One librarian told us that she insists that kids take one more "meaty" book for each *Nancy Drew* they check out. Our feeling is that reading nonliterature is a whole lot better than not reading at all. We also think the *Nancy Drew–Hardy Boys* series craze usually is temporary. However, there are series that offer a bit more challenge than the two mentioned here. One is *The Great Brain* series by John Fitzgerald. The other is the series marketed by Knopf under the name of *Capers* with titles by popular authors like Jane Yolen and William Hooks. It may be possible to steer a youngster to these books if you feel he is staying with book junk food too long.

To sum up about tens—every child is different. The books we are going to talk about are suitable for ten-year-olds and up. Some tens will read them, some will go beyond them, some will not be ready for them. If your child is having trouble reading, or simply wants to linger with the familiar or the "easy read" for a little longer, by all means look back at the eight- and nine-year-old list at the end of Chapter VI. Remember, ten seems to be the place in childhood where boys and girls may pause to take a breather before getting on with the tumultuous business of becoming adolescents.

THE SEARCH FOR SELF

Anyone who has spent time with a ten-going-on-eleven will notice that there begin to be changes. These changes become even more marked at eleven. Eleven-year-olds quarrel, are moody. They dream of being famous. And they may suddenly lose the energy to concentrate on schoolwork. Between ten and twelve is the era of the secret club, the exclusive peer group, the sudden —and sometimes inappropriate—new friendship. It's a time of a new kind of fascination with bodily functions, particularly sexual ones, and a new and intense interest in romance and adventure. For many kids, books begin to take on a richer and deeper meaning, and they become more aware of style and more sensitive to the content and the message of the book. They are also beginning to be more aware of the author behind the book. Katherine Paterson, Virginia Hamilton, Lloyd Alexander, Lois Duncan, John Bellairs, and Judy Blume all have their following.

Mystery and fantasy continue to be popular, but now more adult themes and so-called "problem" books become popular. This isn't so much a seeking after the bizarre as it is a need to explore life and begin to face adult issues.

For other children in this age group, preadolescence may be a period when they suddenly (and usually temporarily) stop reading. At the same time they rebel in this way, they may begin questioning other parental values. Curiously, this questioning is part of their new search for a deeper personal moral code. Friends, too, come under scrutiny; what peers do and think gets a new and sharper look.

If you were to give a name to these changes that begin to take place anywhere from the latter part of the tenth year on up, you might call them *The Search for Self.* It's around this age that boys and girls begin asking *Who am I? How do I fit into the world?* During these years, a child may try on a number of hats in an effort to find standards and ways of behaving that he or she can live with comfortably.

To children seeking answers to their selfhood, books are necessary and important experiences. They can play a vital role in the sorting-out process. Through a book like Scott O'Dell's *Island of the Blue Dolphins* a child can have a window into another culture and a different lifestyle. Books like *Are You There, God?—It's Me, Margaret* by Judy Blume can answer some of a youngster's questions about emerging sexuality in a way that gives information and independence without risk. Books like *The Mulberry Music* by Doris Orgel can bring comfort by mirroring the preadolescent's own feelings or confusions about death. A book like *Mrs. Frisby and the Rats of NIMH* by Robert

Illustration by Zena Bernstein from *Mrs. Frisby and the Rats of NIMH* by Robert O'Brien.

O'Brien will awaken a youngster to issues in the real world through the medium of fantasy. And reading aloud books like *Huckleberry Finn* by Mark Twain and *Sounder* by William Armstrong can help kids make a bridge between childhood and adult moral choices.

Certainly no one should live entirely through books, or for that matter any other medium. But there's nothing wrong with living vicariously at certain times. This is one of the times. Books for ten- to twelve-year-olds provide a way to learn about certain aspects of life without actually experiencing them. They help children have literary experiences that enrich their lives and at the same time sort out ideas in a way that is meaningful, but also safe.

THE RELUCTANT READER

But what if your ten- to twelve-year-old has not, up to now, fully discovered the joys of reading?

Over and over again teachers and librarians say that one

way to get kids reading is through their special interests. Whether he's interested in stamp collecting or snakes, magic or mime, the child who gets a book that feeds an interest is much more likely to get caught up in the process of reading.

Also, the point can't be made often enough—reluctant readers can be encouraged to read by dipping into books mentioned in previous chapters, books like *The Sword in the Tree* by Clyde Bulla, *James and the Giant Peach* by Roald Dahl, or the *Encyclopedia Brown* mysteries. Don't think of these choices as a reflection on a child's reading ability. After all, don't you sometimes want to read a light mystery instead of that serious tome you checked out of the library?

THE TURNED-OFF READER

Some parents complain that their ten to twelve has lost interest in books, that the former bookworm has suddenly turned away from reading.

A temporary turn is certainly nothing to be concerned about. It may simply be that real life has, for the moment, much more drama than anything literature can offer. Chances are that he or she will turn back to reading.

During the turn-off period, it's not a good idea to make reading a bone of contention. You certainly don't want to force books on a reluctant reader; that will only make things worse. However, there are a few ways you can keep the reading habit alive and well.

Most kids this age won't necessarily read what their parents suggest. But they will read a book their friends tell them about. So one thing you can do is to listen to what kids are saying about books and then make those books available. A book like *The Outsiders* by S. E. Hinton that moves swiftly and confronts contemporary issues of in-group, out-group behavior might just bring a turned-off reader back to reading.

You might even want to select a book from the adult shelf, something you and your son or daughter can talk about after you have both read it. One father told us that he sometimes gives a "teaser" review of a book he has enjoyed and then leaves it in a conspicuous spot for his preteen to find. A book like *The Incredible Journey* by Sheila Burnford or *Never Cry Wolf* by Farley Mowat may be just the thing to reawaken flagging book interest, if it is given a little introduction beforehand.

READING ALOUD

What about reading aloud? Should you abandon it at this age? We think not. Reading aloud is a great idea at every age, but especially during a period when independent reading seems to be falling off. You will enjoy it. Your children of almost any age will enjoy it. Your ten to twelve will surely benefit and so will younger sibs. In fact, there is very little that can set or reinforce the lifelong habit of reading as much as this lovely custom.

It's the *language* that we don't fully appreciate when we read to ourselves. One of the great benefits of reading aloud to ten to twelves is that it fits into their increasing sensitivity to nuances of writing. This is the right age for their ears to be tuned up to the subtleties of style. They are more able to get the point or the moral of the story. It's nice to have the whole family in on these "what is the author saying?" discussions.

POETRY

Children of ten to twelve have often acquired a little background in poetry. They may even have written some, and their tastes as well as their own writing will reflect what they've been exposed to.

For example, it was fashionable a few years ago to teach Japanese Haiku in school. And so for a while American kids were turning out seventeen-syllable examples of this ancient form.

However, for many kids of ten and even older, poetry often means humor, which may explain the enormous popularity of an author like Shel Silverstein. Silverstein's bril-

A Light in the Attic

poems and drawings by Shel Silverstein

liant and zany play with language appeals to youngsters and adults alike. If you or your children have not yet discovered his *A Light in the Attic* or *Where the Sidewalk Ends,* there's a treat in store for you.

But humor is only one of the voices of poetry. And both sunny ten-year-olds and more brooding elevens and twelves may be ready for poetry of content and seriousness. They may suddenly be open to the lure of metaphor and cadence. Reading good poetry can't help but educate one's ears to the possibilities of language. If you're looking for reasons, you could probably make a case for reading poetry as a way of teaching writing. But the best reason for including poetry in a child's reading diet has to do with quite another kind of learning. It's the abstract quality of poetry that is so appropriate for youngsters of this ten-to-twelve group. They are ready to tackle those spaces between concrete thoughts, even if it requires a leap.

One way to enjoy poetry is in an anthology. Anthologies are put together in various ways. Sometimes the poems are grouped by subject matter. In *My Mane Catches the Wind,* compiled by Lee Bennett Hopkins, the subject is horses. More typically, anthologies are a collection of works that give the reader a sample of the styles of a number of poets. The best collections don't make a distinction between poets who write for adults and poets who write for children. Good poetry is good poetry.

Another way to approach poetry is by author. Reading the output of a single author is another kind of experience. Kids can pick up on the author's way of writing, and even try a poem or two in the author's style. There's nothing wrong with trying to emulate the rhythm of Edgar Allen Poe's . . .

Once upon a midnight dreary
While I pondered, weak and weary . . .

Copying, as they say, is the sincerest form of flattery. It can also be an intense learning experience!

"Bite into a poem" advises Eve Merriam, whose poetry has enchanted a generation of children. One way to sink your teeth into a poem is to read it aloud. The sounds will stay in the air for everyone's pleasure.

BOOKLIST FOR TEN- TO TWELVE-YEAR-OLDS

It's almost impossible to pick one book that speaks to all the needs, dreams, and desires of children in these years of the Search for Self. But if we were to choose one book for a ten to twelve stranded on that proverbial desert island, it would probably be *Tuck Everlasting* by Natalie Babbitt.

Books About Selfhood

Tuck Everlasting by Natalie Babbitt. Farrar, Straus and Giroux, 1975. Winnie Foster lives at the edge of an ancient wood. Her family has owned this land for generations, but the Fosters do not go into the wood. Small wonder, then, that they do not know about the great oak tree and the secret that lies in the spring that bubbles up from its roots.

One day Winnie looks at her life and finds it wanting. She feels alienated from her parents and a prisoner of a too-narrow, childish world. She decides to run away. Her path of flight takes her through the wood. There she meets young Jesse Tuck, and soon after, his brother Miles, and Mae, his mother. It is quickly made clear to Winnie that this is no ordinary family gathering. Nor are the Tucks a typical family. All of them have, by accident, drunk from the spring and have become touched with the magic of everlasting life.

Because the Tucks are forced to share with her their momentous secret and because she is the only one who knows, Winnie stays temporarily in their custody. They take her to their home, where she is accepted as a new and loved child and enfolded in a magical cocoon of love and acceptance that is every child's fantasy of family life. In this dream-like place, the wise and gentle Tuck explores with Winnie the nature of life and death. What he tells her about the magic of the spring is both miraculous and terrifying.

Although she feels some pangs of homesickness, Winnie stays with the Tucks. She has fallen in love with the handsome (and unattainable) Jesse. Neither the Tucks nor Winnie realizes that a mysterious stranger has followed them and will use them and the secret of the wood for his own evil purposes. What follows is an adventure that ultimately brings Winnie face to face with death and difficult choices. But in the long run it is she who powers the events that lead to her saving those she loves and gaining a measure of control over her life.

Tuck Everlasting is everything a good story should be. And it meshes superbly with the ten-to-twelve's search for self. Winnie's running away is the stirring of rebellion. Her discovery of the golden boy Jesse goes to the heart of the yearning for romance, but the fact that she can never marry him is perfect; she does not have to face adult choices yet. Her surrogate parents, the Tucks, are fantasy parents, perfect and understanding. And they will live forever, not grow older and die, as real parents do.

Finally, while it is Mae Tuck who saves Winnie from the evildoer, it is Winnie who in the end is able to save the Tuck family. In doing so she breaks the law and confounds her family. But there is great moral choice being exercised here, and children will weigh what Winnie did over many rereadings.

Tuck Everlasting can be read aloud and enjoyed by the whole family, or it can be savored privately. Like other fine children's literature, it is for everyone.

Blowfish Live in the Sea by Paula Fox. Bradbury, 1970. Carrie's half-brother Ben is searching for something. In locating the father he never knew, he begins to become a whole person, and can continue toward selfhood. The marvel here is the characterizations and the author's ability to put herself into the heart and mind of Carrie. Also: *One-Eyed Cat.* Bradbury, 1984.

Bridge to Terabithia by Katherine Paterson. Crowell, 1977. Leslie and Jess are from different backgrounds but they form a close friendship and create an imaginary, secret kingdom. The girl's tragic accidental death marks the end of childhood for Jeff, but their shared experiences help him bear the loss.

The Cat Ate My Gymsuit by Paula Danziger. Delacorte, 1974. Entering junior high school is one of the traumas of this age group. In this on-the-mark novel, an understanding teacher helps a young girl over her feelings of insecurity about her new school situation. The girl has the courage to return the favor when the teacher is fired and she fights for reinstatement. Also: *Can You Sue Your Parents for Malpractice?* Delacorte, 1979. Officially, this is considered a "teenage novel." But the vocabulary can be handled by most ten- to twelve-year-olds who are interested in fourteen-year-olds, love, and authentic sights and sounds of junior high. Written by a former teacher with a wonderful ear. Also: *It's an Aardvark-Eat-Turtle World.*

Circle of Fire by William H. Hooks. Atheneum, 1983. A novel set in the South explores the operations of the Ku Klux Klan against a group of gypsies. Young Harrison has to test family loyalties against his moral convictions in this original and moving story, about a boy growing up in the thirties, that airs some important ethical issues. Also: *Crossing the Line.* Knopf, 1978. Harrison and his friends meet a strange old woman, whose link with the legends of the area bring them close to the supernatural and offer them new understanding of their roots. A passage to personhood, southern style, and a generous evocation of place.

Dear Mr. Henshaw by Beverly Cleary. Morrow, 1983. Leigh Bates is the new kid in school. An absent father (the result of a divorce) and problems with a lunch-bag thief cause Leigh to begin to share his troubles with an author to whom he has been writing fan letters. Mr. Henshaw becomes his mentor—or at least Leigh thinks he is. This correspondence rings absolutely true. Before it's over, the post office is not the only beneficiary. Both Leigh and his parents have done some growing up. The laconic voice of Mr. Henshaw is perfect here. By the author of the Ramona books.

The Great Gilly Hopkins by Katherine Paterson. Crowell, 1978. Gilly is a foster child. Full of spunk, she conducts her search for selfhood and a permanent family with humor and verve. Her condition mirrors the growing pains of many preteens who, even in a stable family, begin to feel alienated from their parents. Gilly's struggle to find herself is their struggle too.

Hazel Rye by Vera and Bill Cleaver. Lippincott, 1983. Eleven-year-old Hazel, her father's pal, plans to be a school dropout and to grow rich driving a taxi and selling her orange grove. When she hires a boy to restore the grove to fertility, he arouses her interest in nature and in reading. Gradually, she changes her goals. A sensitive, humorous tale of an original girl and her search for self.

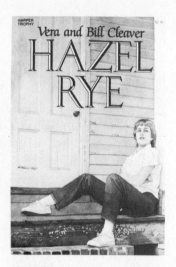

Homecoming by Cynthia Voigt. Atheneum, 1981. Thirteen-year-old Dicey and her brothers and sister have been abandoned by their mother. Dicey takes on the responsibilities of the family. She is determined to keep the four of them together and to find a home and roots. In an odyssey that is often an allegory of the passage from childhood to adulthood, Dicey and her siblings travel and learn, are threatened and make happy discoveries. At last, in a satisfying conclusion, they have their homecoming. For good readers. Also: *Dicey's Song,* about the same family, and *Jackaroo.*

Nobody's Family Is Going to Change by Louise Fitzhugh. Farrar, Straus and Giroux, 1974. A girl who wants to be a lawyer and a boy who wants to be a dancer star in a quite wonderful book about the hopes and dreams of eleven-year-olds and about "inner progress before outer progress." Never preachy. Basis for the musical *The Tap Dance Kid.* Also: *Harriet the Spy.* Harper & Row, 1964.

Nothing's Fair in Fifth Grade by Barte De Clements. Viking, 1981. When grossly fat Elsie comes into the fifth grade, the students react with taunts and hostility. Elsie is made more miserable and antisocial than she was already. But Jenny, the narrator of the story, keeps her eyes open and learns a few things. With her new knowledge she is able to help Elsie curb her appetite and begin to go to work on her problems. During this interchange the selfhood of both girls is enhanced.

Simon by Molly Cone. Houghton Mifflin, 1970. A Walter Mitty–like fantasy life accompanies Simon's actual experiences until he has no further need for fantasy. A book full of insights and marked by a humaneness that is unusually appealing. Spells out the loneliness kids this age feel even with loving parents.

Sounder by William Armstrong; illustrated by James Barkley. Harper & Row, 1969. A poor black sharecropper and his family are caught in a cycle of poverty that leads the father to steal and deprives the family of his presence. Both Sounder, the great coon dog, and his master are wounded and share a similar sad fate. The beauty of the book lies in its rich rendering of the boy, who, in spite of the heartbreak around him, manages to cope and to grow.

Superfudge by Judy Blume. Dutton, 1980. Peter is already burdened by a younger brother when his family announces that there is another baby on the way. With her characteristic ear for family dialogue, Judy Blume takes the reader through a fifth-grader's life and relationships, especially that time when he comes to grips with the reality of his parents' sexuality. Dads, Moms, Grandmas, and little brothers and sisters all come under the author's loving and witty magnifying glass. Ten-year-olds who are average readers will manage this one nicely, and be enriched by its careful rendering of the fun and pain of finding one's way in a family.

The Two Thousand Pound Goldfish by Betsy Byars. Harper & Row, 1982. A boy invents a horror script about a two-thousand-pound goldfish. The ongoing story he works on helps to sustain him as he lives through abandonment by his mother and the illness of his grandmother. The author's perception about the boy's use of the fantasy script to both distract and save himself is something children will understand.

The Unmaking of Rabbit by Constance Greene. Viking, 1973. A warmly appealing account of how a boy not only discards the hated nickname Rabbit, but also develops new insights about himself and his problems.

Words by Heart by Ouida Sebestyen. Little, Brown, 1980. A young black girl, driven by a hunger for books and learning, memorizes most of the Bible. This is a story about finding

oneself in a world of prejudice and remaining compassionate and loving, true to the words learned "by heart."

Zeely by Virginia Hamilton. Macmillan, 1967. Eleven-year-old
Geeder Perry meets Zeely Taber, six-and-a-half-feet tall
and beautiful as a Watutsi queen. In fact, she may be a
Watutsi queen, Geeder decides. Her made-up story has
consequences. In her trip back from fantasy Geeder learns
how to separate the real from the imaginary and finds a true
heroine in the process of finding herself. Also: *M. C. Higgins
the Great.* Macmillan, 1974.

Breaking Away and Coping

In many cultures puberty requires a test of fitness. In Australia
young people of the aboriginal tribes take a "walkabout" in
which they go into the wilderness and try to survive, armed only
with a weapon. Native American tribes had similar rites, as did
other ancient peoples. It may be that these ceremonies, with
their recognition of the onset of adult responsibility, in some
way tap into a developmental need of human beings. Certainly
young people of today are drawn to books that are about some
sort of test of the ability of a person close to their age, trying to
survive, usually in a hostile or elemental environment. Books
like *My Side of the Mountain* by Jean George speak eloquently to
this theme.

Call It Courage by Armstrong Sperry. Macmillan, 1968. Mafatu
has always been afraid of the sea. How he meets the challenge to his manhood and conquers his fear forms a gripping tale of courage that will appeal to youngsters this age.

The Cay by Theodore Taylor. Doubleday, 1969. Phillip is thrust
into a dependent relationship with a black man when the
two of them are cast upon a Caribbean island as the result
of a shipwreck. Slowly the boy learns to value people on a
basis other than race. A look at prejudice that will make a
real impression.

From the Mixed-up Files of Mrs. Basil Frankweiler by E. L. Konigs-
burg. Atheneum, 1968. You could say this is the urban
version of the native "walkabout." When Claudia Kincaid
decides to leave home and family, she does it in style—and

with her brother Jamie for company. The two runaways settle in at the Metropolitan Museum of Art where a bath in the elegant museum fountain is just one of the ways to "make do." While these precocious and intriguing kids are in hiding, they stumble on an artistic mystery and stay in the museum long enough to solve it. Funny and yet serious, this is a good choice for a youngster who has been to the museum—or one who hasn't.

Island of the Blue Dolphins by Scott O'Dell. Houghton Mifflin, 1960. This book is based on the true experiences of a young woman in the 1800s. Karana, the girl, is a native of the islands off the coast of California. She is marooned when she leaves the ship carrying her and her people from the island and swims to shore to find her younger brother. The subsequent death of her brother forces on her a totally solitary struggle for survival, plagued by wild dogs, visits from Aleutian otter hunters, and a series of natural disasters that forces her to use all the skills passed down to her by her hunter-gatherer forebears. There's an almost mythic quality to Karana's lonely "walkabout." A lovely book, and a Newbery winner.

Julie of the Wolves by Jean George. Harper & Row, 1973. This novel, which won the 1973 Newbery award, is also about survival and coming of age. It chronicles a thirteen-year-old Eskimo girl's decision to get away from a forced marriage and to fulfill her dream of living in San Francisco with her pen pal. Making her way across the tundra, she establishes a lifesaving friendship with a pack of wolves, and meets once again the father she thought was dead. There's almost unbearable sadness in part of this story. But in the end, Julie is able to come to terms with both her own culture and her future. The descriptions of animal life and the sense of place are masterfully done, and the universality of its message sets this book apart.

My Side of the Mountain by Jean George. Dutton, 1959. Teenage Sam Gribley is looking for his roots in the form of land abandoned by his forebears. The Gribley land sits in a remote part of the Catskills and it is to this place that Sam goes, determined to live out a year in his ancestral acres as a mountain boy. Children will be delighted with his supportive family, who beam on this venture. Off he goes, and the adventures of his year and the wild creatures he meets living off the land make this a book with special appeal for nature lovers. It's also, incidentally, full of useful information on wild foods, survival techniques, and how-to. Look for the movie, too. One of the best by a noted author of books about the outdoors.

A Year in the Life of Rosie Bernard by Barbara Brenner. Harper & Row, 1971. Rosie's mother has died and she goes to live with her grandparents. Her spunky and sometimes hilarious struggle with a new school, her mixed feelings about her dual religious heritage, and her need to come to terms with a stepmother when her father remarries are all components of growing up with which many children will be familiar.

Contemporary Life

Books that mirror their lives and thoughts are always of interest to children, but perhaps never more so than as they move toward adolescence. These books about contemporary life are all distinguished by literary merit and a variety of subject matter of interest to ten- to twelve-year-olds.

Ace Hits the Big Time by Barbara Beasley Murphy. Delacorte, 1982. Here are gangs and would-be gangs on New York's west side, in a fast-moving story full of suspense, surprise, and comedy.

Al(exandra) the Great by Constance Greene. Viking, 1982. Here's a perfect example of a book for "tens" that tells about other family styles (divorce, stepfamily) in a more or less optimistic way. Values-packed, one book about Al will develop a craving for another. Fortunately, the craving can be satisfied with *A Girl Called Al* and others in the series.

Anastasia Krupnik by Lois Lowry. Houghton Mifflin, 1979. Every youngster should meet Anastasia, a ten-year-old whose life mirrors the joys and sorrows of family life. In this first novel about Anastasia, she grows to understand the older generation (her grandmother) and finds the maturity to accept a new generation (a baby brother). It's all wrapped in a delightful package and we promise that reading Anastasia is like eating peanuts. Luckily, there are other Anastasia books.

Arthur, for the Very First Time by Patricia MacLachlan; illustrated by Lloyd Bloom. Harper & Row, 1980. Youngsters will love the adults and the kids in this fresh and humorous book. They'll also pick up some insightful clues to both animal and human behavior. By an author who always offers something original.

The Best Christmas Pageant Ever by Barbara Robinson. Harper & Row, 1972. The Herdmans may be "the worst kids in the history of the world," but their antics at the Christmas pageant turn into one of the funniest books for young people we've ever read. Not only is it funny, it's wise too. Give it as a gift for Christmas, Chanukah, or any other time of the year.

A Book for Jodan by Marcia Newfield. Atheneum, 1975. Jodan's father and mother split up and the reader gets to experience it. This is already a major first, since most separations in children's books happen offstage. We live through Jodan's cycle of guilt, anger, and frustrations. Finally, her security begins to be rebuilt when her father makes for her a quite marvelous "book" that is reproduced in the back of this one and is sure to make any child feel good about himself and parent. This book has a wide age range—could be read to a child of seven and independent readers up to eleven or even twelve will get something out of it.

The Buffalo Nickels Blues Band by Judie Angell. Bradbury, 1982. An engrossing tale of an interesting assortment of sixth graders—black and white—who make a success of their band.

A Bundle of Sticks by Paul Rhoads Mauser; illustrated by Gail Owens. Atheneum, 1982. Ten to twelve seems to be the age when bullying runs rampant. In this story the boy who is being bullied goes to a martial arts school. Here he learns techniques so he can defend himself. But he also learns a philosophy that allows him to handle conflict in a new way.

Child of the Morning by Barbara Corcoran. Atheneum, 1982. Susan loves dancing. But she has a problem with recurrent spells of dizziness after a slight accident. The dizzy spells don't go away, and she finally is diagnosed as an epileptic.

Children who have had a physical problem or know someone who has had one will appreciate this well-told story.

Come Sing, Jimmy Jo by Katherine Paterson. Lodestar Books/Dut-
ton, 1985. Eleven-year-old James Johnson comes from a
family of country singers. When the family's new agent
accidentally hears James sing, he is thrust into a new life as
part of the group. He must change his name to Jimmy Jo,
conquer his shyness, and above all, leave his beloved
Grandma and home to go on the road. It's an education
both for him and the reader. The music of this wonderful
book will linger long after you close its pages. How we
actually hear that singing is part of the magic this author is
a master at conjuring.

Confessions of a Prime Time Kid by Mark Jonathan Harris. Lothrop,
Lee and Shepard, 1985. Kids often wonder what it would
be like to be rich and famous. In this interesting and believable story, thirteen-year-old Margaret O'Brien Muldaur
writes her memoirs and tells it like it is. Meg is a TV super-
star, caught up in the high-powered world of options, resi-
dents, and ratings. The family dynamics are great—brother
Kelly's attempt to break into TV; Howie's struggle to help
stagestruck youngsters; and the father's belated attempts to
get to know his daughter. All well done.

Conrad's War by Andrew Davies. Crown, 1978. Something different—a kids' book written by a playwright. This may account
for the "you are there" dialogue in this offbeat book about
a boy at war with his parents—and the world. A witty adventure that kids will both laugh at and be sobered by.

Dear Lovey Hart, I Am Desperate by Ellen Conford. Little, Brown,
1975. Carrie takes on the advice column for her school
newspaper and discovers that there are many real problems
out there. This is a meaningful novel about how other
young people feel about a variety of issues. Also: *And This
Is Laura*. Little, Brown, 1977.

Dorp Dead by Julia Cunningham. Pantheon, 1965. Gilly is a wiry
orphan with one friend, a dog named Mash. The story begins when Gilly is apprenticed to Mr. Kobalt, the town
eccentric. Her harrowing adventures in his service and her
ultimate escape are spun out in a way to satisfy completely

this age group's thirst for adventure. Also: *Burnish Me Bright.* Pantheon, 1970.

Earthquake by Matt Christopher; illustrated by Ted Lewin. Little, Brown, 1975. A boy runs away and encounters many hazards, including an earthquake. What makes this one interesting is the boy, who is identified as a slower learner. Short chapters make this a less intimidating book for younger or reluctant readers. Also: *The Fox Steals Home.*

The Egypt Game by Zilpha Wheatley Snyder. Atheneum, 1976. A quirky new girl in town and an imaginative play based on the sixth grade's study of Egypt release much drama. But when the oracle starts getting out of hand, it's time to analyze what's happening. Authentic in feeling, this book is by an author who obviously knows kids this age.

Family Secrets by Susan Shreve; illustrated by Richard Cuffari. Knopf, 1978. A wonderfully humane and truthful book, so deftly written that the reader believes he/she is hearing a real boy speak of his secret thoughts and upsetting experiences. These short, gripping vignettes give children an absorbing model for living. The illustrations match the compassionate text.

The Hocus-Pocus Dilemma by Pat Kibbe; illustrated by Dan Jones. Knopf, 1978. A very funny account of a family's encounters with the occult, as told by the youngest daughter, B. J., would-be magic-maker. Kibbe's family is totally believable, as well as pleasantly zany. Also: *My Mother the Mayor— Maybe.* Knopf, 1982.

Home Is Where Your Feet Are Standing by Patricia Windsor. Harper & Row, 1975. Ten-year-old Colin is always alert to the "scent of possibilities." And so when odd things start happening in the English cottage where he and his American family are living, he decides he has something called "poltergeist disease." This book will suit readers looking for offbeat humor and sensitive to an original style.

How to Eat Fried Worms by Thomas Rockwell; illustrated by Emily McCully. Watts, 1973. Billy bets his friend that he can eat fifteen worms. In a *yuck!* situation that will tickle every ten-year-old's appetite for gross humor, Billy tries to get them down. This is a very popular book among this age group, and for good reason. It's right on the mark situation-wise, and the kids are *real.*

The Incline by William Mayne. Dutton, 1972. The incline is the railroad that takes the stones from the quarry up the mountain. In this taut and symbolic novel it is also the difficult road toward adulthood traveled by Mason Ross. Set in the 1900s in England, *The Incline* is for mature readers who enjoy books of substance. Also: *Pig in the Middle.* Dutton, 1967.

It Can't Hurt Forever by Marilyn Singer; illustrated by Leigh Grant. Harper & Row, 1978. Eleven-year-old Ellie has a heart problem that requires an operation. The author manages to make a novel about such a life situation interesting, informative, and not too heavy. Empathy is what this one is about.

It's Not the End of the World by Judy Blume. Bradbury, 1972. As usual, Judy Blume "tells it like it is." In this case, it's divorce. With Judy's help, children learn that it's not necessarily the end of the world.

Last Was Lloyd by Doris Buchanan Smith. Viking, 1981. Lloyd is fat. He can't run and he has no friends. And his mother babies him. But before this satisfyingly plotted novel is finished, readers of every shape and size will be rooting for Lloyd in his battle for maturity and control of his life. Hooks in beautifully with children's push toward independence and their preoccupation with their appearance.

Listen, Cat by Emily Neville. Harper & Row, 1963. New York City is the setting, but Dave Mitchell's fourteen-year-old experiences will be familiar to youngsters all over the country. His affection for a stray tom cat, his shy friendship with a girl, and his mixed feelings about his father are all on target.

The Loner by Esther Weir. David McKay, 1963. A picture of a very different sort of life, one that many children will never see. A boy is alone, without family or friends. He is a crop-picker, a migrant worker who follows the seasons. Abandoned by his latest set of exploiters, he is found by a woman who is a sheepherder. An uneasy friendship develops between the two. The novel is about how they come to trust each other, and how the boy ultimately proves himself to the woman and to himself. This is not a particularly upbeat book, but it is one of true grit.

The Moves Make the Man by Bruce Brooks. Harper & Row, 1984. When Jerome, the black narrator of this unusual first novel, sees Bix, the incredible baseball player, the issue seems to be sports. Being better than the white boy is Jerome's fantasy and he works at it. But when he finally meets Bix, everything changes. Basketball is the metaphor here for a brilliant show of many real life issues, and the author keeps the ball in play beautifully as he bounces among them.

The Night Swimmers by Betsy Byars. Delacorte, 1980. Their mother is dead and Retta has difficulties as person in charge of her two young brothers. Convincing dialogue and interactions make this a vivid story, alive with the sound of children's real voices in an unusual setting. Also: *Cracker Jackson,* Viking, 1985.

Nobody's Baby Now by Carol Lea Benjamin. Macmillan, 1984. An overweight girl acquires a better self-image through her relationship with her depressed grandmother.

The Outsiders by S. E. Hinton. Viking, 1967. The "greasers" battle their affluent enemies and some serious repercussions follow. The scenario is somewhat reminiscent of *West Side Story.* It's a real favorite among eleven- and twelve-year-olds.

The Preacher's Kid by Rose Blue; illustrated by Ted Lewis. Watts, 1975. This is an absorbing story of racial prejudice centered on the problems a white minister and his family face in their community. Written with clarity and compassion.

A Ring of Endless Light by Madeleine L'Engle. Farrar, Straus and Giroux, 1980. An absorbing realistic novel, fourth in a series about friends, family, dolphins, and death. No condescension here in the author's approach to life's serious questions. Thoroughly contemporary and moving.

Robbie and the Leap Year Blues by Norma Klein. Dial, 1981. Eleven-year-old Robbie has a lot to cope with. There's taking care of his divorced mother, and school, and sports, and adjusting to his father's new girlfriend. And now on top of it all there are girls! And they're talking *marriage!* Not too heavy and probably just right for tens and elevens.

The Secret Life of the Underwear Champ by Betty Miles; illustrated by Dan Jones. Knopf, 1981. Larry tries to keep his under-wear-modeling TV job a secret from the rest of the baseball team! A very funny book that will delight readers. Also: *Sink or Swim.*

The Summer of the Swans by Betsy Byars. Viking, 1971. A Newbery Award book that accurately reflects the many moods of emerging adolescence. A thirteen-year-old girl fears that her mentally handicapped younger brother is lost. A boy whom she has disliked comes to her aid.

Thirteen Ways to Sink a Sub by Jamie Gilson; illustrated by Linda Strauss Edwards. Lothrop, Lee and Shepard, 1982. It's a caper a minute when the fourth grade gets a "sub." Point scores between class and substitute teacher seesaw back and forth, but the book itself is a winner.

The Toothpaste Millionaire by Jean Merrill; illustrated by Jan Palmer. Houghton Mifflin, 1974. Rufus becomes a million-aire when he decides to sell homemade toothpaste far below the price of the commercial stuff. But being a million-aire is not all glitter and glow. The red tape starts to en-velop his enterprise. Preteens will get a vicarious thrill as Rufus takes on the commercial establishment in the "tooth-paste war." A Horatio Alger story with a humorous twist.

What I Really Think of You by M. E. Kerr. Harper & Row, 1981. For good readers, here's the world of the Pentecostal taber-nacle, the preacher's Sunday morning TV shows, and the lives of young Opal and Jesse—brilliantly revealed through M. E. Kerr's usual sharp perception and skillful dialogue. Also: *Dinky Hocker Shoots Smack,* Harper & Row, 1972. *Is That You, Miss Blue?* Harper & Row, 1975.

Body Language

Kids of ten and up are powerfully aware of their growing bodies and yearning to understand them. As they approach puberty, both girls and boys become fascinated by the subjects of men-struation, childbirth, and other manifestations of sexuality and reproduction. Even if they already know the facts, they want to read and know more. They go over and over the same territory, mining it for any information that will help explain to them their new feelings and how to handle them.

The sexual curiosity of ten- to twelve-year-olds is normal—and important. It's one way humans prepare themselves for mature sexual identification. Kids may giggle and wisecrack about sex, but, in fact, they are working hard to put together the facts and the feelings. They want to read not only what sex and love is all about but what people feel and do about it.

It would be ideal if children could put sex and love in perspective with all the best and most appropriate information. But in a world where the nearest adult porno palace may be around the corner, and where TV offers steamy how-to lessons in every sexual practice, it's unrealistic to think we can shelter ten- to twelve-year-olds from information we'd rather they didn't have. What we *can* do is to help make good books like the following list available and be there ourselves for questions and discussion.

Are You There, God?—It's Me, Margaret by Judy Blume. Bradbury, 1970. Margaret is a typical suburban eleven-year-old, neither bizarre nor tragic. Not hers the high drama of rape, alcoholism, terminal disease, or a broken family. Her concerns are, quite simply, with growing up. She worries about when she will develop a bosom and begin to menstruate. She is concerned with fitting in with her peers, and she is reevaluating loyalty, empathy, friendship, and family feeling.

> Judy Blume has become something of a cult figure among the young, because she so accurately homes in on their concerns, and in bringing them into the open helps to sort them out. This book, one of her earlier works, is distinguished by its taste as well as its honesty. Few parents have to urge a boy or girl ten to twelve to read Judy Blume. It's a rite of passage, and for good reason.

Body Sense, Body Nonsense by Seymour Simon; illustrated by Dennis Kendrick. Lippincott, 1982. A well-known science educator and author looks at questions children have about their bodies and bodily health. He explains some, debunks others in a sort of guessing game format that readers of this age will enjoy.

Love and Sex in Plain Language by Eric Johnson. Harper & Row, 1977. Just what the title implies—a refreshingly frank discussion about sex that may put to rest some of preteens' anxieties and questions.

Oh, Boy! Babies! by Alison Cragin and Jane Laurence Mali; photos by Katrina Thomas. Little, Brown, 1981. This is officially an adult book, but one so special that we think youngsters will find it absorbing and enriching. The excellent photos and natural speech and action of the boys in the book will spellbind their peers and enlarge their knowledge of babies as fascinating human beings.

Philip Hall Likes Me, I Reckon Maybe by Bette Greene; illustrated by Charles Lilly. Dial, 1974. An on-again, off-again crush, typical of this age, is portrayed with telling effect, as is the ambivalence of boys as they confront gang disapproval for friendship with a girl.

Sticks and Stones by Lynn Hall. Follett, 1972. A sensitive portrayal of a seventeen-year-old's discovery of a homosexual friendship and of the destructive force of community prejudice. Told with quiet compassion and recognition that love comes in many ways.

A Very Touchy Subject by Todd Strasser. Delacorte, 1985. This book by a young author believably describes how it is for boys dealing with growing up and sexual feelings.

What Makes Me Feel This Way? Growing up with Human Emotions by Eda LeShan. Macmillan, 1972. A good introduction to understanding our feelings, explained in everyday language, with lots of anecdotal stories to illustrate a range of emotions.

Fantasy

Ten- to twelve-year-olds may be caught up with the real world, but they still fantasize. And they enjoy books of fantasy to take them out of themselves and into other times and places. Reading fantasy is to older children what fantasy play is to the young child. Many psychologists feel that this continuing exercise of the imagination is one of the keys to problem-solving skills in later life. Even if this were not so, the truth is that fantasy books are a form of reading that seems to be enjoyed by everyone.

Some children of this age are ready for the big leaps—into *The Hobbit* by J. R. R. Tolkien or *Mrs. Frisby and the Rats of NIMH* by Robert O'Brien. Others want to stick with somewhat simpler fantasy plots like *The Indian in the Cupboard* by Lynn Reid Banks or the *Oz* series by Frank Baum. But whether they like their fantasy simple or complex, historical, contemporary, or futuristic, somewhere they should be exposed to what someone has referred to as "the fairy tales of puberty."

We've already mentioned the modern classic fantasy of self-realization, *Tuck Everlasting.* Here are some other fantasies we think should not be missed.

Abel's Island by William Steig. Farrar, Straus and Giroux, 1976. If kids haven't read this one by the time they're ten, by all means introduce them. A charming, meaningful tale about a mouse marooned on a desert island who learns about what it means to cope.

Alice's Adventures in Wonderland by Lewis Carroll; drawings by Sir John Tenniel. St. Martin's, 1977. Some librarians regard Alice as an acquired taste. But we think ten- and eleven-year-olds are mature enough to appreciate some of the satire and humor in this charming classic. Read it aloud for the joy of the language!

Amy's Eyes by Richard Kennedy; illustrated by Richard Egielski. Harper & Row, 1985. The story of an orphan girl who turns into a doll and of her sea captain "brother" who is a doll turned human. No description of the admittedly fantastic plot can do justice to this author's way with words. So richly evocative the book may well be a new classic. And the illustrations by Richard Egielski are a perfect match. Also: *Inside My Feet: The Story of a Giant* illustrated by Ron Himler. Harper & Row, 1979.

Beauty: A Retelling of the Story of Beauty and the Beast by Robin McKinley. Harper & Row, 1978. A retelling of the story that reinvests it with significance and wonder and points up the many issues inherent in the original—greed and vanity as well as decency and love. Also: *The Blue Sword.* Greenwillow, 1982. A girl leading a sheltered life in a mythical colony is kidnapped by a native king with magical powers and discovers that she has magic of her own.

The Borrowers Afloat by Mary Norton; illustrated by Beth and Joe Krush. Harcourt, 1959. Children may have already met these little people in *The Borrowers.* This sequel tells how Pod and friends take to the water in search of a new home.

Charlotte's Web by E. B. White. Harper & Row, 1952. The gentle fantasy about a girl of independence and a spider of equal spirit. For everyone, and especially delightful when read aloud.

Dragon's Blood by Jane Yolen. Delacorte, 1984. A young man named Jakkin trains a dragon for gladiatorial combat in another time and place. A girl named Akki aids and abets him. Also the sequel, *Heart's Blood.* Delacorte, 1984. More fantastic adventures of the boy Jakkin and the girl Akki.

Earthfasts by William Mayne. Dutton, 1967. Two boys meet an eighteenth century drummer boy who has arisen from the earth with a strange candle that triggers a series of odd events.

The Fledgling by Jane Langton. Harper & Row, 1980. Lonely Georgie Hall dreams of flying. When no one in her family understands her yearning, she goes to look for the expert practitioners of the art—the Canada Geese. She meets the Goose Prince, a figment of her imagination. Or maybe not. The reader never knows, as dream and reality flow into one another. A book to read in a hammock on a summer's day.

Freaky Friday by Mary Rodgers. Harper & Row, 1972. A girl is magically transformed for a day into her own mother. The results of this contemporary fantasy are both hilarious and instructive. Also: *A Billion for Boris.* Harper and Row, 1974.

Hemi: A Mule by Barbara Brenner; illustrated by Winslow Higgenbottom. Harper & Row, 1973. An amusing, wise story of a determined mule's search for his friend, a young black boy who has gone off to agricultural college. Hemi's search takes him across the country, through adventures both dangerous and humorous, before the two are reunited.

The Indian in the Cupboard by Lynne Reid Banks. Doubleday,

1981. A boy gets a three-inch-high wooden Indian as a birthday present. When the tiny Indian comes to life, the boy becomes deeply involved in his future. A story that manages to be both moving and believable.

The Lion, the Witch, and the Wardrobe by C. S. Lewis. Macmillan, 1951. Four English children step through a magical wardrobe into the enchanted land of Narnia, where they meet the Lion King Aslan and a wicked White Witch, who manages to delude one of their band into thinking she is on their side. This misconception has grave consequences for all the children, and one new friend is asked to sacrifice his life for them. This classic tale is one of a series called *The Chronicles of Narnia.* Like the other "bests" in the fantasy genre, this one is laced with moral choices clearly translatable to our own time and place. Good for reading aloud as a family as well as being savored privately by a ten-year-old or older child.

Mrs. Frisby and the Rats of NIMH by Robert O'Brien. Atheneum, 1971. A group of superintelligent rats escape from a medical laboratory to help a family of mice. Their devotion and empathy form a modern moral tale that speaks to contemporary issues far beyond animal rights.

The Phantom Tollbooth by Norton Juster; illustrated by Jules Feiffer. Random House, 1961. A trip to a "Land Beyond," but with a difference. This time the boy Milo travels through a magical tollgate, where he and his friends leave Reality, bring back Rhyme and Reason, and altogether have a romp. A modern allegory.

Playing Beatie Bow by Ruth Park. Atheneum, 1982. A fantasy which takes place Down Under, where 14-year-old Abigail glimpses a strange girl playing a game and follows her into the Australia of a hundred years ago. Another and very different way of handling the "time warp" theme, with a little dollop of romance that will appeal to elevens and twelves.

Rabbit Hill by Robert Lawson. Viking, 1944. If somehow a child missed this one before, it's worth looking at now. A map and the author's evocative words conjure a world of moles and toads, mice and rabbits who present a beautiful argument for animals and people living in harmony.

The Return of the Twelves by Pauline Clarke. Coward, McCann, 1963. An adventure of little people who are toy soldiers that once lived in the Brontë house. Max, an eight-year-old, discovers that they have lives of their own and would like to go back where they came from.

Stuart Little by E. B. White. Harper & Row, 1945. Who can believe in a mouse born of human parents? Everyone, when the author is E. B. White and when the tender friendships are so moving.

Tom's Midnight Garden by Philippa Pearce. Lippincott, 1958. Tom is sent away from home because of a temporary family crisis. In his new setting, an old house that his aunt and uncle are renting, he stumbles on a way to go back in time and see the garden of the house and its former occupants as they once were. His nights in the garden become the focus of his stay with the relatives and of his letters to his brother. A surprise ending and a link between past and present make for a satisfying story.

The Twenty-one Balloons by William Pene Du Bois. Viking, 1947. Professor Sherman decides in his retirement to travel around the world by balloon. It's a blast all the way, including a trip to Krakatoa and some earthshaking adventures. A delightful spoof, but the philosophy in these balloons is by no means all hot air! A Newbery Award winner.

Wind in the Willows by Kenneth Grahame; illustrated by Ernest Shepard. Scribner's, Rev. Ed. 1933 (original 1908). A gentle fantasy about a mole and friends who live on a river bank and think like real folks. There are many editions, but we like this original the best.

Wingman written and illustrated by Manus Pinkwater. Dodd, Mead, 1975. Donald Chen (Chen Chi-Wing at home) is the only Chinese-American kid in PS 132. And they're making his life miserable. For relief he retreats into his comic books. One day as he is reading, he conjures Wingman, an armored figment of his imagination. Through his fantasy hero, he is able to both cope with prejudice and to begin to exercise his creativity in school. A lovely, upbeat tale told in simple, short chapters that are easy enough for a ten-year-old to read, yet the ideas are rich with significance for a twelve- or even thirteen-year-old to enjoy.

A Wizard of Earthsea by Ursula LeGuin. Parnassus Press, 1968. Ged, a student wizard, calls up a wizard from the place of the dead. All about a boy coming of age, a quest, dragons, and evil in a mythical land created by a skillful author.

The Wizard of Oz (and others in the series) by L. Frank Baum; illustrated by Evelyn Copelman. Grosset & Dunlap, 1956. The classic tales introduced to many in this generation and the previous one by Judy Garland, Ray Bolger, and Metro-Goldwyn-Mayer. Still fresh and appealing and certainly worth a read.

The Wonderful Flight to the Mushroom Planet by Eleanor Cameron; illustrated by Robert Henneberger. Little, Brown, 1954. A zany professor of astrophysics invites two inventive boys to go on a light-hearted trip to another planet. Also: *Stowaway to the Mushroom Planet.* Little, Brown, 1956.

Myth, Legend, and Folktale

At this age many children begin to be drawn to myth and legend —the days of King Arthur, the Greek heroes and heroines, stories from the Bible. In fact, the clear moral and ethical tone of myths and legends satisfies the developmental need of youngsters ten to twelve to probe values. At the same time legends speak to their yearning for romance.

Aesop's Fables by Fritz Kredel. Grosset, 1963. *The Fox and the Grapes* and other wonderful tales, each with a moral not lost on this age group.

Beginnings: Creation Myths of the World by Penelope Farmer; illustrated by Antonio Frasconi. Atheneum, 1979. More than eighty stories of creation, death, and the end of the world, garnered from all over the globe and presented with handsome woodcuts. Children will be fascinated by the likenesses and differences among cultures.

Book of Greek Myths by Ingri and Edgar D'Aulaire. Doubleday, 1972. Widely acknowledged as one of the best collections for children this age, and a great introduction to the Greeks.

The Book of Three by Lloyd Alexander. Holt, 1964. This fantasy, based on Welsh legend, pits the boy Taran, Assistant Pig-Keeper, against an array of villains that equals any Steven Spielberg flick. But the heroes and heroines are in evidence, too. Anyone, child or adult, with a taste for adventure will enjoy thoroughly Taran's initiation into the real meaning of heroism. This is the first book of a series called *The Prydain Chronicles,* which includes *The Black Cauldron* (on which the movie was based). Also: *Westmark,* Dutton, 1981; and *Time Cat,* Holt, 1973.

The Children's Bible from the Good News Bible in Today's English Version illustrated by Guido Bertello. Collins, 1978. Both the Old and the New Testament stories are presented clearly, with illustrations, maps, and an index.

Fairy Tales of Hans Christian Andersen edited by Bryan Holme; illustrated by Kay Nielsen. Viking, 1981. The classic stories of Andersen, illustrated by an outstanding artist of the early twentieth century.

The Hobbit by J. R. R. Tolkien. Houghton Mifflin, 1938. A tale of dragons, treasure, and quests, about a dwarflike creature and the magical world he inhabits. Not every child's taste, but those who love Tolkien are committed to the cult.

I, Heracles by Elizabeth Silverthorne. Abingdon Press, 1978. An introduction to mythology through Heracles, whose first-person account of his remarkable feats makes it seem as if you are there. Maps help make it clear.

Legend Days by Jamake Highwater. Harper & Row, 1984. An Indian girl's struggle for selfhood and her conflict between the old and the new ways. Part 1 of *The Ghost Horse* cycle.

Mean Jake and the Devils by William H. Hooks. Pictures by Dirk Zimmer. Dial, 1981. The author draws on the folktales he heard growing up in the South to create a "devilish" family that will make children giggle and shiver by turns. Short chapters make easier reading for reluctant older readers as well as for adventurous younger ones.

The People Could Fly: American Black Folk Tales by Virginia Hamilton; illustrated by Leo and Diane Dillon. Knopf, 1985. A retelling of folktales from several sources, with meaty comments and notes that add another dimension to old favorites like Br'er Rabbit. Illustrations by two award-winning illustrators.

Robin Hood: His Life and Legend by Bernard Miles; illustrated by Victor Ambrus. Rand McNally, 1979. The inside story of Robin Hood, enriched by historical detail and bold, swashbuckling illustrations. This version has a Maid Marian that *Ms.* would approve of.

Seasons of Splendor: Tales, Myths and Legends of India by Madhur Jaffrey; illustrated by Michael Forman. Atheneum, 1985. The author leads the reader through the Hindu year with a series of stories attached to various festivals. For good readers and/or twelves and over.

Tales of Pan by Mordicai Gerstein. Harper & Row, 1986. What better way to get your first taste of the Greeks than through Mordicai Gerstein's light-hearted story of *Pan*? The author's irreverent fun does not detract, but in fact adds to, the story of the folks on Mount Olympus.

Where the Buffaloes Begin by Olaf Baker; drawings by Stephen Gammell. Warne, 1982. Little Wolf, age ten, sees the mighty buffaloes come crowding out of the lake in this Native American legend, magnificently illustrated.

The Wizard Children of Finn by Mary Tannen. Knopf, 1981. An enormously popular tale of an enchanted boy who makes friends with a brother and sister. The three are spirited back through time to ancient Ireland. Based on an ancient legend.

Zlateh the Goat and Other Stories by Isaac Bashevis Singer. Harper & Row, 1966. Seven tales out of middle European daily life that have a flavor all their own.

· · ·

Science Fiction, Mystery, and the Supernatural

Beloved Benjamin Is Waiting by Jean Karl. Dutton, 1978. When Lucinda's mother and father abandon her, she goes to live in a cemetery, and there makes contact with an alien being communicating from inside the statue of a dead boy.

The Dark Is Rising by Susan Cooper. Atheneum, 1973. Will Stanton begins a dark adventure on his eleventh birthday when he discovers that he is the last of the Old Ones, immortals dedicated to fighting the forces of evil.

A Deadly Game of Magic by Joan Lowery Nixon. Harcourt, 1983. A girl and her friends find themselves trapped in a dangerous game with a murderous magician whose motivations are shrouded in mystery. Good for goose bumps.

A Gift of Magic by Lois Duncan. Little, Brown, 1971. A brooding mansion that serves as a girls' school, a weird headmistress, and some students with ESP create a setting marvelously chilling. Duncan is popular with this age group, and for good reason: she is a high priestess of the supernatural. Also: *Stranger with My Face,* Little, Brown, 1981 and *Down a Dark Hall,* Little, Brown, 1974.

The Ghost of Thomas Kempe by Penelope Lively; illustrated by Anthony Maitland. Dutton, 1973. Who or what is responsible for the odd happenings in James's new home? The ghost of a seventeenth-century sorcerer emerges and tries to make the boy his apprentice. Amusing.

Ghosts I Have Been by Richard Peck. Viking, 1975. It's 1913 in the Midwest. A quartet of characters share daring adventures, including exorcising a ghost. Also: *The Ghost Belonged to Me.* Spooky and funny.

The Ghosts of Departure Point by Eve Bunting. Lippincott, 1982. A group of teenagers killed in fatal auto accidents comes back as ghosts to haunt the living. Surprise ending.

House with a Clock in Its Walls by John Bellairs. Dial, 1973. An orphaned boy, a house with a tick, and both evil and good wizards. The characters in this book are most skillfully drawn; the klutzy boy will win hearts.

Long After Midnight by Ray Bradbury. Bantam, 1976. This fine collection of stories by a gifted science-fiction writer explores a variety of subjects. In one, two drifters in space search through the dead cities of Mars for a fabled Blue Bottle. In another, a man journeys back into the past to commit the perfect crime of revenge. Good for reading aloud and a perfect "pocket" book to take on a trip. Also: *Dandelion Wine*, Bantam, 1969.

Mystery of the Plumed Serpent by Barbara Brenner; illustrated by Blanche Sims. Knopf, 1980. Elena and Michael Garcia are twins who have keen noses for mystery. The clues they discover lead them to ancient Mexican treasure. Children will be caught up in this fast-paced mystery that is well researched, well written.

Mystery on Bleecker Street by William Hooks. Knopf, 1980. A delightful caper of an odd couple, young Chase and his Gray Panther friend Babette. Lots of suspense, mystery, and humor spice this fast-paced yarn for middle years children not quite ready for fat novels.

No Such Thing As a Witch by Ruth Chew. Hastings House, 1980. Nora and her brothers are sure the lady next door is a witch. And she certainly acts like one. But in this fast-paced, funny, easy-to-read story enchantment is wrought with a plate of fudge and a handful of exotic animals. Children will love the playful, spirited writing in this popular series. Also: *What the Witch Left* and others.

The Westing Game by Ellen Raskin. Dutton, 1978. An eccentric millionaire dies and leaves a peculiar group of heirs to uncover certain circumstances before they can claim the inheritance. The intriguing component of this mystery is its "puzzle" quality.

White Mountains by John Christopher. Macmillan, 1967. Three children form a revolutionary cadre against alien invaders who are dominating earth.

Wild Jack by John Christopher. Macmillan, 1974. A young man on the outs with the government of the twenty-third century meets an outlaw band run by a sci-fi Robin Hood.

A Wrinkle in Time by Madeleine L'Engle. Farrar, Straus and Giroux, 1962. Two children search for their missing scientist father in a time warp and are subjected to great danger. The dialogue is superb. The humor and the rich weave of plot and idea made this a Newbery book in the year of its publication. But it is as good today as when the previous generation enjoyed it. A timeless wonder of a book.

Other Times, Other Places

"There is no frigate like a book, to take you miles away." So said Robert Louis Stevenson quite some time ago. It's an idea that still holds true, and certainly for this age group. Whether the people you get to know in a book are miles away in real space or whether they are simply people from a different background or time, books can help develop an understanding of their lives.

Children of this age can find out the facts about how other people live from good nonfiction, like *Ishi: Last of His Tribe* by Theodora Kroeber. Another kind of resonance comes from reading fiction written by an author who knows a setting intimately and is able to share with the reader a special imaginative vision of history. Here are some noteworthy examples of fiction and nonfiction that embody a sense of time and place.

Across Five Aprils by Irene Hunt. Follett, 1965. The emotional conflicts of a family living through the Civil War. Based on the author's family records, there are accurate eyewitness reports of battles and other incidents that give this fictional story added power.

Anne of Green Gables by L. M. Montgomery. Buccaneer Books, 1908. The odyssey of an orphan girl in Canada who finds happiness and a new family is a classic that is going into its fourth generation of readers. Some children may find it a bit soupy and old-fashioned, but we think that as an evocation of another time, it holds up.

Beyond the Divide by Kathryn Lasky. Macmillan, 1981. Just another covered wagon story? By no means. This vivid account of the perilous journey of a fourteen-year-old girl and her father has been called a "transcendent novel." So it is —full of danger, courage, and unforgettable people.

Blue Willow by Doris Gates; illustrated by Paul Lantz. Viking, 1940. Janey Larkin is ten—and caught in the Depression. She and her family are migrant workers. Her one treasured possession is a blue willow plate. A dishonest work boss almost causes her to lose it, and with it, her one link with better times. Family life in the thirties in a poignant story that has outlasted the era it tells about.

A Boat to Nowhere by Maureen Crane Wartski. Westminster Press, 1981. The story of the flight of a dispossessed Vietnamese family and how the spirit of the grandfather helps the family to survive.

Caddie Woodlawn by Carol Ryrie Brink. Macmillan, 1935. An "oldie" in the *Little House on the Prairie* tradition. A prairie girl has the adventures associated with the settling of the West. Children of today like to read about pioneer days, particularly when the heroes are in their age groups.

Clan of the Cave Bear by Jean Auel. Crown, 1980. Although this is an adult novel, the subject of ancient peoples is so intriguing that good readers ten and up may be willing to wrestle with the vocabulary. The information is cast in an adventure-story format. A great way to learn about prehistory!

Coming-and-Going Men: Four Tales by Paul Fleischman. Harper & Row, 1985. Four travelling men pass through New Canaan, Vermont, in the 1800s. They are catalysts for four tales of suspense, beautifully crafted and full of the marvelous word magic that is a trademark of this author.

Commodore Perry in the Land of the Shogun by Rhoda Blumberg. Lothrop, Lee and Shepard, 1985. Commodore Perry is credited with opening Japan to the West. In this account we get the feeling of those dramatic days in 1853 when "the black ships of the evil men" arrived. This extraordinarily handsome book will captivate young readers who like their history laced with anecdote and liberally sprinkled with beautiful art.

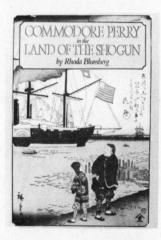

A Day No Pigs Would Die by Robert Newton Peck. Knopf, 1972. A thirteen-year-old boy takes on the duties of a man on a

Shaker farm in the 1920s. Life and death and the pain of growing up in a harsh time are all beautifully portrayed by an author who knows this setting well.

Dragonwings by Lawrence Yep. Harper & Row, 1975. A novel about a young Chinese immigrant who survives the San Francisco earthquake and fire.

The Endless Steppe by Esther Hautzig. Crowell, 1968. A ten-year-old Polish girl and her family are relocated from Poland by the Russians just before World War II. The true experiences of this Jewish family in a labor camp in Siberia give a picture of a world seldom glimpsed. But it is the family's relationships, their humor, and their incredible ingenuity as they face almost insurmountable problems that make this an unforgettable story.

Great Civilizations of Ancient Africa by Lester Brooks. Four Winds, 1971. A handsomely designed and well-written book that helps to fill the great gap in the knowledge of most people concerning African history and culture. An appendix containing a time-line relating African events to those in western history is included.

Halfway Down Paddy Lane by Jean Marzollo. Dial, 1981. A girl from the present is time-warped to 1850, encounters the brutality of mill life for the Irish immigrants, and falls in love with the boy who will be her great-grandfather. Fascinating and informative, this well-written account of that world will provide new insights for today's preteens.

The House of Dies Drear by Virginia Hamilton. Macmillan, 1968. A family moves into the former home of an abolitionist. The house is complete with tunnels and secret passages, and a possible ghost. But this one isn't simply a mystery. It's resonant with history and alive with wonderful characters. Also: *Sweet Whispers, Brother Rush.* Philomel, 1982.

Introducing Shirley Braverman by Hilma Wolitzer. Farrar, Straus and Giroux, 1975. Here is World War II seen through the eyes of a young girl growing up in Brooklyn. "Ancient history" comes alive through this author's gift for language.

Ishi: Last of His Tribe by Theodora Kroeber. Parnassus, 1964. This documentary takes a look at the one survivor of a once powerful North American Indian tribe. Originally an anthropological study, it has become a young people's classic.

Johnny Tremain by Esther Forbes. Houghton Mifflin, 1943. A sullen boy with a crippled hand finds himself in the middle of the intrigue of the American Revolution. The reader and Johnny meet Paul Revere, John Hancock, and others. A dandy yarn and a wonderful way to learn about our country's beginnings.

Jump Ship to Freedom by James Lincoln Collier. Delacorte, 1981. A fourteen-year-old slave escapes from a harsh master and attempts to buy freedom for himself and his mother. An unusual look at slavery as it was practiced in 1787.

Kon-Tiki by Thor Heyerdahl. Rand McNally, 1950. A true account of the author's voyage across 4,000 miles of Pacific Ocean on a balsa raft to prove his theory that the Polynesians are descended from the peoples of pre-Inca Peru.

Little Women by Louisa May Alcott. Little, Brown, 1868. It's hard to know where to list this lovely classic. It's a glimpse of another time and place, a model of the search for self, a story about friendship and death and growing pains and family. The fact that there are at least ten editions still in print should tell us something about the sticking power of this classic.

The Night Journey by Kathryn Lasky; drawings by Trina Schart Hyman. Warne, 1982. This is a tale of a Jewish family's escape from Russian pogroms. Only once in a while does a book come along that offers so much—not only a suspenseful story but amazingly real people to know and care about. Even the drawings seem to glow.

My Brother Sam Is Dead by James Lincoln Collier and Christopher Collier. Four Winds, 1974. Tragedy strikes a family during the Revolutionary War when one son joins the rebels and the rest of the family tries to stay neutral. This book is full of drama and emotional impact and laced with accurate historical detail. It is bound to give a young person a deeper understanding of the many issues involved in taking up a cause, and has much relevance for today. Also: *The Bloody Country.* Four Winds, 1977.

Prairie Songs by Pam Conrad; illustrated by Darryl S. Zudick. Harper & Row, 1985. Life in a sod house on the Nebraska prairie at the turn of the century, told from the viewpoint of a twelve-year-old girl. In vivid and evocative prose the reader experiences the wide, empty spaces dotted with a few families miles apart, but rich with experiences—death, birth, Indians, and the excitement of a newcomer who brings books to the prairie.

Roll of Thunder, Hear My Cry by Mildred D. Taylor. Dial, 1976. Cassie Logan is an independent black girl living in Mississippi in the Depression. Surrounded by white neighbors who despise her and her family, living in fear of the night-riders, Cassie and her brothers struggle to retain their integrity and to grow up independent. This truthful book, by a black author, is truly a "must" for every American.

The Secret Garden by Frances Hodgson Burnett. Lippincott, 1911. A willful English girl goes to live in a manor house on the moors. Adventure and ambiance make this a classic, and although some few children will consider it old-fashioned, it is in fact a wonderful lead-in to Dickens and Jane Austen. Also: *A Little Princess.* Grosset & Dunlap, 1965.

The Slave Dancer by Paula Fox. Bradbury, 1973. Fourteen-year-old Jessie is a captive on a slave ship, forced to play the fife to keep the slaves exercising on the long trip to the new world. A well-written story by a distinguished author.

Smith by Leon Garfield; illustrated by Anthony Maitland. Pantheon, 1967. A twelve-year-old pickpocket, a mysterious document, and a murder supply the plot. But it's the colorful writing that is the key to enjoyment here. Youngsters will learn more about eighteenth-century London from listening to "Smut," than from a dozen encyclopedias.

A Spirit to Ride the Whirlwind by Athena Lord. Macmillan, 1982. This book, suitable for good readers, is a look at a little-known segment of the past. A Child Study Association prizewinner, it tells of a young woman's passage to adulthood through her experiences as a textile worker in the 1830s.

Tikhon by Ilse-Margaret Vogel. Harper & Row, 1984. A Russian fugitive hiding in Germany in World War II wins a young girl's heart. Poignant.

The Upstairs Room by Johanna Reiss. Crowell, 1972. Annie de Leeuw is eight years old when the Nazis invade Holland. As a Jew, her life is at risk. But she is hidden by a courageous

Dutch family in the upstairs room of their farmhouse. A true story of the experiences of the author.

Walking up a Rainbow by Theodore Taylor. Delacorte, 1985. Susan Carlisle, right-on pioneer teenager, enters the reader's life with a bang in this adventure packed story of life on the trail to California in the 1850s. The story is often grim and bloody, but Taylor is a fine storyteller and the spunky character of the heroine make this a good alternative to the soupy teenage romances.

The Wild Children by Felice Holman. Scribner's, 1983. Twelve-year-old Alex is left behind when his family is arrested in Russia after the revolution. On the way toward a new life, he falls in with a band of homeless children. This is a fictional story based on the *bezprizorni,* the wild children who roamed Moscow during the 1920s.

The Witch of Blackbird Pond by Elizabeth G. Speare. Houghton Mifflin, 1958. Sixteen-year-old Kit Tyler sails to Connecticut in 1687. Her friendship with a local woman embroils her in the witchcraft craze of the time and results in her trial on charges of witchcraft.

Biography and Autobiography

If one of the questions children of this age ask is, "Who am I?" surely another one must be, "Who are you?" Some children of ten to twelve are fascinated with the lives of real people. They may find someone they want to read about through a science or social studies class, at the movies, or watching TV. Some latch on to a name in the news. However they arrive at biography, it's a worthwhile genre to explore and can often trigger a child's desire to write about his or her own life.

How deep the plunge into biography often depends on the subject matter. Some ten-year-olds will struggle through a book like baseball player Pete Rose's, *My Life in Baseball.* Other youngsters will snatch up the biography of a rock star or movie hero. But it's nice for them to know that there are many kinds of famous people.

Unfortunately, many so called junior biographies of historical and contemporary figures in the arts, politics, and science are

—let's face it—boring. The following books have been carefully selected from among those by writers who have managed to invest this genre with life and verve. They are all distinguished for their readable style and the selection of an interesting subject.

Abe Lincoln Grows Up by Carl Sandburg. Harcourt, 1926. New edition, 1985. In this case, there's nothing like going to the expert. For clarity, for interesting detail, it's *the* Lincoln biography to be read for the language as much as for the fine attention to detail.

Alexander Calder and His Magic Mobiles by Jean Lipman and Margaret Aspinwall. Hudson Hills, 1981. This book is a lovely window into the life of an artist. Creativity at work, and a different sort of biography.

And Then What Happened, Paul Revere? by Jean Fritz; illustrated by Margot Tomes. Coward, McCann, 1973. How the famous ride took place and what Paul and friends were really like. A close-up view of Revolutionary America full of charming detail and humor, and so authentic you can smell it. Also: *The Double Life of Pocahontas,* Putnam, 1983; *Make Way for Sam Houston,* Putnam, 1986. *Can't You Make Them Behave, King George?* Coward, McCann, 1977.

Black Troubadour: Langston Hughes by Charlemae Rollins. Rand McNally, 1970. A sensitively written book about the great black poet and his search for identity. Always interesting and often inspiring.

Darwin and the Voyage of the Beagle by Felicia Law; illustrated by Judy Brook. Deutsch, 1985. Drawing on the diaries of both Darwin and Captain Fitzroy, the author offers an interesting picture of both men and some of what went on during the fateful voyage.

Frederick Douglass: Slave, Fighter, Freeman by Arna Bontemps. Knopf, 1959. Portrait of an illustrious black leader by a popular writer of books for young people.

The Golda Meir Story by Margaret Davidson. Scribner's, 1976. A thoughtful look at a remarkable world figure. Important messages here for girls in this story of a right-on woman. Also: *Louis Braille,* Hastings, 1972. The story of the boy who invented books for the blind.

In Their Own Words: A History of the American Negro by Milton Meltzer. Harper & Row, 1964. The concept of their own words is what distinguishes this well-compiled history of a people. Also: *The Jewish Americans: A History in Their Own Words,* Harper & Row, 1982; *Mark Twain, A Writer's Life,* Watts, 1985.

Little Men in Sports by Larry Fox; illustrated with photos. Norton, 1968. The lives of Bobby Riggs, Phil Rizzutto, Mario Andretti, and others who became sports heroes in spite of their size. May be especially meaningful to a youngster who is small for his age.

Magic Johnson by Marshall Burchard. Putnam, 1981. This biography of Ervin (Magic) Johnson, Los Angeles Lakers basketball star, is part of the series called *Sports Heroes.* They are heavily (so far) oriented toward male sports figures, but they're well done and youngsters in this age group, when sports is apt to be an intense interest, can indulge their mania.

Meet the Remarkable Adams Family by Lillian Bragdon. Atheneum, 1967. A lively and readable account of one of our Founding Fathers and his many offspring. A good choice for a youngster who may have gotten interested in the Adamses through watching *The Adams Chronicles* on TV.

On the Frontier with Mr. Audubon by Barbara Brenner; illustrated with photographs. Coward, McCann, 1977. Here is the famous artist-naturalist through the eyes of his thirteen-year-old apprentice. The diary device works, and the complex founder of the conservation movement emerges as a fascinating human being.

The Secret Ship by Ruth Kluger and Peggy Mann. Doubleday, 1978. Ruth Kluger was a member of a secret organization (the Mossad) formed in World War II to get Jews out of Hitler's Europe. Her account of her life during this period reads like a novel, and the simple, terse style is perfect for a ten-year-old, but has content enough for twelves.

Shark Lady: True Adventures of Eugenie Clark by Ann McGovern; illustrated by Ruth Chew. Four Winds, 1979. The underwater world revealed through the biography of a marine scientist. Children of both sexes will relate to the exciting life of the woman who works with sharks and is at home in the ocean's depths.

Streams to the River, River to the Sea: A Novel of Sacagawea by Scott O'Dell. Houghton Mifflin, 1986. In this taut novel the author speaks in the voice of Sacagawea. The story, rich with authentic detail, shines as another way in which literature and history can come together.

Three Who Dared by Tom Cohen. Doubleday, 1979. The true stories of three civil rights activists working against segregation in the South during the 1960s. The lives of Henry Aronson, John O'Neal, and Eric Weinberger help children to understand a dramatic time in American history.

Wild Animals, Gentle Women by Margery Facklam; illustrated with photos and line drawings. Harcourt, 1978. Everybody in the family will enjoy this beautifully crafted book about ten women who have made their careers in "animal watching." From Jane Goodall and her chimpanzees to Ruth Harkness and the panda, there's never a dull moment.

Young and Female edited by Pat Ross. Random House, 1975. Vivid excerpts full of wit and courage from the lives of a group of American women.

Poetry

Here is a modest list of poetry books, each one of which would be a good addition to the family library.

Far and Few by David McCord; illustrated by Henry B. Kane. Little, Brown, 1952. Gems from a contemporary poet.

Hailstones and Halibut Bones by Mary O'Neill. Doubleday, 1961. Everyone, from kindergarten to college, will enjoy this one.

I Never Saw Another Butterfly: Children's Drawings and Poetry from Terezin Concentration Camp edited by Hana Volavkova. Schocken, 1978. This is strong stuff—a book of poems written by victims of the Nazis. But for children who are ready for it, it is a moving and powerful adjunct to contemporary history.

If I Were in Charge of the World and Other Worries by Judith Viorst; illustrated by Lynn Cherry. Atheneum, 1981. Gripes and bouquets, to life and to almost everything under the sun. By the author of *Alexander's Terrible, Horrible, No Good, Very Bad Day.*

Miracles collected by Richard Lewis. Simon & Schuster, 1966. In this distinguished collection, children themselves are the authors. Kids will enjoy reading poetry written by their peers, and this is the cream of the crop. Also: *There Are Two Lives: Poems by Children of Japan.* Simon & Schuster, 1970.

My Mane Catches the Wind: Poems About Horses compiled by Lee Bennett Hopkins; illustrated by Sam Savitt. Harcourt Brace Jovanovich, 1979. Lovely poems that speak to the powerful appeal of horses to this age group. Also: *Moments: Poems About the Seasons* illustrated by Michael Hague. Harcourt Brace Jovanovich, 1980.

Nightmares: Poems to Trouble Your Sleep by Jack Prelutsky. Greenwillow, 1979. Just what the title implies. Tens and up will shiver gleefully as they read about things that never were.

On City Streets selected by Nancy Larrick; photos by David Sagerin. Evans, 1968. A splendid selection of urban poems.

The Other Side of a Poem edited by Barbara Abercrombie; illustrated by Harry Bertschmann. Harper & Row, 1977. Contemporary poets speak of animals and other things.

Reflections on a Gift of Watermelon Pickle edited by Stephen Dunning, Edward Luedders, and Hugh Smith. Lothrop, Lee and Shepard, 1967. This anthology, illustrated with photographs, has been lovingly selected from among America's best-loved poets. A contemporary classic.

Something New Begins by Lilian Moore; illustrated by Mary Jane Dunton. Atheneum, 1982. Shining new and burnished bright poems by a remarkable poet. Every child who hears the deceptive simplicity and singular imagery in these poems will be exposed to new standards of excellence and to fresh visions of everyday experiences.

Strings selected by Paul Janeczko. Bradbury, 1984. These poems focus on the family. Some are serious, some not. All are lovely, but will require some thinking about from kids younger than twelve.

Talking to the Sun selected by Kenneth Koch and Kate Farrell; illustrated with photographs. The Metropolitan Museum/ Holt, 1985. A lovely idea—to pair poetry and paintings on subjects such as Love, Children, and Nature. The selections of both art and literature are all first rate and the color reproductions are exceptional.

A Way of Knowing by Gerald McDonald; illustrated by Clare and John Ross. Crowell, 1959. Although it is subtitled "A Collection of Poems for Boys," we could find nothing limiting in the poetry. Maybe it's a question of the difference between 1959 and the 1980s. Anyway, here's a fine collection for both sexes.

Where the Sidewalk Ends by Shel Silverstein with his drawings. Harper & Row, 1974. Thoroughly original approaches to everything from wearing Band-aids to sibling rivalry. Also: *The Light in the Attic,* Harper & Row, 1981. More of same, but a smitch more sophisticated.

Friendship

In terms of friendships, this time from ten to twelve is one of great change. Peer pressures, clubs and cliques, out-groups and in-groups all loom large in children's lives. Because identifying with a group and making choices is so important, the books about the subject are important, too.

Almost a Hero by Clyde Bulla. Dutton, 1981. In this short, powerful book a boy brought up in an orphanage goes back for revenge as a teenager, and meets a friend who helps change his mind. The short chapters and terse vocabulary make this a good choice for ten-year-olds, and for reluctant readers who are older.

The Cat Ate My Gymsuit by Paula Danziger. Delacorte, 1974. Friendship is a two-way street, and this is beautifully illustrated in the relationship of a young girl and her junior high teacher. The teacher helps the girl cope with feelings of insecurity and gives her new perspectives on acting on one's beliefs. When the teacher is fired, the girl fights for her reinstatement.

Cider Days by Mary Stolz. Harper & Row, 1978. Polly and Kate are best friends who are separated when Kate moves from Vermont to California. Polly needs to find another friend, and eventually she does. Along the way there's a warm and realistic story about families, making friends, growing up, as well as a perceptive look at how it feels to be an immigrant. Also: *Ferris Wheel*, Harper & Row, 1977.

The Devil in Vienna by Doris Orgel. Dial, 1978. Two young Viennese girls—one Jewish, one a Hitler youth—manage to maintain their friendship in the face of anti-Semitism and the Nazi scourge in the Austria of 1938. A reaffirmation of love and bravery in the face of indifference and betrayal during a terrible time in history.

Dexter by Clyde R. Bulla. Crowell, 1973. On one level this is a book about friendship between Dave, a farm boy, and a new neighbor. On another level it's an animal story, about a remarkably courageous horse named Dexter. And on still another level it's about loyalty and commitment, death and abandonment. Taken all in all, this small volume, typical of this author, is all about Life.

The Loner by Esther Weir. David McKay, 1963. A young migrant worker boy follows the seasons, alone, without family or friends. He strikes up an unusual friendship with a woman sheepherder and learns how to be a friend and to accept friendship.

Nobody's Baby Now by Carol Lea Benjamin. Macmillan, 1984. Olivia, overweight and unhappy, finds herself through helping her depressed grandmother.

Nothing's Fair in Fifth Grade by Barte De Clements. Viking, 1981. When Jenny befriends the school outcast, Elsie, she finds the going rough. But sticking by Elsie proves in the long run to benefit both girls.

The Pigman by Paul Zindel. Harper & Row, 1968. Two lonely young people meet an eccentric old man—and find each other and some hard-won maturity. This novel is one of the best of the so-called teenage novels, but an eleven or twelve who is a good reader can get a lot out of it.

Soup by Robert Newton Peck; illustrated by Charles Gehm.

Knopf, 1974. The friendship between two boys, done with humor and feeling. Also: *Soup's Drum* illustrated by Charles Robinson. Knopf, 1980.

Thank You, Jackie Robinson by Barbara Cohen; illustrated by Richard Cuffari. Lothrop, Lee and Shepard, 1974. A Brooklyn Dodger fan and a black man share baseball and form a friendship. Also: *King of the Seventh Grade.*

You Two by Jean Ure; illustrated by Ellen Eagle. Morrow, 1984. Two girls of quite different backgrounds become best friends. Recommended by the Child Study Association.

War and Peace

Many psychologists have discerned in children of the nuclear age a feeling of hopelessness about the future. One way youngsters can cope with war and peace issues is to read about these subjects in good fiction and nonfiction.

Anne Frank: The Diary of a Young Girl. Doubleday, 1967. The authentic diary of a victim of the Holocaust will tell children much about Nazism and its effects. Anne Frank's belief in the innate goodness of people is an inspiring message for young and old alike.

Hiroshima no Pika written and illustrated by Toshi Maruki. Lothrop, Lee and Shepard, 1982. Author-illustrator Toshi Maruki heard this story in 1953 from a survivor of Hiroshima. It was not until twenty years later that she was able to find a form in which to tell this tale of the impact of the bomb on one Japanese family. Powerful and upsetting, *Hiroshima no Pika* is nevertheless an important statement about the horror of nuclear war.

I Never Saw Another Butterfly: Children's Drawings and Poems from Terezin Concentration Camp 1942–1944 edited by Hans Volavkova; translated by Jeanne Newcova. McGraw-Hill, 1964. The title tells it all. Heartrending, but guaranteed to make a youngster think.

My Brother Sam Is Dead by James Lincoln Collier and Christopher Collier. Four Winds, 1974. Tragedy strikes a family during the Revolutionary War, when one son joins the rebels and the rest of the family tries to stay neutral. This book is full of drama and emotional impact and laced with accurate historical detail. It is bound to give a young person a deeper understanding of the many issues involved in taking up a cause, and has much relevance for today. Also *The Bloody Country,* Four Winds, 1977.

The Pushcart War by Jean Merrill. Addison-Wesley, 1964. A war between the pushcart peddlers of New York City, complete with a shoot-out with hi-tech pea shooters. A farce that says much about war by an author whose offhand style appeals to kids.

Summer of My German Soldier by Bette Green. Dial, 1973. This realistic and often bleak novel tells of a girl's friendship with a Nazi prisoner of war in the United States. Small-town attitudes are examined as is the cruelty of some parents. A good reader eleven and up will find this book a powerful and memorable experience.

The Upstairs Room by Johanna Reiss. Harper & Row, 1972. Annie de Leeuw is eight years old when the Nazis invade Holland. As a Jew, her life is at risk. But she is hidden by a courageous Dutch family in the upstairs room of their farmhouse. A true story of the experiences of the author.

Who Comes to King's Mountain? by John Beatty. Morrow, 1975. Young Alec is a scout for Francis Marion, The Swamp Fox, who was a guerrilla leader of our own history. The Revolutionary War provides the backdrop for this swashbuckling adventure.

Wolf of Shadows by Whitley Strieber. Knopf, 1985. A book about two survivors of a nuclear war who join with a wolf pack to search for survival in the wild. Told simply and with great understanding of animals, this book on a grisly subject manages to be both tender and hopeful.

Death and Dying

Children of eleven and up are beginning to be increasingly aware of their own mortality and that of their loved ones. Books can offer support and insights as they struggle with the concept of death.

Beat the Turtle Drum by Constance Greene. Viking, 1976. Joss, a girl in love with horses, plans to rent a horse for her birthday. But her beautiful plan ends in tragedy when she is killed in a fall. This tender book explores the death of a family member and its impact on the other people in the family.

Bridge to Terabithia by Katherine Paterson. Crowell, 1977. Leslie and Jess are from different backgrounds but they form a close friendship and create an imaginary, secret kingdom. The girl's tragic accidental death marks the end of childhood for Jess, but their shared experiences help him bear the loss.

The Empty Window by Eve Bunting; drawings by Judy Clifford. Warne, 1982. A young boy tries to capture a wild parrot for a dying friend. Readers will understand the confused emotions of the narrator of this absorbing story. Moves swiftly to an unexpected ending.

Grandma Didn't Wave Back by Rose Blue. Watts, 1972. When Debbie finds her grandmother beginning to act strangely, she's upset and puzzled. This chronicle, not of death, but of an aging person's loss of faculties and its impact on the whole family, rings true on every page. This is an important book for kids (or anyone) to read. It's one that will not be forgotten in a hurry.

A Matter of Time by Roni Schotter. Collins, 1980. A moving, compassionate story of a young girl who copes with her own problems and her mother's impending death. An ABC Afternoon Special and a much talked-about first novel.

The Mulberry Music by Doris Orgel. Harper & Row, 1971. A tender account of a young girl's first experience of death— the death of a beloved grandmother. The reality of the characters, the swift, suspenseful pace, the unusual resolution, all create an uncommonly moving story. The honest facing of grief somehow helps the reader as well as the girl to accept the inevitable.

A Taste of Blackberries by Doris Buchanan Smith. Crowell, 1973. Death comes suddenly and unexpectedly to a boy named Jamie when he is stung by a bee. His friend, the narrator of the story, tells what happened and how he feels about it. A distinguished novel which is also about an important issue, the death of a contemporary.

There Are Two Kinds of Terrible by Peggy Mann. Doubleday, 1977.

When Robbie breaks his arm, that's terrible. But he learns that there is another kind of terrible when his mother dies of cancer. An intensely accurate reflection of feelings, this book explores how difficult it is for remaining family members to reestablish their relationships with one another after a death.

Where the Lilies Bloom by Bill and Vera Cleaver. Lippincott, 1969. A death in the family and an unforgettable young heroine who struggles to keep her family together. The prose is like mountain music, made for reading aloud. Also *Trial Valley,* Lippincott, 1977.

Animal and Nature Stories

A connection with nature and caring about the creatures with whom we share the planet is a function of maturing as a human. The instinct to relate to wild things and to pets is very strong in many children during the years from ten to twelve. A love of horses, or snakes, or the whole outdoors is common. It can be nurtured by books such as those listed here.

All Things Bright and Beautiful by James Herriot. St. Martin's, 1974. The author is a veterinarian in a village in Great Britain. But this book is much more than a career guide for youngsters itching to care for animals. It's a collection of stories of warmth, wit, and compassion that are not only about animals but about people of all descriptions. Herriot's decency and humaneness comes shining through every one of them. Much better than the TV series!

The Black Stallion by Walter Farley. Random House, 1941. The romance and adventure of a boy and a wild stallion thrown together as the result of a shipwreck. Children will recognize the plot from the highly successful movie, but the book is another and equally satisfying experience.

The Call of the Wild by Jack London. Grosset & Dunlap, 1965. One of the quintessential dog books and a tale of derring-do and adventure that every child should be exposed to. Also *White Fang,* MacMillan, 1935.

Every Living Thing by Cynthia Rylant; illustrated by S. D. Schindler. Bradbury, 1985. A slow-learning boy finds a slow-moving turtle and their friendship enriches both of them. That's just one of twelve stories just right for ten year olds, about animals and people. The satisfying thing about these stories is that they are about people and animals who feel *real* to the reader. The author pulls no punches, problem-wise. And yet in every case the interaction between human and animal results in something warm, touching, and positive.

Gentle Ben by Walter Morey; illustrated by John Schoenherr. Dutton, 1965. An Alaskan brown bear kept in captivity is visited and tamed by a boy who names him Ben and rescues him from his imprisonment. The friendship between boy and beast and the boy's long struggle to protect the bear from the hunters makes a compelling story full of authentic Alaskan ambiance. Also: *Kavik the Wolf Dog,* Dutton, 1968.

The Gorilla Signs Love by Barbara Brenner. Lothrop, Lee and Shepard, 1984. Sixteen-year-old Maggie wins a science prize which takes her to Africa, where she discovers a lowland gorilla with a talent for sign language. Filled with authentic detail on gorilla research, this novel combines romance, animal rights issues, and rich nature settings.

The Horselover's Handbook by Leda Blumberg; photos by Murray Tinkelman. Avon, 1984. Do you know how to cool down a horse after a ride? The "rules of the road" in riding a trail? This and more is what this factual, practical book offers. Obviously written by a horselover.

In Search of a Sandhill Crane by Keith Robertson. Viking, 1973. Young Link Keller is by no means a nature buff. But he changes during the course of a summer spent fulfilling an assignment from his uncle to get photographs of sandhill cranes in a wilderness setting in Michigan.

The Incredible Journey by Sheila Burnford; illustrated by Carl Berger. Little, Brown, 1961. Three dogs and a cat set out on a journey. This story is all about devotion, animal lore and love. It's a real tear-jerker, and well worth the cry.

Julie of the Wolves by Jean C. George. Harper & Row, 1972. This is an absorbing adventure of a young Eskimo girl's survival with the help of a wolf family. Deeply moving and scientifically accurate. Also: *My Side of the Mountain,* Dutton, 1975.

A Killing Season by Barbara Brenner. Macmillan, 1981. A sixteen-year-old whose parents have died in a fire comes to terms with her surviving brother and her own life through her work with black bears in the Pocono mountains of Pennsylvania. Good details of bear research woven into an intriguing story.

Lassie Come Home by Eric Knight. Holt, 1940. Joe Carraclough is a Yorkshire lad whose father raises collies. Lassie is Joe's personal dog, and dog and master have a rare relationship. When things get rough financially for the Carraclough family, Lassie must be sold. But there is no way that this dog will be kept from the one she loves. The original on which the Lassie series was based.

Misty of Chincoteague by Marguerite Henry. Rand McNally, 1947. There is hardly a child who won't be Misty-eyed after reading this tender classic about a family that acquires a Chincoteague pony for its own. Still holds up after twenty-two printings! The perfect book for the lover of horses. Also: *King of the Wind,* Rand McNally, 1948.

Never Cry Wolf by Farley Mowat. Little, Brown, 1963. A biologist is sent into the northern wilds to observe wolf behavior and therein lies a funny, poignant, and true story of bureaucratic bungling, mistaken science, human foibles, and the "gross" humor so dear to the hearts of this age group. Check out the recipe for mouse soup, for instance, offered in the interests of science! A great book, which was made into a movie.

Old Yeller by Fred Gipson. Harper & Row, 1964. Travis is a fourteen-year-old living in the Texas hill country. Old Yeller is his hound dog, and the hero of this moving story of the relationship between a boy and his dog.

The Pond by Robert Murphy. Dutton, 1964. Joey lives in Vermont in 1917. His concerns are fishing for bass, watching the otters and mink, and talking to Shake, the hermit. This is a quiet book about a boy of Vermont working toward maturity and a new understanding of animals and nature.

Rascal: A Memoir of a Better Era by Sterling North. Dutton, 1963. Maybe it was a better time. Or maybe it just seems so, in this splendid story of a boy who keeps a pet raccoon. There's warmth of family here and a terrific sense of place. But it's the animal that steals the show.

The Return of the Buffalo by Jack Denton Scott and Ozzie Sweet. Putnam, 1976. Where and how the buffalo disappeared as well as their natural history is presented in a beautiful format, with stunning photography and a memorable text. The team of Scott and Sweet produces consistently fine books on nature for this age. Also: *The Book of the Pig,* Putnam, 1984.

Illustration by John Schoenherr from *Rascal* by Sterling North.

A Snake-Lover's Diary by Barbara Brenner. Harper & Row, 1970. Based on the author's son and his interest in snakes, this fictional diary with its authentic photos has all the excitement of a true story. Informative and accurate, it will delight all young "snake-lovers."

The Story of Doctor Dolittle by Hugh Lofting. Lippincott, 1920. Dell, 1948. The celebrated doctor of animals—part James Herriot, part professor of wizardry—and his wonderful menagerie of animals. No sign that the doctor will be going into retirement in the foreseeable future.

Superpuppy: How to Choose, Raise, and Train the Best Possible Dog for You by Jill Pinkwater and D. Manus Pinkwater. Seabury, 1977. A popular author of fiction tells everything you need to know about dogs in a readable and humane style. A classic on the subject for this age group.

What Is Your Cat Saying? by Michael Fox. Coward, McCann, 1983. The author is a well-known veterinarian and student of canine and feline behavior. Here he focuses on cats. For a child with a feline pet, this book will prove fascinating. Also: *What Is Your Dog Saying?* by Michael Fox and Wende D. Gates. Coward, McCann, 1977.

Where the Red Fern Grows by Wilson Rawls. Doubleday, 1961. A different kind of dog story, alive with a sense of raw nature in a backwoods society, brutal at times, but true in the best literary sense. How Billy Colman trains his dogs to win, and the tragedy that awaits them, makes gripping drama.

The Yearling by Marjorie Kinnan Rawlings. Scribner's, 1962. The story of a young boy and the sacrifice he must make of his pet deer. Set in the Florida swamplands, and told in elegant, compassionate language. For good readers who can manage a long book.

Information, Please

Many children ten to twelve have already developed hobbies and have special subjects that they seem to gravitate to. Sometimes, if the interest is casual, a good book can help to fan the flame. Books provided by a thoughtful parent or teacher can be the follow-up that cements an interest in place.

A book like *Our Earth* by Huck Scarry is one example of an informational book on a wide range of subjects. A teacher we know, who used it in a fourth-grade class, reports that the youngsters pored over it and kept coming back to it at various times during the term.

Keep in mind that no matter how esoteric a youngster's interest, a book can usually be found. Check the subject catalog in your local library, or look in the reference book *Subject Guide to Books in Print.*

Behind the Headlines by Betty Joe English. Lothrop, Lee and Shepard, 1985. What goes on behind the scenes at a big city newspaper? This book gives a personalized and vivid portrait of how a daily paper gets put together.

The Book of How to Be Naturally Geographic by Neill Bell. Little, Brown, 1983. Mapping is an important and often neglected skill that children this age are ready to tackle. Maps and games are only two of a number of interesting ideas in this book. It could put geography on the map in your house.

The Changing Desert by Ada and Frank Graham. Sierra Club/ Scribner's, 1981. Two well-known naturalists write about desert habitats, animals, and desert ecology in a way that helps a youngster to relate to her own environment and to one of the unique ecosystems of the world. Also: *Bears in the Wild,* Delacorte, 1981.

Chemically Active! Experiments You Can Do at Home by Vicki Cobb. Lippincott, 1985. Over thirty detailed, *safe* experiments to do at home—and at the same time learn the principles of chemistry from a science teacher-writer noted for her lively style. Also *Science Experiments You Can Eat,* Lippincott, 1972 (Spanish version, too).

Chimney Sweeps by James Cross Giblin; illustrated by Margot Tomes. Crowell, 1983. Children will relate to this short, well-researched history of a profession, because it is one that traditionally employed children. The author skillfully weaves the facts together and clears the cobwebs from a seldom swept corner of history. Also: *Walls: Defenses Throughout History,* Little, Brown, 1985.

The Creative Kids Guide to Home Computers by Fred D'Ignazio. Doubleday, 1981. A book for computer buffs that shows some of the things you can do with computers. For the reader who can follow directions for something as complex as making a robot, this is good solid information.

Dinosaurs of North America by Helen Roney Sattler. Lothrop, Lee and Shepard, 1981. An excellent and thorough look at dinosaurs of this country, incorporating some of the newer theories about these popular creatures.

Drawing from Nature by Jim Arnosky. Lothrop, Lee and Shepard, 1982. How-to drawing book that hits a common interest of this age group.

Drawing Horses and Foals by Don Bolognese. Watts, 1977. Those who love horses will also want to draw them. A good book on this captivating subject.

Eavesdropping on Space: The Quest of Radio Astronomy by David C. Knight. Morrow, 1975. The story of radio astronomy, its beginnings, and where it was up to ten years ago.

Flim-Flam! by Randi James. Harper & Row, 1980. For the believer and the skeptic both, a book that debunks psychic phenomena. Pair this book with *Sixth Sense* and you may be able to get a family debate going!

Here Come the Robots by Joyce Milton. Hastings House, 1981. A fascinating subject to some kids, looked at from several perspectives.

Hidden Worlds by Seymour Simon. Morrow, 1983. Breathtaking pictures explore the hidden worlds of the eye of a mosquito, a bullet in flight, and earth from a satellite. Truly a fantastic voyage, explained by the author in his usual clear style.

History of Art for Young People by H. W. Janson with Samuel Cauman. A noted art historian and scholar offers kids a serious book on art, complete with over four hundred illustrations of excellent quality, seventy-six of them in full color. Although the text can't be described as lively, it is clear and readable and the book makes a good resource for the whole family.

How Did We Find Out About Outer Space? by Isaac Asimov. Walker, 1977. Part of a series which includes *How Did We . . .* books about the sea, dinosaurs, and comets.

I Am Not a Short Adult by Marilyn Burns. Little, Brown, 1977. One of a series of sprightly nonfiction books, this one is loaded with information that should satisfy the thirst of this age group for information about themselves. Other titles in the series are *Blood and Guts* (about the body), *The Reasons for Seasons* (weather), *The I Hate Mathematics Book* (which may just make a ten- to twelve-year-old love math), and the new *Gee! Why* (a series of experiments in science and art).

Into Winter: Discovering A Season by William Nestor. Houghton, Mifflin, 1983. Information and nature activities for the whole family.

Jewish Holidays by Margery Cuyler. Holt, 1978. The story behind each of the major Jewish holidays, written in a clear and interesting way. Among the best and most complete books on this subject.

KidSpeak About Computers by Joanne Oppenheim. Ballantine, 1985. This unique book explores through interviews with computer-literate kids the complicated relationships between kids and computers. In their own words kids tell us how they have learned to use computers, how this has changed their lives, and what they think about and expect from the high-tech world they will grow up in.

Life on Earth by David Attenborough. Little, Brown, 1981. A beautifully illustrated natural science book based on the TV series. A good family resource.

Love and Sex in Plain Language by Eric Johnson. Harper & Row, 1977. Just what the title implies. A refreshingly frank discussion about sex that may put to rest some of a preteen's anxieties and questions.

Macmillan Illustrated Almanac for Kids by Ann Elwood, Carol Orsag, and Sidney Solomon. Collier-Macmillan, 1981. One of those collections of surprising and amazing facts so dear to the hearts of all of us, and particularly satisfying to this age group's love of the astonishing and "gee whiz" kind of fact.

Our Earth by Chuck Scarry. Wanderer Books, 1982. A potpouri of information on everything—atoms, geology, a little physics—coupled with an excellent visual presentation. A book to be enjoyed by ages eight to eighty.

Pack, Band, and Colony: The World of Social Animals by Herbert Kohl and Judith Kohl; illustrated by Margaret La Farge. Farrar, Straus and Giroux, 1983. A most wonderful book that takes the reader right into the animals' lives.

Paddle-to-the-Sea by Holling Clancy Holling. Houghton Mifflin, 1941. A Native American boy carves a toy canoe and launches it in Lake Nipigon. The pictures and text follow it through all the Great Lakes, and finally into the Atlantic. Lots of information on shore and water life, in a large format book, generous with pictures. This design, similar to that of the newer book *Our Earth,* is particularly appropriate for nonfiction for children of ten to twelve. Although this one may not be readily available in your bookstore, search it out. It's a classic, as are Holling's other works. Also: *Pagoo* (story of a Hermit Crab). Houghton Mifflin, 1957.

Pyramid by David Macaulay. Houghton Mifflin, 1975. This detailed explanation of how and why the Egyptians built pyramids is a favorite with this age group. Fascinating cutaways lend themselves to use as models for building your own pyramid. Also: *Cathedral: The Story of Its Construction,* Houghton Mifflin, 1973, and *Castle,* Houghton Mifflin, 1977.

All of these books fit naturally into subjects being studied in school by ten- to twelve-year-olds.

The Science Book by Sara Stein. Workman, 1980. This is a book of how-to, from building a worm farm to making your hair stand on end.

Sixth Sense by Larry Kettelkamp. Morrow, 1970. ESP is a subject dear to the hearts of many in this age group. This author approaches it in a thoughtful, scientific way.

Sports Cards: Collecting, Trading, and Playing by Margaret McLoone and Aline Siegel. Holt, 1979. An unusual subject, treated fully and interestingly. For the child with this special interest.

A Twister of Twists, A Tangler of Tongues by Alvin Schwartz; illustrated by Glen Rounds. Lippincott, 1972. Can you imagine an imaginary menagerie manager? Here's a collection of witty and clever tongue twisters guaranteed to while away a rainy weekend or to help youngsters forget about their braces!

The View from the Oak by Judith and Herbert Kohl; illustrated by Roger Boylen. Scribner's, 1977. A peek into the private world of animals that will appeal to mature youngsters who like to think about aspects of animal behavior and share some of the more philosophical speculations of ethologists.

Writing for Kids by Carol Lea Benjamin. Crowell, 1985. A children's writer with good credits tackles the subject of teaching writing. "Anyone can write" is her thesis, and kids who try her lighthearted exercises will believe it, and may truly become "scribblers." Teachers might try this one in writing classes, too.

The Young Rockhound's Handbook by W. R. Shedenhelm. Putnam, 1978. If the interest in geology is already there, this will be a welcome addition to the collector's library. If it isn't, this book could certainly awaken a kid's curiosity.

Series

One good book deserves another. Unfortunately, not all individual books in a series are always of equal merit. The Hardy Boys and Nancy Drew books are widely read by this age group, as are the books based on the gimmick of "choosing your own adventure." Few of these books that we've seen do much for a child's appreciation for the language, and a steady diet of them alone is better than not reading—but not a whole lot better.

Here are some series that are entertaining *and* have literary merit. They are all available in paperback.

The Astonishing Stereoscope (and others) by Jane Langton; illustrated by Erik Blegvad. Harper & Row, 1971. The Hall children of No. 40 Walden Street, Concord, specialize in mischief, mystery, and problem solving. Along the way they and the reader always learn a little about history and science and a lot about values. Part realism, part surrealism, totally delightful.

The Black Stallion (and others) by Walter Farley. Random House, 1941. This is the first and most famous of the adventures of a boy and the wonderful horse shipwrecked with him. There are eighteen others; and unlike many series, the literary quality is pretty uniformly high.

The Borrowers (and others) by Mary Norton; illustrated by Beth and Joe Krush. Harcourt, 1952. There are not many Borrowers left, but in this series the miniature race of people continues to live and fascinate new generations of children. Fantasy that appeals to a wide range of ages.

Five Children and It (and others) by E. Nesbit; with illustrations by H. R. Millar. Puffin, 1959. This first book about five English children and a sand fairy was originally published in 1902. The series survives because of its enduring magic, the universal theme of three wishes, and its treatment of the consequences of one's choices. Children who have seen *E.T.* will recognize some of his characteristics in the Psammead. The series is good fantasy reading for ten to twelves.

A Girl Called Al (and others) by Constance Greene; illustrated by Byron Barton. Dell, 1969. Al is "a little on the fat side and a nonconformist." The narrator of these stories is her best friend, and the underlying theme of two girls on the edge of adolescence is warmly and engagingly told. Kids will feel that they know Al and her friend forever after reading one book—but they'll want to go on to some of the others, like *Al(exandra) the Great*.

Go Jump in the Pool! by Gordon Korman. (Apple) Scholastic,

1979. Part of the *Bruno and Boots* series. Bruno and Boots are two friends who attend a decidedly unfancy prep school called MacDonald Hall. After they lose a swim meet with their bitterest competitor, they get involved with a haphazard scheme to finance their own pool. Fast-paced and contemporary, this series rings true, as well it should. It is written by a young man who completed the first one as a seventh-grade English project!

The Great Brain (and others) by John D. Fitzgerald; illustrated by Mercer Mayer. Dial, 1967. Tom Fitzgerald, alias the Great Brain, is a rapscallion of the first order. He's also smart (he skipped fifth grade) and crafty. His business is scheming, but he's not averse to helping people and solving mysteries. His admiring brother is the narrator. They're hilarious, besides being well written.

Civil War Secret Agent by Steve Perry. Bantam, 1984. Part of the *Time Machine* series. All the books in the *Time Machine* series require the reader to make choices. In this one, you become a Civil War Secret Agent and have a chance to meet Harriet Tubman and to help her underground freedom fighters. Although each book is part game, the historical facts are accurate and the plot moves along briskly. Readers who like to immerse themselves in a story as in another world may be less happy with this series than the kids who like their books as puzzles.

Books for Reading Aloud

Here are a few books that are appropriate for reading aloud to ten to twelves. Some of them are classics that may be a little too difficult for a child to tackle on his own. A few contain material that benefits from having a grown-up perspective. And one is simply for family laughs together.

Anne Frank: The Diary of a Young Girl by Anne Frank. Doubleday, 1967. Everyone knows the story of the young Dutch girl living in the attic hidden from the Nazis. In spite of Anne's terrible fate, this is a book of faith in the ultimate goodness of people and a splendid book to read aloud and talk about together.

Author's Choice edited by Gillian Avery, et al. Crowell, 1971. Modern authors whose names readers will recognize have picked their favorite stories and the results make a good anthology for reading aloud. Also: *Author's Choice 2.*

The Bat-Poet by Randall Jarrell; illustrated by Maurice Sendak. Macmillan, 1963. One of the loveliest of this poet's works, and a book to buy and cherish. It's all about a bat who wants to be a poet. In the process of creating poems about his friends—the mockingbird and the other creatures of the woods—he learns much about the creative process and shares it with the reader.

Great Expectations by Charles Dickens. Penguin, 1982. A great cast of characters makes this a "must." Reading Dickens aloud is a treat, not so much for the plots but for the matchless descriptions. And let's not forget the romance and terrific sense of place. Also: *A Tale of Two Cities,* Grosset & Dunlap, 1982, and *A Christmas Carol,* Buccaneer Books, 1981.

Huckleberry Finn by Mark Twain. Grosset & Dunlap, 1981. This classic begs to be read aloud. The odyssey of a nineteenth-century country boy's search for himself has plenty of implications for today. And his relationship with the black slave Jim can be food for many family discussions. Also: *The Prince and the Pauper,* Buccaneer, 1982; *Tom Sawyer,* Putnam, 1981; and *Life on the Mississippi,* Buccaneer, 1983.

I Am the Cheese by Robert Cormier. Pantheon, 1977. A strange and somewhat downbeat book, filled with ambiguity. The story of haunted Adam, and what they do to him and his father needs sharing and talking about. Also: *The Chocolate War,* Pantheon, 1974, and *After the Chocolate War,* Pantheon, 1984.

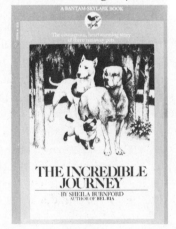

The Incredible Journey by Sheila Burnford. Little, Brown, 1961. Three dogs and a cat set out on a journey. This one is all about devotion, animal lore, and love. There won't be a dry eye in the house, and it's all worth it.

Never Cry Wolf by Farley Mowat. Little, Brown, 1963. A young
biologist goes out on the tundra in search of wolves. An
often hilarious tale of bureaucratic foul-ups that was made
into a movie. Also: *Owls in the Family,* Little, Brown, 1961.

The Owl Hoots Twice at Catfish Bend by Lucien Burman. Wieser and
Wieser (and Avon), 1961. The family will hoot with delight
at this humorous saga of Doc Raccoon and the other inhabitants of Catfish Bend.

Rebecca by Daphne du Maurier. Doubleday, 1948. A haunting
tale of mystery and romance that will keep everyone spell-
bound on those long winter's nights.

Spartacus by Howard Fast. Buccaneer Books, 1982. The hero of
an ancient resistance movement, as told by a master storyteller. This book was made into a movie and hits the spot
with youngsters (and oldsters) who like adventure and history combined. Also: *Citizen Tom Paine,* Grove, 1983.

Treasure Island by Robert Louis Stevenson. Grosset & Dunlap,
1947. A glimpse of another time
and place, and a story somewhat
familiar to children through its
many editions and adaptations.
The original is more difficult to
read but is worth going back to,
and can be found in a Scribner's
edition with *Kidnapped* and other
classics; illustrated by N. C.
Wyeth.

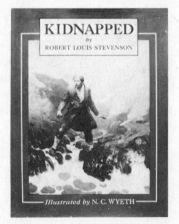

Watership Down by Richard Adams.
Macmillan, 1975. Even younger members of the family will
get something out of this adult saga of a journey of a group
of rabbits to find a safe place. A fantasy based on a careful
study of rabbit behavior, it's the sort of book a ten to twelve
might never read on her own. Read aloud, it's a literary
experience for the whole family.

· · ·

ONWARD AND UPWARD WITH BOOKS

After twelve some kids head straight for the adult bookshelves. Some pause for awhile at the section marked YA (Young Adult) and read the classic examples of this genre—like William Golding's *Lord of the Flies,* J. D. Salinger's *Catcher in the Rye,* and Alice Childress's *A Hero Ain't Nothin' but a Sandwich.* These titles are typical of the modern classics that a kid of thirteen or older may read, either in school or on his own. Other YA readers may begin to be attracted to the adult, popular novels of writers like Stephen King and Sidney Sheldon. Their books have been described as soap operas in book form, but they appeal to some adolescents' tastes for the racy and the bizarre.

Many parents worry about exposing adolescents to the frank language and the sometimes questionable values of "pop" adult novels. While we can't recommend them as literature, we really don't see the harm, unless a youngster is going to binge on this kind of book only. In that case, it's apt to give a youngster a somewhat distorted view of what real people think, do, and say. It's like watching nothing on TV but *Dynasty* and *Dallas.*

What about the teenage novel?

Until recently, there was a tendency among reviewers (and even writers) to dismiss this category as a manufactured one, created by the marketing division of publishing companies. In fact, teenage fiction has become a legitimate and useful bridge between children's books and adult literature. It offers mature concepts, good plots, and some of the best writing in the field. Teenage fiction at its best gives young people themes and content especially appropriate to the ages and stages of adolescence. At its worst, as in many of the so-called romance novels, it is pap written to a formula, the Nancy Drew of the teenager.

Here are just a few fine authors of good YA novels that you may want to suggest to a thirteen-year-old or older child.

Betsy Byars	Doris Orgel
John Donovan	Katherine Paterson
Norma Klein	Marjorie Sharmat
John Knowles	Todd Strasser
Norma Fox Mazer	Barbara Wersba
Gloria Miklowitz	Paul Zindel

REMINDERS FOR CHOOSING BOOKS FOR TEN- TO TWELVE-YEAR-OLDS

- Children this age need books that explore morals and values.
- Nonfiction can be as important as fiction in expanding horizons and interests.
- Fantasy and legend speak to creativity and problem-solving.
- Reading aloud as a family activity is still a sound idea.
- Discuss books and encourage a child to make independent choices.

TEN BOOKS EVERY TEN- TO TWELVE-YEAR-OLD SHOULD KNOW

Are You There, God? It's Me—Margaret by Judy Blume
The Book of Three (The Prydain Chronicles) by Lloyd Alexander
Bridge to Terabithia by Katherine Paterson
Island of the Blue Dolphins by Scott O'Dell
The Lion, the Witch, and the Wardrobe by C. S. Lewis
Mrs. Frisby and the Rats of NIMH by Robert O'Brien
My Side of the Mountain by Jean George
Roll of Thunder, Hear my Cry by Mildred Taylor   The Midnight Fox by Betsy Byars
Tuck Everlasting by Natalie Babbitt   Wingman by Daniel M. Pinkwater
A Wrinkle in Time by Madeleine L'Engle   On My Honor by Marion D. Bauer

The Incredible Journey by Sheila Burnford   Where the Red Fern Grows
II. by Jane Wagner   by Wilson Rawls

WHAT HAPPENS NOW?

After age twelve, parents don't usually have much to say about their children's choices in books. Even before twelve, the search for self may signal a reluctance to listen to parents in the matter of books. What her peers are reading may have far more influence on your child's reading habits than you will. One parent told us that neither of his children read a single book that he recommended when they were between the ages of ten and sixteen!

Not to worry. The whole idea of this book has been to give

youngsters the kinds of books that will not only mesh with their development, but will also develop taste. Adolescence is probably the time for a parent to step back and let the taste that they've set in place go to work. Some choices you'll applaud. Others you may deplore. But if you let this relatively benign rebellion take place, chances are it will come out right in the end.

CHAPTER IX

Sources and Resources

When a young child reaches out for a picture book with *Big Bird* or the *Cabbage Patch Kids* on the cover, he is actually doing something very important; he's connecting his interest with a book. Even if he can't read yet, he is having a literary experience.

Today it's more and more possible for young children to connect with books. Almost every supermarket, drugstore, and toy store has a rack full of children's material. But unfortunately, the artistic and literary quality of books that reach the greatest number of children is often the most limited. Like many other items mass produced and competing for shelf space, mass market books are dependent on instant recognition and impulse appeal. As a result, many of them are manufactured rather than written, with licensed characters dominating the scene. *The Three Bears* has been bumped off the rack by *The Care Bears* and their clones. Cutesy spin-offs of pop TV and movie shows are the "stars" of books with little regard for plot or theme.

If *Strawberry Shortcake* is on the cover of a book, does it matter what's inside? Absolutely. And here's why. Mass market books are the first (and sometimes the only) books millions of children own. It's through such early books that they have their first experiences with the printed page, and with the rhythm of words and the images they convey. Junk books are like junk food; they don't much help to develop a taste for better things.

We're not saying that all the books in the dime store or supermarket are worthless. Some discount stores do carry some books of higher quality. And for many young children even a banal or cutesy book can be a stepping stone to better books of more lasting value. But it's a good idea when you're in the supermarket to be aware that the books most readily available there are not necessarily the best ones you can buy, even for the price.

Someday, we hope, book publishers will find a way to bring the best in children's books into easily affordable bindings and wider circulation. In the meantime, if you're looking for most of the books reviewed in this volume, you probably won't find them in the supermarket or discount store. You're going to have to be resourceful.

Let's take a look at some of the ways to get children together with books and related literature.

BORROWING BOOKS

Public Library

When's the best time to start taking a child to the library? Today, if not sooner. When your child is still in a stroller, roll on down. There's no better way to establish the library link than by using the library yourself.

If you haven't been to the public library since your last project for science class, you're in for a shock. Despite the budget cutbacks and shortened hours, most libraries have turned into multimedia centers. They don't just circulate books; they loan records, computer software, videotapes, and films. Many small libraries are linked to larger regional systems. So, even if your local collection has slim pickings, you may be able to send for special requests through interlibrary loans.

Young children, of course, need your help in finding a few books to take home. Older children may need plenty of browsing time. Try to hang back a bit and give them some space to investigate. We're not saying abandon ship and leave them adrift. Children of seven, eight, and even older often need help in making a meaningful selection. One librarian complained that as soon as kids can read, many parents just drop them at the library's doorstep for the afternoon or evening.

Whether your library fills a city block or comes to you once a week in the form of a traveling bookmobile, introduce yourself and your children to the best book resource person of all, your librarian.

Busy though they may be, most librarians will put paperwork aside when people turn to them for advice. If you're fortunate enough to have a children's librarian on staff, then you've got a resident expert who can play an important role in bringing books and children together. As specialists, children's librarians spend part of their time reading and selecting books for their collections, so they know both what's new and what's old. That's why they can say to your child, "If you liked that mystery, you'll love this one!" or "I know you're interested in UFO's and we must get . . ."

If your child is reluctant to break the ice with the person behind the desk, open the channels of communication by asking some questions yourself. By fourth or fifth grade your sons and daughters will probably be ready to do their own asking. They may actually turn from you as their book advisor. This doesn't mean that all adult opinion is now suspect. In fact, it may be the perfect time to step back a bit and let the librarian take over.

The librarian at the local library is likely to be regarded by your youngster as an unbiased source of reading material. His/her taste, once tested and found reliable, is likely to be followed even when a parent's suggestion is ignored. Take heart, part of growing up is learning to know who to turn to for information and assistance. The librarian who answers children's questions and needs can play a significant role in shaping an appetite for books and a taste for reading that goes beyond the children's room.

If you're new to the scene, be sure to check your library's

calendar of events. Many children's librarians offer story hours for preschoolers. Most have special reading programs for schoolage children during summer vacation. Others run film festivals, puppet shows, book sales, craft classes, and family story hours. If your library doesn't offer any of these services, maybe you can organize other interested parents and volunteer your time and talent to launch such programs. Your participation is a way you can show your own child how much you value books and libraries—and serve your community as well.

School Librarian

If your child's school has a library, it's likely to have the best children's collection in town. Schools vary in the way they use such resources. Most of them permit young students to borrow one or two books a week. Slightly older students are introduced to the way the library works. Students are taught how to use the card catalogue and other resource materials. Classes may "go to library" once a week to select books and/or students may use the library as the need arises.

Like public libraries, a school library may be better called a multimedia center. Many have fine collections of records, film strips, movies, audiocassettes, video films, computers, and software. For the most part all of this equipment is intended for classroom use.

In some communities parents and children are allowed to borrow both print and electronic material overnight and during weekends. Other schools run summer programs with the emphasis on entertainment and pleasurable reading. Unfortunately, the vast majority of schools lock the library every weekend and all summer. Rather than staffing the library even on a part-time basis, the richest resource in town is off limits during the time when kids have time on their hands. This does seem a terrible waste that parent/teacher organizations should be able to remedy. Even limited hours with a teacher/librarian and volunteer parent aides would be better than *no* hours from June to September. Here's another area where parents' interest and pressure could bring about change.

Some communities use older students to assist with shelving books, repairing ripped pages, and helping younger visitors find books. Providing older kids with work with a purpose gives them valuable learning experiences. They begin to know their way around the library and its Dewey Decimal System. It also gives them a taste of being socially responsible and serving their community.

Author! Author!

In many school and public libraries children have their first opportunity to meet and speak to real authors and artists. Young children are often confused about how books are made. They don't understand that there are real people—an author and an illustrator—behind books. But when they do get the idea, they are thrilled. Then books begin to have another dimension. They look for authors by name and follow the works and careers of their favorites.

Parents can help to encourage the reader-author connection in a number of ways. Through their parent/teacher organizations they can arrange for authors and illustrators to come to the schools. There are author-in-the-school programs in many communities. They're often sponsored by state Councils on the Arts and are a worthwhile investment for a school district or parent group to sponsor.

In such programs the author comes to the school a number of times and interacts with students. Youngsters get a sense of what an author is and what he/she does. Authors discuss the process of writing and help children with their own work. Since reading helps writing and vice versa, both skills benefit from these programs. Although these programs are most often set up for nine- to twelve-year-olds, some authors (and artists) are working with first and second graders.

Fan Mail

Another way to make the author connection is through the fan letter. Youngsters ten to twelve tend to be very people-oriented. When your ten-year-old announces that "————— was the best book I ever read!" you might suggest that the author might like to hear that.

Some schools make a point of having students write to authors. Often this activity is part of a unit on writing. More often it is connected with Language Arts. The best kind of fan letter is the one that's encouraged, but not mandated. A "canned" letter copied from one the teacher put on the board is not enjoyed by either sender or receiver. On the other hand, a spontaneous outpouring of enthusiasm, even sloppily written, probably goes a long way to entrench the book connection. One school prints Valentines for its primary grade youngsters to write on and send to their favorite authors. Another school makes a bulletin board of pictures and bio material on selected authors.

Authors like to hear from children and will usually answer fan letters. Your child can send letters to the author's publisher, who will send them on to the author's home. Or check your library's reference shelf for *Something About the Author.* It includes authors' biographical sketches and mailing addresses.

BUYING BOOKS

Building Your Child's Library

All children should have some books of their own. They don't need shelvesfull. In fact, it may be that a few well-chosen titles at each age are more memorable than dozens of the quick-pick second rate variety that can be looked at and then left. To the child a meaningful book grows more meaningful as it's reread and savored. Since you're the one who's going to do the rereading, taking the time to be selective has long-term value. One of the best ways to choose is to borrow first from the library. A book that needs renewing frequently is obviously a good candidate for purchase.

You may be surprised to find that a full-color picture book costs as much as fifteen dollars. Is that outrageous? Well, compared to what? Many toys cost far more than a book, and lose their novelty more quickly. Books are a bargain; they can keep on going. And many wonderful titles are now available both in hardcover and paperback editions. The difference in price is dramatic. For the most part, the only difference between the original and paperback edition is the less durable cover and paper the book is printed on. Sometimes, the quality of the paper affects the color of illustrations, but not significantly in most cases. Obviously, your child's paperback library can grow for a fraction of the cost of hardcover editions. These less costly libraries may not hold up for your children's children, but they will certainly do the job for this generation. Two sources that list paperback editions are *Paperback Books in Print* and *Books in Print* (Titles). Both of these are usually available at your library or at any good-size bookstore.

In our own families each birthday and holiday season was always punctuated with one hardcover edition of a book that formed the core of the child's personal library. For our grown children such books remain treasured possessions of childhood. Opening them today is perhaps as pleasurable, or more so, than it was twenty years ago. The pictures and words of *Blueberries for Sal* and *The Runaway Bunny* evoke the same delight they did years ago with the added sense of joy in revisiting old friends that still speak to the heart.

Books also make a good gift for other kids. And if you're not sure which book a youngster has, a gift certificate to a well-stocked local bookstore will give the young reader the thrill of picking her own.

Few toys or other childhood mementos are as enduring. These will be shared with yet another generation on their way to becoming literate.

The Bookstore

All too few communities have bookstores devoted to the needs of children. But should you have one in your neighborhood, it will make a real difference in your youngster's book habits. A knowledgeable bookstore salesperson will allow a child to browse, will offer sound advice, and will know what to suggest for which age.

Our own Bank Street College Bookstore is a familiar gathering place for children of all ages. Younger children come in with their parents and look over the stock and choose with parents' help. But kids of ten to twelve arrive with their allowances in their jeans, knowing exactly what they want—which is often a copy of Shel Silverstein's *A Light in the Attic* or the latest Lois Duncan book. If you ask these kids where they got the ten or twelve dollars that it costs to get a Shel Silverstein, you can hear stories that suggest that they are learning about priorities and that, in these cases, books are at the top of the priority list.

Of course, not everyone has access to a bookstore with a section for children. Many give a nod to kids with the same sorts of books they carry in the supermarket. However, if you know what you want by title and author, they may be able to order for you. If you are having trouble finding a bookstore to help, write to:

American Booksellers Association
122 East 42nd Street
New York, NY 10017

It can give you the names and addresses of the nearest bookstore that will take your orders. Or check with your local librarian for advice on buying.

OTHER SOURCES

Book Clubs

Your child's teacher may circulate book club order forms with student newspapers. Scholastic, Xerox, and others publish paperback editions of many excellent books. Since they sell such mass quantities, they can offer them at reasonable prices. So these are good buys! The teacher who runs such programs may receive dividend books and posters for the classroom. If your school doesn't offer these services, check with the teacher. She may be willing to do so or you might have your parent/teacher organization to volunteer to do the bookkeeping and distribution several times a year. This is a great way to provide quality and quantity to your child's library at a fraction of the cost of hardcover editions.

Mail-Order Book Clubs

You'll see ads in magazines for book clubs that send your child selections. Most of them sell special hardcover editions, sold at significantly lower prices than they would cost in the bookstore. Generally they do the picking and the shipping, so what they select is what you get. You have few if any choices. Naturally, children relish receiving packages in the mail, so this arrangement may be just right for preschoolers and children in the early grades. Older children prefer having a say in their book choices. As with all mail-order clubs, be sure to read the fine print before signing on. There may be a minimum number you must order a year and limited time for returning books you don't want.

Here are a few clubs you should know about:

Caedmon
1995 Broadway
New York, NY 10023
Original hardcover books and reprints of classics with cassettes

Grolier Enterprises, Inc.
Sherman Turnpike
Danbury, CT 06816
(203) 792-1200
Beginning Readers Program
Disney's Wonderful World of Reading

Junior Literary Guild
Customer Service
245 Park Avenue
New York, NY 10167
Hardcover book selections for ages three to sixteen

Scholastic Book Services
50 West 44th Street
New York, NY 10036
Clubs that distribute paperbound reprints of originals for grades kindergarten to twelfth

Xerox Educational Publications
245 Long Hill Road
Middletown, CT 06457

Weekly Reader Children's Book Clubs for ages three to eleven
Paperback Book Clubs for grades Kindergarten to twelfth

Shop by Phone, Home Computer, or Mail-Order Catalogue

You can also buy books without ever leaving home. Check your
Sunday paper's book review section for an 800 number that
takes orders on all current books reviewed. With a credit card
and a call, a company like Book Call (1-800-255-2665) will gift
wrap and ship your orders anywhere in the world. Or, if you
have a computer and modem, you'll find a children's book section at CompuStore through CompuServe or The Source.

One idea that seems to be gaining popularity is buying
reprints of really old classics. Two companies that can supply
catalogs and books in this category are:

Dover Books
180 Varick Street
New York, NY 10014

Peter Smith
Junior Books
6 Magnolia Avenue
Magnolia, MA 01930

Museums

Some of the loveliest bookshops today are part of the museums
you'll be visiting with your children. Their books are usually
carefully selected for accuracy as well as beauty and relate to the
museum collection. Compared to other souvenirs of a day's
outing, the book can extend the experience and enlarge the
child's view of what was seen in the museum. You may leave a
science museum with a small field book about rocks, stones, or
dinosaurs. Or after a trip to a reconstruction like Williamsburg,
a novel set in Colonial times will have new dimension. Take the
time to browse in the bookshop for regional folktales when you
travel. It's a lovely way of bringing home a piece of your family
outing and connecting it to books.

Book Fairs

One of the best ways to raise money for your parent/teacher organization, community center, or youth group is to run a book fair. Not only will you make a profit, you'll be giving children and parents an opportunity to look at and buy books from many publishers.

Running a book fair demands a lot of paperwork and time. Children place orders for books on display and pay for their purchases. After all orders are taken, the book dealer ships the books to your committee and books must be distributed. Most groups like to run book fairs just before the holiday gift-buying season. There's no doubt that's a good time for selling, but book buying should not be a seasonal affair. Chances are it would be just as successful in spring or fall.

Unfortunately, not all book fair dealers offer quality books. Many pack up books that you can find in any dime store. So they're not providing your audience with choices worth the bother. Such companies may offer you a bigger percent of the profits, but that's not the way to go. Better to sell fewer books of quality than to promote second-rate reading material.

Check with your school librarian for the names of companies in your area who will supply books for fairs. One company that has a special department set up to coordinate book fairs is:

Waldenbooks
201 High Ridge Road
Stamford, CT 06904
(203) 356-7797 or 7599

Ask the librarian if she'll go over the booklist with your book committee to help you decide on which dealer to go with.

Other Ideas

Another way to run a book fair is to coordinate it with the visit of an author or authors. Seeing and hearing an author whets the child's appetite for the author's books. Then if you have the books there, with the author ready to autograph them, you're all set. Most publishers will be glad to work with schools on such a program, and to ship books on a consignment basis. Many PTAs run this kind of function as an annual event. Some coordinate it with writing programs ongoing in the school. One Texas school district makes it a week-long affair. Illinois schools have had state-wide Writing-Author-Book festivals, as do some New York and New Jersey schools. The Philadelphia Children's Reading Round Table chooses a book by a Philadelphia author and illustrator and features it in city bookstores each month.

Book Swaps

Consider running a book swap section at your book fair or at the school or public library. Kids do outgrow some books, families move, and shelf space is limited in most homes today. A book swap is an ideal way to trade up on books they've finished and have no continuing interest in owning.

Your library may have some old books they're ready to take off the shelf. Check the garage and attic. At the book swap kids are expected to bring in a book in exchange for taking a book. You may want to classify books by size or quality. One hardcover book may be worth two paperbooks. Or you may want to keep it simple—bring one and get one.

THE MEDIA

You can hear good children's books read on radio—particularly public radio. *Kids America* on National Public Radio has a regular feature called "Paging Dr. Book" on which Dr. Rita Book prescribes books for all kinds of problems and interests. And you can see contemporary and classic children's stories come to life on your TV screen. It's true that you have to do a little dial turning. But on the whole, it's worth the effort.

The media connection can work both ways. Seeing something on TV or hearing it on radio may stimulate the reading of a book. And books can make TV watching and radio listening more selective.

Here are a few TV programs to watch for that may help to further the book connection:

Wonderworks

ABC Afterschool Specials

Reading Rainbow (Public TV)

CBS Children's Specials
The Living World
National Geographic Specials
Main Street (NBC)
Voyage of the Mimi

Audiocassettes and Records

There are some really fine readings of children's books and stories available on records and cassettes. These are bound to augment your library and in many cases they may be an introduction to a book that your child might not otherwise see. Some of the records and cassettes even come *with* the book. Audio material is available for a wide age range—from preschool to adult. And with a set of earphones and the new mini cassettes, your offspring can be listening to a favorite story even as she walks the dog!

Here are a few sources for audio material that offer catalogs:

Caedmon Records
1995 Broadway
New York, NY 10023

Caedmon will even sign you up on a literary subscription plan. You choose the budget and age group, they will make selections from a core list and send them at intervals.

Educational Activities, Inc.
P.O. Box 87, Dept. PC
Baldwin, NY 11510

Records on a variety of subjects.

Educational Record Center
472 East Paces Ferry Road
Atlanta, GA 30305
(800) 438-1637
(404) 233-5935

Records for the youngest member of the family, including readings of *The Velveteen Rabbit*. Also: Read and Hear record and book combinations for babies.

Folkways
632 Broadway
New York, NY 10012

Old and new classic children's songs and literature on record or cassette. Some you may know from when you were a kid, like Woody Guthrie's *Songs to Grow On.* Also Spanish translations of old favorites.

Listening Library, Inc.
One Park Avenue
Old Greenwich, CT 06870

Both books and cassettes. Good contemporary classics like Arnold Lobel's *Mouse Tales.*

Quality Paperback Book Club
Camp Hill, PA 17102

The Little Prince, James and the Giant Peach, and *Spoken Sendak* are among the offerings.

Spoken Arts
310 North Avenue
New Rochelle, NY 10802
(914) 636-5481

Books, cassettes, and recordings for older kids, featuring famous artists like Julie Harris reading *The Diary of Anne Frank.*

Videocassettes

If you have a VCR at home, it can be another way to introduce children to books. Many classics, traditional and contemporary, have found their way into this new medium. Videocassettes can be purchased or rented. Often a child who has seen *The Black Stallion* or *Heidi* on the VCR will then look for the book at the library. Some videocassettes have the book and cassette as a package. We recommend getting both, so the VCR version doesn't take the place of reading.

· · ·

Computer Software

Neither computer disks nor cassettes are a substitute for reading books. At their best, they are nice adjuncts to a reading experience, particularly for older kids. *Hitchkiker's Guide to the Galaxy* (Infocom), for instance, is something between a book and a puzzle and is fun for a kid who has already seen the show on TV and/or read the book. *Fahrenheit 451* (Spinnaker) is a computer game which takes off from the book by Ray Bradbury. Both of them are "edufun." But they are not books, nor are they intended to be. As for computer books for the younger fry, we haven't seen any computer software that a small tyke can snuggle up to like she can with a book.

Magazines for Children

Think about a subscription to a kid's magazine as one of the ways in which you can implant good reading habits. Here are just a few of the many good kids' magazines.

Boys Life
Published by Boy Scouts of America
Box 61030
Dallas/Ft. Worth Airport, TX 75261

Children's Digest
Box 567B
1100 Waterway Blvd.
Indianapolis, IN 46296
(Ages eight to twelve)

Cobblestone: The History Magazine for Young People
Cobblestone Publishing
20 Main Street
Peterborough, NH 03458-9976
(Ages eight to twelve)

Cricket Magazine
Box 100
La Salle, IL 61301
(Ages eight to twelve)

Ebony Jr!
820 S. Michigan Avenue
Chicago, IL 60605
(Ages six to twelve)

Faces
Cobblestone Publishing in cooperation with American Museum of Natural History
20 Main Street
Peterborough, NH 03458-9976

Highlights for Children
Box 269
2300 W. Fifth Avenue
Columbus, OH 43216
(Ages four to twelve)

Humpty Dumpty's Magazine for Little Children
Children's Better Health Publications
P.O. Box 567B
Indianapolis, IN 46206

Owl: The Outdoor and Wildlife Discovery Magazine for Children
Scholastic Home Periodicals
P.O. Box 1925
Marian, OH 43302
(Ages eight to twelve)

National Geographic World
Department 00880
17th and M Streets, N.W.
Washington, DC 20036
Natural science, sports, even collectors'
cards for middle years kids from the folks who
bring adults *National Geographic.*

Ranger Rick's Nature Magazine
National Wildlife Federation
1412 16 Street, N.W.
Washington, DC 20036

Scholastic Magazines
50 West 44th Street
New York, NY 10036
Magazines for Kindergarten to twelfth grade levels

Stone Soup
Box 83
Santa Cruz, CA 95063
A magazine by children

3–2–1 Contact
P.O. Box 2933
Boulder, CO 80322
Info on computers and related science subjects
for eight- to twelve-year-olds.

Parent Sources of Information About Books

The Children's Book Council
67 Irving Place
New York, NY 10003
Posters, bookmarks, the calendar of children's
books, library for research.

Appraisal
Children's Science Book Review Committee
Boston University School of Education
Science and Mathematics Program
605 Commonwealth Avenue
Boston, MA 02215
Reviews of science books for children.

Child Study Association
610 West 112th Street
New York, NY 10025
Reviews, annual review publication, annual award.

Council on Interracial Books for Children
1841 Broadway
New York, NY 10023
Specialized reviews on ethnic material.

Booklist
Published by American Library Association
50 East Huron Street
Chicago, IL 60611
Reviews adult trade and juvenile books.

Horn Book
Park Square Building
31st Street and James Avenue
Boston, MA 02116
Articles on children's books, authors, and illustrators; reviews.

Parents Choice
Box 185
Waban, MA 02168
Reviews of all children's media.

Some Major National Awards for Children's Books

The Newbery Medal and Honor Awards. Presented annually by the American Library Association for distinguished contributions to children's literature published in the United States. First medal was presented in 1922.

The Caldecott Medal and Honor Awards. Annually to illustrators of the most distinguished picture books published in the United States. Named for British illustrator Randolph Caldecott.

The Laura Ingalls Wilder Medal. Named for author of the *Little House* series and presented every five years to author or illustrator who has made a lasting contribution to children's literature.

Boston Globe/Horn Book Awards. Annual awards to an author for an outstanding work of fiction, nonfiction, and to an illustrator for an outstanding work.

National Book Awards. Given annually to United States authors whose books have contributed most significantly to human awareness, national culture, and the spirit of excellence.

William Allen White Children's Book Award. Given annually

since 1953 to an outstanding children's book selected by Kansas children.

The Children's Book Award. Given annually by the International Reading Association to a children's author whose work shows unusual promise.

The Carnegie Medal. Annual award to an outstanding book first published in the United Kingdom.

Hans Christian Andersen International Medal. Presented every two years to a living artist and author for outstanding quality of their total works for children.

Children's Choices. An annual list of favorites selected by children. Published by The Children's Book Council.

Irma Simonton Black Award. Presented annually by Bank Street College of Education for outstanding book selected by literature specialists and children.

Golden Kite Award. Given annually by the Society of Children's Book Writers for a distinguished work of fiction and nonfiction plus an honor book in each category.

The Caldecott Medal Books

The Caldecott Medal, named in honor of nineteenth-century English illustrator Randolph Caldecott, is awarded annually by the Association for Library Service to Children, a division of the American Library Association, to the artist of the most distinguished American picture book for children.

Animals of the Bible	Helen Dean Fish Illustrated by Dorothy P. Lathrop (Lippincott)	1938
Mei Li	Thomas Handforth (Doubleday)	1939
Abraham Lincoln	Ingri and Edgar Parin D'Aulaire (Doubleday)	1940
They Were Strong and Good	Robert Lawson (Viking)	1941
Make Way for Ducklings	Robert McCloskey (Viking)	1942
The Little House	Virginia Lee Burton (Houghton Mifflin)	1943

Many Moons	James Thurber Illustrated by Louis Slobodkin (Harcourt)	1944
Prayer for a Child	Rachel Field Illustrated by Elizabeth Orton Jones (Macmillan)	1945
The Rooster Crows	Maud and Miska Petersham (Macmillan)	1946
The Little Island	Golden MacDonald Illustrated by Leonard Weisgard (Doubleday)	1947
White Snow, Bright Snow	Alvin Tresselt Illustrated by Roger Duvoisin (Lothrop, Lee and Shepard)	1948
The Big Snow	Berta and Elmer Hader (Macmillan)	1949
Song of the Swallows	Leo Politi (Scribner's)	1950
The Egg Tree	Katherine Milhous (Scribner's)	1951
Finders Keepers	Will Lipkind Illustrated by Nicolas Mordvinoff (Harcourt)	1952
The Biggest Bear	Lynd Ward (Houghton Mifflin)	1953
Madeline's Rescue	Ludwig Bemelmans (Viking)	1954
Cinderella	Illustrated and retold from Perrault by Marcia Brown (Scribner's)	1955
Frog Went A-Courtin'	Retold by John Langstaff Illustrated by Feodor Rojankovsky (Harcourt)	1956
A Tree Is Nice	Janice Udry Illustrated by Marc Simont (Harper & Row)	1957

Time of Wonder	Robert McCloskey (Viking)	1958
Chanticleer and the Fox	Barbara Cooney (Crowell)	1959
Nine Days to Christmas	Marie Hall Ets and Aurora Labastida (Viking)	1960
Baboushka and the Three Kings	Ruth Robbins Illustrated by Nicolas Sidjakov (Parnassus)	1961
Once a Mouse	Marcia Brown (Scribner's)	1962
The Snowy Day	Ezra Jack Keats (Viking)	1963
Where the Wild Things Are	Maurice Sendak (Harper & Row)	1964
May I Bring a Friend?	Beatrice Schenk de Regniers Illustrated by Beni Montresor (Atheneum)	1965
Always Room for One More	Sorche Nic Leodhas Illustrated by Nonny Hogrogian (Holt)	1966
Sam, Bangs & Moonshine	Evaline Ness (Holt)	1967
Drummer Hoff	Adapted by Barbara Emberley Illustrated by Ed Emberley (Prentice-Hall)	1968
The Fool of the World and the Flying Ship	Retold by Arthur Ransome Illustrated by Uri Shulevitz (Farrar, Straus and Giroux)	1969
Sylvester and the Magic Pebble	William Steig (Windmill Books)	1970
A Story a Story	Gail E. Haley (Atheneum)	1971
One Fine Day	Nonny Hogrogian (Macmillan)	1972
The Funny Little Woman	Lafcadio Hearn, retold by Arlene Mosel Illustrated by Blair Lent (Dutton)	1973

Duffy and the Devil	Retold by Harve Zemach Pictures by Margot Zemach (Farrar, Straus and Giroux)	1974
Arrow to the Sun	Gerald McDermott (Viking)	1975
Why Mosquitoes Buzz in People's Ears	Retold by Verna Aardema Pictures by Leo and Diane Dillon (Dial)	1976
Ashanti to Zulu	Margaret Musgrove Pictures by Leo and Diane Dillon (Dial)	1977
Noah's Ark	Peter Spier (Doubleday)	1978
The Girl Who Loved Wild Horses	Paul Goble (Bradbury)	1979
Ox-Cart Man	Donald Hall Pictures by Barbara Cooney (Viking)	1980
Fables	Arnold Lobel (Harper & Row)	1981
Jumanji	Chris Van Allsburg (Houghton Mifflin)	1982
Shadow	Blaise Cendrars Translated and illustrated by Marcia Brown (Scribner's)	1983
The Glorious Flight: Across the Channel with Louis Bleriot	Alice and Martin Provensen (Viking)	1984
Saint George and the Dragon	Retold by Margaret Hodges Illustrated by Trina Schart Hyman (Little, Brown)	1985
Hansel and Gretel	Retold by Rika Lesser Illustrated by Paul O. Zelinsky (Dodd,Mead)	1985-Honor

Have You Seen My Duckling?	Nancy Tafuri (Greenwillow)	1985-Honor
The Story of Jumping Mouse	Retold and illustrated by John Steptoe (Lothrop, Lee and Shepard.)	1985-Honor

The Newbery Medal Books

The Newbery Medal, named for eighteenth-century British bookseller John Newbery, is awarded annually by the Association for Library Service to Children, a division of the American Library Association, to the author of the most distinguished contribution to American literature for children.

Adam of the Road	Elizabeth Gray (Viking)	1943
Johnny Tremain	Esther Forbes (Houghton Mifflin)	1944
Rabbit Hill	Robert Lawson (Viking)	1945
Strawberry Girl	Lois Lenski (Lippincott)	1946
Miss Hickory	Carolyn Bailey (Viking)	1947
The Twenty-One Balloons	William Pene Du Bois (Viking)	1948
King of the Wind	Marguerite Henry (Rand McNally)	1949
The Door in the Wall	Marguerite de Angeli (Doubleday)	1950
Amos Fortune, Free Man	Elizabeth Yates (Dutton)	1951
Ginger Pye	Eleanor Estes (Harcourt)	1952
Secret of the Andes	Ann Nolan Clark (Viking)	1953
. . .And Now Miguel	Joseph Krumgold (Crowell)	1954
The Wheel on the School	Meindert DeJong (Harper & Row)	1955

Carry On, Mr. Bowditch	Jean Lee Latham	1956
Miracles on Maple Hill	Virginia Sorensen (Harcourt)	1957
Rifles for Watie	Harold Keith (Crowell)	1958
The Witch of Blackbird Pond	Elizabeth George Speare (Houghton Mifflin)	1959
Onion John	Joseph Krumgold (Crowell)	1960
Island of the Blue Dolphins	Scott O'Dell (Houghton Mifflin)	1961
The Bronze Bow	Elizabeth George Speare (Houghton Mifflin)	1962
A Wrinkle in Time	Madeleine L'Engle (Farrar, Straus and Giroux)	1963
It's Like This, Cat	Emily Neville (Harper & Row)	1964
Shadow of a Bull	Maia Wojciechowska (Atheneum)	1965
I, Juan de Pareja	Elizabeth Borton de Trevino (Farrar, Straus and Giroux)	1966
Up a Road Slowly	Irene Hunt (Follett)	1967
From the Mixed-Up Files of Mrs. Basil E. Frankweiler	E. L. Konigsburg (Atheneum)	1968
The High King	Lloyd Alexander (Holt)	1969
Sounder	William H. Armstrong (Harper & Row)	1970
Summer of the Swans	Betsy Byars (Viking)	1971
Mrs. Frisby and the Rats of NIMH	Robert C. O'Brien (Atheneum)	1972
Julie of the Wolves	Jean Craighead George (Harper & Row)	1973
The Slave Dancer	Paula Fox (Bradbury)	1974
M. C. Higgins, the Great	Virginia Hamilton (Macmillan)	1975
The Grey King	Susan Cooper (Atheneum)	1976

Roll of Thunder, Hear My Cry	Mildred D. Taylor (Dial)	1977
Bridge to Terabithia	Katherine Paterson (Crowell)	1978
The Westing Game	Ellen Raskin (Dutton)	1979
A Gathering of Days	Joan W. Blos (Scribner's)	1980
Jacob Have I Loved	Katherine Paterson (Crowell)	1981
A Visit to William Blake's Inn: Poems for Innocent and Experienced Travelers	Nancy Willard (Harcourt)	1982
Dicey's Song	Cynthia Voigt (Atheneum)	1983
Dear Mr. Henshaw	Beverly Cleary (Morrow)	1984
The Hero and the Crown	Robin McKinley (Greenwillow)	1985
Like Jake and Me	Mavis Jukes (Knopf)	1985-Honor
The Moves Make the Man	Bruce Brooks (Harper & Row)	1985-Honor
One-Eyed Cat	Paula Fox (Bradbury)	1985-Honor

Classics of Children's Literature

There is a powerful body of writing loosely known as "Classics of Children's Literature." As a rule these writings cut across several stages of childhood, and many would be considered to be for "all ages," defying any attempt to age relate them. They are pieces of writing characterized by fine style, originality of concept, and universal appeal. They have withstood the test of time and remain fresh and vigorous as each new generation meets and is refreshed by them. Here is our list of classics:

Illustration by W. Heath Robinson from *The Water Babies* by Charles Kingsley.

Aesop's Fables		
Arabian Nights Tales		
Fairy Tales	Charles Perrault	1697*
Robinson Crusoe	Daniel Defoe	1719
Gulliver's Travels	Jonathan Swift	1727
Mother Goose Rhymes		
Household Tales	Wilhelm and Jacob Grimm	1812
Swiss Family Robinson	Johann Wyss	1813
Fairy Tales	Hans Christian Andersen	1835
The Pied Piper of Hamelin	Robert Browning	1842
A Christmas Carol	Charles Dickens	1843
A Book of Nonsense	Edward Lear	1846
The King of the Golden River	John Ruskin	1851
Hiawatha	Henry Wadsworth Longfellow	1855
The Water Babies	Charles Kingsley	1863
Hans Brinker	Mary M. Dodge	1865
Alice in Wonderland	Lewis Carroll	1865
Little Women	Louisa May Alcott	1869
At the Back of the North Wind	George MacDonald	1871
Peterkin Papers	Lucretia P. Hale	1874
Adventures of Tom Sawyer	Mark Twain	1875
The Boys' King Arthur	Sidney Lanier	1880
Pinocchio	Carlo Collodi	1880
Heidi	Johanna Spyri	1880
Treasure Island	Robert Lewis Stevenson	1881
Nights with Uncle Remus	Joel Chandler Harris	1883

*Dates are for first publication in English.

The Merry Adventures of Robin Hood	Howard Pyle	1883
The Adventures of Huckleberry Finn	Mark Twain	1884
Child's Garden of Verses	Robert Louis Stevenson	1885
Blue Fairy Book	Andrew Lang	1889
The Tale of Peter Rabbit	Beatrix Potter	1893
The First Jungle Book	Rudyard Kipling	1894
Just So Stories	Rudyard Kipling	1897
Bob, Son of Battle	Alfred Ollivant	1898
Peter Pan	James M. Barrie	1906
The Wind in the Willows	Kenneth Grahame	1908
The Secret Garden	Frances H. Burnett	1911
The Story of Dr. Dolittle	Hugh Lofting	1920
Smoky, the Cowhorse	Will James	1926
Millions of Cats	Wanda Gag	1928
Little House in the Big Woods	Laura I. Wilder	1932
The Story of Babar	Jean de Brunhoff	1933
Mary Poppins	Pamela I. Travers	1934
Caddie Woodlawn	Carol R. Brink	1935
Good Master	Kate Seredy	1935
Five Chinese Brothers	Claire H. Bishop	1938
Mr. Popper's Penguins	Richard and Florence Atwater	1938
The Hobbit	J. R. R. Tolkien	1938
Madeline	Ludwig Bemelmans	1939
Thimble Summer	Elizabeth Enright	1939
Blue Willow	Doris Gates	1940
The Moffats	Eleanor Estes	1941

The Little House	Virginia L. Burton	1942
Johnny Tremain	Esther Forbes	1943
Homer Price	Robert McCloskey	1943
Rabbit Hill	Robert Lawson	1944
Strawberry Girl	Lois Lenski	1945
King of the Wind	Marguerite Henry	1948
Door in the Wall	Marguerite De Angeli	1949
Benjamin Franklin	Ingri and Edgar D'Aulaire	1950
Pippi Longstocking	Astrid Lindgren	1950
Charlotte's Web	E. B. White	1952
Winnie-the-Pooh	A. A. Milne	1954
Beezus and Ramona	Beverly Cleary	1955

INDEX OF AUTHORS AND ILLUSTRATORS

INDEX OF TITLES

ILLUSTRATION CREDITS

1. From *Why Mosquitoes Buzz in People's Ears* by Verna Aardema. Pictures © 1975 by Leo and Diane Dillon. Reproduced by permission of the publisher, Dial Books for Young Readers.

11. From the cover illustration of *A Horse and a Hound, a Goat and a Gander* by Alice and Martin Provensen, copyright © 1980 by Alice and Martin Provensen, The Scribner Book Publishing Companies, Inc.,

16. From the cover illustration for *Outside Over There,* copyright © 1981 by Maurice Sendak, Harper & Row Publishers, Inc.

31. From the cover illustration for *Tomie de Paola's Mother Goose,* illustrations copyright © 1985 by Tomie de Paola, G.P. Putnam's Sons.

37. From the cover illustration for *The Very Hungry Caterpillar* by Eric Carle, published by Philomel Books, copyright © 1969.

42. From *Reading* by Jan Ormerod, copyright © 1985 by Jan Ormerod; reprinted by permission of the publisher, Lothrop, Lee & Shepard, a division of William Morrow & Company, Inc.

48. From the cover illustration for *Where's Spot* by Eric Hill, published by G.P. Putnam's Sons, copyright © 1980 by Eric Hill.

50. From the cover illustration for *Max's New Suit* by Rosemary Wells, copyright © 1979 by Rosemary Wells, reproduced by permission of the publisher, Dial Books for Young Readers.

53. From the cover illustration for *Goodnight Moon* by Margaret Wise Brown, illustrated by Clement Hurd, copyright © 1947 by Harper & Row Publishers, Inc., renewed 1975 by Roberta Rauch and Clement Hurd.

55. From *Ten, Nine, Eight* by Molly Bang, copyright © 1985 by Molly Bang, reprinted by permission of the publisher, Greenwillow, a division of William Morrow & Company, Inc.

69. From the cover illustration for *Cars and Trucks and Things that Go* by Richard Scarry, published by Random House, Inc., copyright © 1974 by Richard Scarry.

84. From the cover illustration for *Frog and Toad Are Friends* written and illustrated by Arnold Lobel, copyright © 1970 by Arnold Lobel, Harper & Row Publishers, Inc.

88. From the cover illustration for *Daddy* written by Jeanette Caines, illustrated by Ron Himler, pictures copyright © 1977 by Ron Himler, Harper & Row Publishers, Inc.

90. From the cover illustration for *Blueberries for Sal* by Robert McCloskey, copyright 1948, renewed © 1976 by Robert McCloskey, reprinted by permission of Viking Penguin, Inc.

96. From *Truck* by Donald Crews, copyright © 1980 by Donald Crews, reprinted by permission of the publisher, Greenwillow, a division of William Morrow & Company, Inc.

98. From *The Snowy Day* by Ezra Jack Keats, copyright © 1962 by Ezra Jack Keats, reprinted by permission of Viking Penguin, Inc.

108. From the cover illustration for *Caps for Sale* written and illustrated by Esphyr Slobodkina, copyright © 1940, 1947, renewed 1968 by Esphyr Slobodkina, Harper & Row Publishers, Inc.

108. From the cover illustration for *Frederick's Fables* by Leo Lionni, published by Pantheon, a division of Random House, Inc., copyright © 1985 by Leo Lionni.

117. First page illustration from *El cuento de Fernando* by Munro Leaf, illustrated by Robert Lawson, published by Viking Penguin, 1936. Copyright © Estate of Nina F. Bowman.

125. From the cover illustration for *Bedtime for Frances* written by Russell Hoban, illustrated by Garth Williams, pictures copyright © 1960 by Garth Williams, Harper & Row Publishers, Inc.

127. From the cover illustration for *Round Trip* by Ann Jonas, copyright © 1983 by Ann Jonas reprinted by permission of the publisher, Greenwillow, a division of William Morrow & Company, Inc.

128. From the cover illustration for *Henny Penny* by Paul Galdone, copyright © 1968 by Paul Galdone, reprinted by permission of Clarion Books/Ticknor & Fields, a Houghton Mifflin Company.

131. From the cover illustration for *Anno's Counting Book* by Mitsumasa Anno (Thomas Y. Crowell), copyright © 1974 by Fukuinkan Shoten, Harper & Row Publishers, Inc.

134. From *Faces* by Barbara Brenner, photographs by George Ancona. Photographs copyright © 1970 by George Ancona. Reproduced by permission of publisher, E.P. Dutton, a division of The New American Library.

140. From the cover illustration for *Wolf's Favor* by Fulvio Testa, copyright © 1986 by Fulvio Testa, reproduced by permission of the publisher, Dial Books for Young Readers.

143. From the title page illustration for *Amos and Boris* by William Steig, copyright © 1971 by William Steig, Farrar, Straus & Giroux, Inc.

146. From the cover illustration for *Arnold of the Ducks* written and illustrated by Mordicai Gerstein, copyright © 1983 by Mordicai Gerstein, Harper & Row Publishers, Inc.

156. From the cover illustration for *Mrs. Peloki's Class Play* by Joanne Oppenheim, illustrated by Joyce Audy dos Santos, illustration copyright © 1984 by Joyce Audy dos Santos; reproduced by permission of the publisher, Dodd, Mead & Company, Inc.

166. From the cover illustration for *Large as Life: Nighttime Animals* written by Joanna Cole, illustrated by Kenneth Lilly, published by Alfred A. Knopf, Inc., a division of Random House, Inc., illustration copyright © 1985 by Kenneth Lilly.

167. From the cover illustration for *Some Busy Hospital* by Seymour Reit, illustrated by Carolyn Bracken, illustration copyright © 1985 by Carolyn Bracken, used by permission of Western Publishing Company, Inc.

171. From the cover illustration for *Little Bear* written by Else Holmelund Minarik, illustrated by Maurice Sendak, pictures copyright © 1957 by Maurice Sendak, Harper & Row Publishers, Inc.

176. From an illustration from *James and the Giant Peach* by Roald Dahl, illustrated by Nancy Eckholm Burkert, published by Alfred A. Knopf, Inc., a division of Random House, Inc. copyright © 1961.

180. From an illustration from *Higglety Pigglety Pop! or There Must Be More to Life* by Maurice Sendak, copyright © 1967 by Maurice Sendak, Harper & Row Publishers, Inc.

194. From an illustration from *And Then What Happened, Paul Revere?* by Jean Fritz, illustrated by Margot Tomes, published by Coward, McCann & Geoghegan, copyright © 1973, illustrations Margot Tomes, used by permission of G.P. Putnam's Sons.

203. From an illustration from *Mean Jake and the Devils* by William H. Hooks, illustrated by Dirk Zimmer, illustrations copyright © 1981 by Dirk Zimmer, reproduced by permission of the publisher, Dial Books for Young Readers.

204. From the cover illustration for *Snow White and the Seven Dwarfs* by the Brothers Grimm, illustrated by Nancy Ekholm Burkert, published by Farrar, Straus & Giroux; illustration copyright © 1972 by Nancy Ekholm Burkert.

205. From an illustration for *The Garden of Abdul Gasazi* by Chris Van Allsburg, copyright © 1979 by Chris Van Allsburg, reprinted by permission of Houghton Mifflin Company.

209. From the cover illustration for *Little Raccoon* by Susan Noguere, pictures by Tony Chen. Pictures copyright © 1981 Tony Chen. Reprinted by permission of Henry Holt & Co.

215. From an illustration for *The Great Brain* by John D. Fitzgerald, illustrated by Mercer Mayer copyright © 1967 by John D. Fitzgerald, reproduced by permission of the publisher, Dial Books for Young Readers.

217. From an illustration for *Mrs. Frisby and the Rats of NIMH* by Robert C. O'Brien, illustrated by Zena Bernstein, copyright © 1971 by Robert C. O'Brien, The Scribner Book Publishing Companies, Inc.

219. From the cover illustration for *A Light in the Attic,* Poems and Drawings by Shel Silverstein, copyright © 1981 by Snake Eye Music, Inc., reproduced by permission of the publisher, E.P. Dutton.

224. From the cover illustration for *Hazel Rye* written by Vera and William Cleaver (J.B. Lippincott), jacket copyright © 1983 by Harper & Row Publishers, Inc.

237. From the Book II frontispiece for *Amy's Eyes* written by Richard Kennedy, illustrated by Richard Egielski, illustrations copyright © 1985 by Richard Egielski, reprinted by permission of Harper & Row Publishers, Inc.

240. From the cover illustration for *Stuart Little* written by E.B. White and illustrated by Garth Williams, copyright © 1945 by E.B. White, pictures copyright renewed © 1973 by Garth Williams.

240. From the title page illustration for *The Twenty-One Balloons* by William Pene Du Bois, copyright © 1947 by William Pene Du Bois, renewed © 1975 by William Pene Du Bois, reprinted by permission of Viking Penguin, Inc.

247. From the cover illustration for *Commodore Perry in the Land of the Shogun* by Rhoda Blumberg, Copyright © 1985 by Rhoda Blumberg; reprinted by permission of the publisher, Lothrop, Lee & Shepard, a division of William Morrow & Company.

255. From the cover illustration for *Nightmares: Poems to Trouble Your Sleep* by Jack Prelutsky, illustrated by Arnold Lobel, illustrations copyright © 1976 by Arnold Lobel, reprinted by permission of the publisher Greenwillow, a division of William Morrow & Company, Inc.

264. From an illustration for *Rascal* by Sterling North, illustrated by John Schoenherr, illustrations copyright © 1963 by E.P. Dutton, reproduced by permission of the publisher, E.P. Dutton, a division of New American Library.

268. From the cover illustration for *Castle* by David Macaulay, copyright © 1977 by David Macaulay, reprinted by permission of Houghton Mifflin Company.

272. From the cover illustration for *The Incredible Journey* by Sheila Burnford, illustrated by Carl Burger, copyright © 1960, 1961 by Sheila Burnford; reprinted by permission of Little, Brown and Company, Inc.

ABOUT THE BANK STREET COLLEGE OF EDUCATION

Since its founding in 1916, The Bank Street College of Education has been devoted to the study of how children learn and develop, educating children, training teachers and child-care specialists, and helping families. This is still Bank Street's mission in the 1980s, when child-care professionals the world over equate the Bank Street name with a respected, progressive, and humanistic approach to a child's education.

ABOUT THE AUTHORS

JOANNE OPPENHEIM has been a writer, teacher, consultant, and editor. She has written books, articles, and classroom materials both for and about children, including the popular *Mrs. Peloki* series. A graduate of Sarah Lawrence College and The Bank Street College of Education, Mrs. Oppenheim is presently an associate editor of the Bank Street Media Group and also serves as a consultant to ABC's Afterschool Specials.

BARBARA BRENNER has written over forty books for children, including two ALA Notable Books and one selected by *School Library Journal* as "the best of the best" books for children of the last thirteen years. As a teacher, one of her principal interests has been encouraging youngters to do their own creative writing. Mrs. Brenner has been associated with Bank Street College since 1962 and is presently an associate editor there.

BETTY D. BOEGEHOLD has earned a nationwide reputation in the field of reading. She was Senior Associate Editor of *The Bank Street Readers,* this country's first multi-ethnic and urban-oriented reading series for young children. She is the author of many books for young readers, and is best known for her *Pippa Mouse* series.

ABOUT THE CONSULTANT

DR. CLAUDIA LEWIS is a member of the Bank Street graduate faculty, and has been awarded the title Distinguished Scholar in Children's Literature. She is the author of the classic textbook *Writing for Young Children,* as well as numerous books of poetry and stories for children.